Abstracts of the
DEBT BOOKS
of the
PROVINCIAL LAND OFFICE
OF MARYLAND

Calvert County

Volume II

Liber 11: 1765, 1766, 1767, 1768
Liber 12: 1769, 1770, 1771, 1773, 1774

By
V. L. Skinner, Jr.

CLEARFIELD

Printed for Clearfield Company by
Genealogical Publishing Company
Baltimore, Maryland
2017

ISBN 978-0-8063-5828-4

Made in the United States of America

Introduction

The Provincial Land Office of Maryland was responsible for the dispensing of land from 1634 to 1777. Land was initially acquired by a warrant and was then patented. Information concerning these documents are found in the Warrants and Patents series of the Provincial Land Office located at the Maryland State Archives and are indexed by Peter Wilson Coldham in his five-volume series *Settlers of Maryland*, published by Genealogical Publishing Company.

Land was patented according to the desires of the patentee, and the name given to a patent was not necessarily unique within any particular jurisdiction.

The Lord Proprietor's personal hold on land affairs was much weakened during the royal period from 1689 to 1715. However, it was immediately revived when his proprietary rights were restored in 1715 (Hartsook and Skordas, *Land Office and Prerogative Court Records*). Both the Rent Rolls and the Debt Books date from this restoration period.

The Rent Rolls and the Debt Books are the means by which the Lord Proprietor kept track of the rents due him. Each piece of land granted to a person was subject to a yearly rent according to the terms of the patent.

A Rent Roll consists of entries for each tract of land patented, plus the name of the person for whom it was originally surveyed, the present owner, the acreage, and the rent. Alienations, or subsequent sales and leases of the piece of land, are also included.

A Debt Book consists of a list of persons owning land with the names and rents of each tract that he or she owned, all listed in one place under his or her name.

The Debt Books

The Debt Books are arranged by county, by year, and then by the name of the person paying the rent. There are a total of 54 libers, covering all of the counties. The extant Debt Books for the Western Shore counties are essentially annual, dating from 1753 to 1774. (The Debt Books for 1750 for five Western Shore counties–Anne Arundel, Baltimore, Charles, Prince George's, Frederick–are found in the Calvert Papers, located at the Maryland State Archives.) The extant Debt Books for the Eastern Shore counties are also essentially annual, dating from 1733 to 1775.

Each liber contains information for only one county, but for multiple years. For purposes of identification, each section (i.e., year) of any particular liber is given the denotation of the specific year.

Tracking land ownership over various years is particularly important for intestate estates, land inherited by women, and land that is not specified in a will.

The information in this series is presented in a tabular form:

- liber and folio citation, with any pertinent date.
- name of the person paying the taxes.
- name of the tract of land.
- acreage.

Notes to Reader

The following conventions are used in this book:

1. "The" and "A" at the beginning of any tract name has been omitted.
2. The index contains both tract names and surnames, sorted together.

3.   "Crossed out" entries in the original libers have been included, as such.
4.   Names have been transcribed as they are written; no attempt has been made to standardize any spelling.
5.   Introduction and index pages of the original libers have been omitted.

Abbreviations

AA	Anne Arundel County	o/c	overcharged
ACC	Accomac County	o/o	orphans of
a/s	alias	PA	Pennsylvania
BA	Baltimore County	PG	Prince George's County
CE	Cecil County	PW	Prince William County
CH	Charles County	pt	part of
cnp	name continued on next page	QA	Queen Anne's County
c/o	child/children of	RI	Rhode Island
CR	Caroline County	SM	St. Mary's County
CV	Calvert County	SO	Somerset County
DE	Delaware	s.p.	square poles
DO	Dorchester County	SU	Sussex County
d/o	daughter of	s/o	son of
FR	Frederick County	<t>	torn
h/o	heir(s) of	TA	Talbot County
KE	Kent County MD	tbc	to be charged to
KEDE	Kent County DE	unr	unreadable
KI	Kent Island	VA	Virginia
n/a	not available	w/o	widow of
NE	New England	WO	Worcester County
n/g	not given		

Contents of this volume

This book is the second of two volumes for Calvert County. The debt books for Calvert County cover the following years: 1753, 1754, 1755, 1756, 1757, 1758, 1761, 1762, 1763, 1764, 1765, 1766, 1767, 1768, 1769, 1770, 1771, 1773, 1774.

From the Debt Books entries, several interesting facts are evident: (1) Calvert County had a Free School established by 1753; and, (2) Hunting Town was an established community in 1754; and, (3) Lower Marlbro was an established community in 1753. The leading landowners were: the Mackall family, Thomas Reynolds. Some Calvert County landowners were cited as inhabiting the following jurisdictions: Anne Arundel County, Charles County, Prince George's County, St. Mary's County.

11:1765:0 ...		Acres
~~Roger Brooke s/o Roger~~	~~\<n/g\>~~	~~\<n/g\>~~
Richard Bond	"Small Reward"	6¾
John Dossey	pt. "Robinson's Rest"	66⅔
~~John Gibson~~	~~pt. "Spittle"~~	~~73~~
	~~"Additional Spittle"~~	~~22~~
Lewis Griffith	"All Points"	24
~~William Hudson~~	~~pt. "Magruder" – not charged in 1766~~	~~40~~
~~Dr. Leonard Holliday~~	~~"Arnolds Purchase"~~	~~50~~
Mary Ireland	"Mill Marsh" – not charged in 1765	63
	"No Name" – not charged in 1765	100
~~William Monnett~~	~~"Williams Purchase" – not charged in 1765~~	~~206~~
Walter Murray	"Wolfs Quarter"	300
Thomas Reynolds	"Robinsons Rest" – not charged in 1765	156
~~h/o Maryland Skinner~~	~~pt. "Williams Purchase" – not charged in 1766~~	~~103~~
~~Elizabeth Skinner~~	~~pt. "Williams Purchase" – not charged in 1766~~	~~103~~
11:1765:\<unnumbered\> \<blank\>		
11:1765:1 ...		
Eleanor Alton	pt. "Hardestys Choice"	50
h/o David Arnold	pt. "Henry Chew"	290
	pt. "Abbington"	350
	pt. "Hardestys Choice"	130
w/o Samuel Austin	pt. "Coxes Choice"	140
	pt. "Farme"	20
h/o Michael Askew	pt. "Lawreys Chance"	118
James Alnutt	pt. "Trumans Chance"	153
William Alnutt	pt. "Trumans Chance"	156
	pt. "Agreement"	100
Samuel Austin	pt. "Coxes Choice"	117
Roger Brooke	pt. "Brooke Place Mannor"	1096
John & Isaac Baker	"Devils Woodyard"	150
Jacob Bowen	pt. "Elton Head Manor"	300
John Beveridge	"Dearbought"	21
John Benion	pt. "Desart"	108
Abraham Bowen	pt. "Dividing Branch"	169½
David Bowen	pt. "Dividing Branch"	189

Isaac Bowen	pt. "Dividing Branch"	190
h/o James Brooke	pt. "Brooke Adventure"	350
	pt. "Cedar Branch"	85
Jesse Bowen	pt. "Elton Head Manor"	1167
11:1765:2 ...		
Charles Bowen	pt. "Neighbourhood"	74
Basil Bowen	pt. "Forge"	50
Henry Broome	pt. "Austins Chance"	65
	pt. "Howard & Letchworth"	200
	pt. "Broad Point"	10
	pt. "Austins Addition"	23
William Blackburn	pt. "Back Pasture"	50
h/o James Bowen	pt. "Dividing Branch"	210
h/o Abraham Barnes	"Fishers Orchard"	255
	"Bran Fry"	100
Roger Brooke, Jr.	pt. "Bowen"	70
	"Knoles Branch"	98
	"Tauneys Addition"	123
	"Stones Hills"	50
Edward Blackburn	"Readley"	100
Thomas Broome	"Rich Neck"	52
	"Marys Widowhood"	30
	pt. "Youngs Attempt"	100
	"Hap at a Venture"	50
	pt. "Horse Range"	125
	"Addition to Island Neck"	30
John Broome	pt. "Island Neck"	500
	"Stones Bay"	200
	"Adventure"	82½
	"Broad Point"	140
	pt. "Austins Addition"	23
Ann Bond	"Middle Fuller"	200
	"Lower Fuller"	200
	"Lower Bennitt"	250
Isabell Barton	pt. "Upper Bennitt"	50
11:1765:3 ...		

John Beckett	"Selbys Clifts"	200
	pt. "Mears"	200
	pt. "Gunterton"	250
	pt. "Hardesty"	50
	"Poppy Gray"	40
h/o Richard Blake	pt. "Upper Bennitt"	557
	pt. "St. Edmunds"	200
	pt. "Lordships Favour"	192
	pt. "Neglect"	50
Jesse Bowen	"Lambeth"	94
Mary Bond	pt. "Hogsdown"	275
	"Micharn"	100
	pt. "Brooks Partition"	104
	"Lawrys Chance"	135
Richard Bond	pt. "Laureys Chance"	50
	"Small Reward"	111
Samuel Chew	"Letchworths Chance"	550
	pt. "Upper Bennitt"	456
	"Lane & Gore"	51½
Joseph Chilton	"Teria in Agua"	4
Philip Lloyd Chew	"Popping Jay"	540
Bennett Chew	"Chews Fortune"	49
Josias Crosby	pt. "Archers Hays"	30
	pt. "Goughs Purchase"	60
Michael Caterton	pt. "Lingans Purchase"	125
Richard Chew	"Stallings Lott"	150
	pt. "Robinsons Rest"	250
Henry Cambden	"Highland"	200
	"Chance"	70
11:1765:4 ...		
Young Cox (cnp)	pt. "Littleland"	17
	pt. "Coxes Inclosures"	65
	pt. "Cops Hall"	25
	pt. "Coxes Freehold"	120
	pt. "Merry Green Wood"	163
	pt. "Good Luck"	10

	"Musquetee Point"	46
	"Turners Chance"	50
John Presley	pt. "Batchelors Quarter"	420
John Clare	pt. "Elton Head Manor"	157
	pt. "Laureys Chance"	130
Calvert County School	"Security"	87
	pt. "Orchard"	100
h/o Charles Claggett	"Blinkhorn"	300
	pt. "Foxes Road"	42
	pt. "Allens Neck"	36
h/o Edward Cole	"Brooke Battle"	230
Calvert County	pt. "Inland"	3
Rev. George Cooke	pt. "Prestons Clifts"	239
	pt. "Gore"	100
Isaac Clare	"Horse Path"	200
	pt. "Elton Head Manor"	143
	"Concord"	161
	"Addition to Horsepath"	40
John Culpepper	"Wolfs Quarter"	40
Thomas Crutchley	"Addition"	50
11:1765:5 ...		
Benjamin Dixon	"Middlesex"	100
	"Addition to Middlesex"	95
	"Foxes Walks"	5
h/o William Dorumple	"Hap at a Venture"	150
	"Foxes Road"	150
James Duke	"Brooke Place"	171
Samuel Dare	pt. "Angle"	140
	pt. "Gideon & Clevelys Right"	336
	pt. "Smiths Purchase"	119½
Benjamin Duke	pt. "Rich Levells"	247
	pt. "Inland"	1
	pt. "Brooke Place Mannor"	300
	pt. "Howard & Letchworth"	303
Joseph Dawkins (cnp)	pt. "Friendship" a/s "Copartnership Rectified"	31¼
	"Dicks Cabbin"	50

	pt. "Taylors Joy"	114
h/o James Dodson	"Huckleberry Hills"	50
	"Littleworth"	21
John Dossey	pt. "Mary Green"	63
	pt. "Dear Quarter"	62½
	pt. "Bennetts Desire"	10
Robert Day	pt. "No Name"	150
Benjamin Day	"Frampton"	50
	"Brandon"	57
Nathaniel Dare	pt. "Gideon & Clevelys Right"	160
William Dawkins	"Mary Dukes Doom"	100
11:1765:6 ...		
James Dawkins	"Josephs Place"	200
Mary Dawkins	"Josephs Reserve"	196
Susannah Dare	pt. "Gideon & Clevelys Right"	472
Philip Dossey	pt. "Youngs Mount"	59
	pt. "Youngs Fortune"	40
	"Schoolhouse"	100
	resurvey of several tracts	312
	"Tauneys Addition"	132
	"Brigantines Adventure"	24
William Day	pt. "No Name"	100
Clevely Dare	"Gideon & Clevelys Right"	1199
	pt. "Prestons Clifts"	100
Ellis Dixon	"Hogs Skin Clifts"	100
Thomas Denton	"Island Neck"	99
	"Puddington"	50
John Dare	pt. "Gideon & Clevelys Right"	100
John Dowell	pt. "Swingfears Rest"	50
	pt. "Lingans Purchase"	100
Richard Deale	pt. "Newington"	200
	pt. "Timberwell"	74
James Deale	pt. "Swinfears Rest"	64½
11:1765:7 ...		
Daniel Dossey	pt. "Garden"	67
Philip Dossey, Jr.	pt. "Robinsons Rest"	150

Francis Dossey	pt. "Bennitts Desire"	50
James Dossey	pt. "Garden"	100
	pt. "Robinsons Rest"	64
Jacob Deale	pt. "Upper Bennitt"	75
William Dare	pt. "Swinfins Rest"	250
Thomas Clevely Dare	pt. "Agreement"	150
	"Bite the Biter"	112
Alexander Deale	pt. "Newington"	46
	"Islington"	25
Philip Dowell	pt. "Lingans Purchase"	116
John Dew	pt. "Archers Hays"	43½
James Dossey, Jr.	pt. "Youngs Mount"	100
John Samuel Dossey	pt. "Youngs Attempt"	100
Richard Everist	pt. "Highland"	100
h/o Benjamin Elt	pt. "Elton Head Manor"	336
11:1765:8 ...		
Richard Everist	pt. "Rocky Neck" – for h/o (N) Pardo	50
	"Foxes Walks" – for h/o (N) Pardo	70
Isaac Essex	pt. "Wolf Trap"	55
Robert Ethrington	pt. "Comsey"	92½
Barnaby Eagan	pt. "Brooke Place Manor"	400
h/o George Fowler	pt. "Tillington"	45½
h/o Thomas Freeman	pt. "Rockhold"	135
James Fraser	"Hills Hall"	100
Col. William Fitzhugh	pt. "Elton Head Manor"	2500
	pt. "Miles End"	399½
	pt. "Mills Run"	150
	"Hattons Cave"	70
	"Stafford Freehold"	70
	"Round Ponds"	100
	"Leak" or "Smiths Hills"	100
	"Gore"	70
Joseph Freeman	"Arnolds Purchase"	50
Henry Fryer	pt. "Arnolds Purchase"	50
Robert Freeland (cnp)	"Mackalls Force"	647
	pt. "Freemans Chance"	232

	"Dosseys Folly"	70
	"Burks Purchase"	50
	pt. "Dear Quarter"	100
Sarah Freeland	pt. "Parkers Clifts"	50
	"Good Luck"	150
11:1765:9 ...		
Jacob Freeland	pt. "Letchworths Chance"	179
	"Neglect"	125
John Furguson	pt. "Griffiths & Govers Pasture"	40
	pt. "Skinners Chance"	30
	pt. "Turners Place"	126
Alexander Fraser	"Sterlings Chance"	40
	"Sterlings Nest"	550
Jacob French	pt. "Danvin"	125
Francis Freeland	pt. "Letchworths Chance"	409½
Richard Gibson	pt. "Swinfins Rest"	72
John Gibson	pt. "Spittle"	20
	"Additional Spittle"	50
h/o John Griffith	pt. "Welch Pool"	143¾
	pt. "Skinners Chance"	90
John Gardner	pt. "Johnsons Lott"	100
h/o Samuel Gover	pt. "Aldermason"	150
	"Govers Expectation"	89
	pt. "Welch Pool"	2
Charles Grahame	pt. "Halls Craft"	521
	"Howard"	42
	"Bell"	68
	"Blackwall"	38
	pt. "Hardesty"	180
Joseph Galloway	pt. "Spittle"	20
	"Additional Spittle"	28
Richard Gibson, Jr.	pt. "Lordships Favour"	50
11:1765:10 ...		
Lewis Griffith (cnp)	pt. "Welch Pool"	215
	pt. "Archers Hays"	231
	"Lewis's Slipe & Dews Purchase"	26

	"Long Lane"	63
James Gibson	pt. "Additional Spittle"	88
	pt. "Newington"	22
h/o Robert Gover	pt. "Archers Hays"	190
	"Gough's Purchase" a/s "Goughs Pasture"	50
	"Govers Addition"	167
	"Govers Meadows"	59
	pt. "Dunkirk"	150
	pt. "Exchange"	66
John Griffin	pt. "Robinson"	60
Edward Gantt	pt. "Ordinary"	606
	"Kingsburys Marsh"	130
	"Craft"	90
Ann Griffin	pt. "Grays Chance"	50
Thomas Gray	pt. "Wolton"	75
	"Grays Addition"	109
	pt. "Nortons Purchase"	166⅔
John Gray (Patuxent)	"Marsh Land & Buckhead"	345
	"Hazard"	42
	"Reserve"	50
	"Stinnetts Ramble"	35
	pt. "Brooke Adventure"	100
	pt. "Tonottle" a/s "Tuxbury"	100
Howerton Games	pt. "Johnsons Lott"	50
	"Hazard"	25
Robert Gardner	pt. "Johnsons Lott"	200
	"Wolf Hole"	50
11:1765:11 ...		
Samuel Gray	"Norwood"	200
	"Theobush Maning"	50
	pt. "Austins Chance"	91
John Graves	"Stephens Plains"	50
	"Graves's Rehobeth"	111
Edward Gardner	"Chatham"	80
	pt. "Dorington"	115
	"Short Neck"	76

Benjamin Gardner	pt. "Round Pond Plains"	100
h/o James Tru. Greenfield	pt. "Aldermason"	150
	"Addition"	56½
Mary Graves	"Haphazard"	135
	"Batchelors Hall"	300
	"Timber Neck"	50
	"Clares Littleworth"	43
Esther Gray	"Fishing Creek"	165
	"Chaplain"	100
	"East Fishing Creek"	50
	"Nutts Clifts"	150
	"East Chaplain"	100
h/o Job Hunt	pt. "Upper Bennitt"	195
	pt. "Robinson"	13
	pt. "Lordships Favour"	9
James Heigh	pt. "Beakly"	300
	"Fosters Purchase"	150
	pt. "Roberts Chance"	34
	"James Chance"	40
	"James Addition"	21
	"Samuels Addition"	15
	"Clarks Hills"	19
	"Little Land"	11
	"Heighs Addition"	15
	"Brooke Place"	300
11:1765:12 ...		
Thomas Hollingshead	pt. "Kents Freehold"	250
Richard Hall	"Halls Hills" tbc W. Ireland in 1766	650
Dr. John Hamilton	"Branford"	150
	pt. "Hardestys Choice"	150
	pt. "Henry Chew"	75
	"Little Ganey"	42
	"Grantham"	200
	"Sams Addition"	78
William Harrison	pt. "Brookes Discovery"	200
	pt. "Islington"	282

Henry Hardesty	pt. "Den"	37
	pt. "Nickolds Chance"	55
Joseph Hardesty	pt. "Den"	37½
	pt. "Nicholls Chance"	55
	"Nelsons Reserve"	22
William Hardesty	pt. "Lordships Favour"	75
William Hickman	pt. "Newington"	220
	pt. "Islington"	260
John Hance	pt. "Newington"	9
	"Johns's Neglect"	128
	"Illingsworths Fortune"	65
Henry Howes	pt. "Refuse"	50
	"Jensbeys Lott"	46
	"Purchase"	23
Thomas Hunt	pt. "Lordships Favour"	50
11:1765:13 ...		
William Harrison, Jr.	pt. "Laureys Reserve"	75
	"Brooke Discovery"	126
	pt. "Coxes Freehold"	128
Henry Harrison	pt. "Swinfins Rest"	100
Thomas Holland	pt. "St. James's Enlarged"	1138
	pt. "Alexanders Hope"	38
George Hall	pt. "Chance"	25
h/o Jacob Hooper	pt. "Taylors Joy"	250
William Harris	pt. "Durain"	200
	pt. "Illingsworths Fortune"	100
	pt. "Littleworth"	150
	pt. "Tillington"	73
	pt. "Letchworths Chance"	275
Susannah Hoxton	"Homesham"	117
Ann Holland	pt. "Abbington"	150
Newman Harvey	pt. "Turners Place"	126
Benjamin Hance (cnp)	"Parkers Clifts"	100
	pt. "Warington"	175
	pt. "Agreement"	50
	"Busseys Garden"	175

	pt. "Illington"	250
	"Sewalls Purchase"	30
	"Hance Lane"	20
	pt. "Newington"	3
	"Purchase"	154
	"Warings Chance"	56
	pt. "Cedar Branch"	240
	resurvey of several tracts	119½
Benjamin Harris	pt. "Expectation"	100
11:1765:14 ...		
William Harris, Jr.	"Addition"	100
James Henley	"Smuggs Folly"	80
Joseph Hance	"Warbleton"	404
	pt. "Stockley" a/s resurvey of several tracts	100
David Hellen s/o John	pt. "Elton Head Manor"	200
	"Friendship"	100
	"Jermin Quarter Enlarged"	143
William Hudson	pt. "Arnolds Purchase"	100
	pt. "Magruder"	40
James Hellen	pt. "Truswell"	150
Samuel Hance	pt. "Theobush Maning"	189
Walter Hellen	pt. "Hoopers Neck"	275
Robert Jenkins Henry	pt. "St. James's"	300
Thomas Hellen	pt. "Warring"	121
	pt. "Bowdleys Chance"	75
	"Busseys Lott"	75
	"Hellens Lott"	12
Dr. Leonard Hollyday	"Buzzard Island"	700
	"Addition"	51
Edmund Hungerford	"Hogskin Neck"	100
	"Stephens Land"	100
	"Purchase"	24
	pt. "Desart"	100
Philip Huntt	pt. "Lordships Favour"	100
11:1765:15 ...		

Richard Hellen	"Trustwell"	150
	"Milton Lott"	100
	"Persie"	100
	"Harrow on the Hill"	80
	pt. "Rich Levells"	20
h/o Richard Johns	pt. "Billingslys Farme"	136
	"Purchase"	100
	pt. "Youngs Desire"	12
William Ireland, Jr.	pt. "Spittle"	70
	"Additional Spittle"	22
Mary Ireland	pt. "Elton Head Manor"	200
	"Irelands Hope"	50
	pt. "Prestons Clifts"	108
	pt. "Angle"	88
John Ireland	pt. "Tillington"	189
	"Wolfs Trap"	45
Thomas Johnson	"Brewhouse"	260
John Johnson	"Elizabeth"	200
	pt. "Gift"	70
	pt. "Preston Clifts"	314
William Johnson s/o Jeremiah	pt. "Exchange"	150
Dr. Edward Johnson	"Preston"	200
	"Moffitts Mount"	200
	"Moods Adventure"	50
	"Hays March"	18
	pt. "Poor Land"	185
h/o John Kent	pt. "Rockhold"	160
11:1765:16 ...		
James Kirshaw	pt. "Prevent Danger"	100
John Kirshaw	pt. "Prevent Danger"	50
Francis Kirshaw	pt. "Sharpes Outlett"	100
Joseph Kent	pt. "Timberwell"	326
h/o James Leach	"Leaches Freehold"	125
John Laurence	"Laureys Addition"	145
	pt. "Islington"	50

William Lyles	pt. "Red Hall"	150
	pt. "Slipe"	8
	pt. "Sumers Pasture"	170
h/o Lewis Lewin	pt. "Redd Hall"	37½
Mary Lyles	pt. "Swingfears Rest"	50
John Leveal	"Whittles Rest"	210
Robert Lyles	pt. "Red Hall"	100
Sarah Lane	pt. "Homesham"	233
Samuel Lyles	pt. "Laureys Chance"	50
Jeremiah Maulden	pt. "Parkers Clifts"	250
Thomas Marshall, Jr.	"Coxes Folly"	50
	pt. "Farme"	19
11:1765:17 ...		
Thomas Marshall 3rd	pt. "Coxes Choice"	50
	pt. "Coxes Choice"	93
Thomas Manning	pt. "Theobalds Manor"	112
	pt. "Gunsbey"	168
w/o William McDowell	pt. "Coles Clifts"	50
h/o James Mackall	"Cage"	250
	"Busseys Lott"	100
	"Mackalls Desire"	10
h/o Thomas Morgan	pt. "Devise"	79
	pt. "Grays Chance"	350
	"Fellowship"	160
John Mackall	pt. "Morgan"	60
	pt. "Littleworth"	60
	pt. "Mary Green"	55
	"Horse Range"	180
	"Clagetts Desire"	376
	"Desert"	350
James Morsell	"Rattle Snake Hills"	120
	"Chance"	70
	"Labour in Vain"	100
Rousby Miller	pt. "Orchard"	253
Barbara Mackall (cnp)	"Brooke Partition"	200
	pt. "Hallowing Point"	200

	pt. "Chance"	75
	pt. "Coursey"	46½
Ann Mills	pt. "Woolton"	25
	pt. "Catch"	50
11:1765:18 ...		
Benjamin Mackall	"Copartnership"	182
	"Chance"	232
	pt. "Hallowing Point"	200
	"Seamores Neck"	382
	pt. "Horse Range"	165
	pt. "Sharpes Outlet"	100
	"Thorough Bridge"	250
	"Brooke Choice"	146
	pt. "Dividing Branch"	179
	pt. "Trouble"	27
	pt. "Moroccco" – in corn	50
	"Jarusalem"	124
	"Addition to Sharpes Outlet"	112
	pt. "Read"	46½
	pt. "Read & Magruder"	92½
	pt. "Swintons Adventure"	25
Walter Murray	pt. "Parkers Clifts"	100
	"Foxes Road"	100
	"Wolfs Quarter"	300
	"Smiths Hogpen"	319
	pt. "St. Leonards" – in corn	175
	"Taylors Disposal"	270
	pt. "Stones Hills"	25
	"Purchase"	22
James John Mackall (cnp)	pt. "Lower Bennett"	500
	pt. "Theobuch Manor"	100
	"Corn Hill"	350
	pt. "Alexanders Hope"	200
	pt. "Grays Chance"	200
	pt. "Bone Road"	89
	"Gunsbey"	38

	"Cold Harbour"	100
	pt. "Brooke Place"	432
	pt. "Stones Bay"	225
	"Piney Point"	50
	"Exchange"	350
	"Laureys Point" pt. "Laureys Rest"	100
	"Littleworth"	77
	"Cold Cubey"	200
	pt. "Angle"	350
	pt. "Laureys Rest"	295
	"Foxes Walks"	40
	"Bram Hall"	500
	"Neglect"	30
	pt. "Godsgrace"	617
	"Meads"	166
	pt. "Evans Land"	200
	pt. "Coles Clifts"	150
	pt. "Preston Clifts"	63
11:1765:19 ...		
John Norfolk	"Kidds Levells"	84
	pt. "Ireland Plains"	27
	pt. "Ridge"	100
	pt. "Refuse"	100
	"Refuge"	14
James Norfolk	pt. "Peahens Rest"	50
Margarett Parran late Rawlings	"Bethens Loss"	50
	pt. "Elton Head Manor"	300
	"Cumton"	75
	"Rawlings's Purchase"	60
	"Dearbought"	200
Elizabeth Prindowell	pt. "Parkers Clifts"	100
	pt. "Roberts Addition"	5
	pt. "Roberts Chance"	5½
	pt. "Beakley"	66⅔
Leonard Prindowell (cnp)	pt. "Roberts Addition"	10
	pt. "Chance"	11

	pt. "Beakley"	133⅓
Mary Parker	"Clay Hammond"	380
	"Wilsons Commond"	29
John Peters	pt. "Upper Bennett"	50
	pt. "Kents Freehold"	50
	pt. "Lordships Favour"	100
	pt. "Danvin & Clares Hundred"	280
William Patterson	pt. "Stones Bay"	75
	pt. "Evans Land"	65
Alexander Parran	"Point Patience"	360
	"Addition"	19
11:1765:20 ...		
Hutcheson Parker	pt. "St. Leonards" – in corn	175
	"Bulmores Branch"	50
	pt. "Stones Hills"	25
Young Parran	pt. "Denit"	349
	"Preston"	400
	pt. "Winfields Resurvey"	207
	"Prestons Neglect"	200
	pt. "Bermingham"	25
	pt. "Parrans Park"	150
	pt. "Morgan"	45
	"Brooke Plains"	100
	pt. "Inland"	2
	"Discovery"	99
Samuel Parran	pt. "Winfields Resurvey"	207
	pt. "Bermingham"	25
	pt. "Morgan"	45
	pt. "Parrans Park"	150
	pt. land without name	100
John Robinson (Halls Creek)	pt. "Johnsons Farme"	150
	pt. "Turners Place"	100
	pt. "Griffiths & Govers Pasture"	20
Thomas Rhodes	"Black Robin"	38
Samuel Robinson (cnp)	"Emersons Addition"	20
	pt. "Halls Hills"	85

	"Braughton Arpley"	73
Daniel Ross	pt. "Robinsons Rest"	200
John Robinson	pt. "Magruder"	175
Daniel Rawlings	pt. "Elton Head Manor"	200
11:1765:21 ...		
Thomas Reynolds (cnp)	pt. "Robinson"	191
	pt. "St. Edmunds"	150
	pt. "Robinsons Rest"	368
	pt. "Good Luck"	100
	"Adjoinder" a/s "Adjunction"	10
	pt. "Brookes Discovery"	64
	"Crowders Lott"	60
	"Reserve"	300
	"Foxes Chance"	72
	"Rich Hill"	5½
	"Foxes Home"	30
	"Sterlings Perch"	300
	pt. "Lordships Favour"	285
	pt. "Neglect"	60
	pt. "Coxes Inclosure"	70
	pt. "Foxes Freehold"	142
	"Troublesome"	50
	"Bennetts Refuge"	33
	pt. "Hopewill"	36
	pt. "Abbington Manor"	769
	"Angle Lane"	37
	"Stallings Lott"	31
	pt. "Meadows"	132
	"Thomas & Williams Chance"	101
	pt. "Thatchcomb"	114
	pt. "Lingans Purchase"	8
	pt. "Brooke Neck"	150
	"Stallings Swamp"	10
	pt. "Spittle"	90
	pt. "Hogsdown"	25
	"Meadows"	54

	"Hopewell"	58
	"Bite"	5
h/o John Somerwell	pt. "Gore"	200
	"Goldens Folly"	75
James Somerwell	"Tobys Quarter"	100
	"Rockey Neck"	50
	pt. "Allens Neck"	164
	"Narrow Neck & Gore"	18
	"Swamp"	67
h/o Maryland Skinner	pt. "Newington"	94
	pt. "Millers Folly"	250
	pt. "Williams Purchase"	103
11:1765:22 ...		
John Simmonds	pt. "Rich Bottom"	25
	"Short Hills"	40
h/o Leonard Skinner	"Borders"	77½
	pt. "Dodsons Desire"	25
	pt. "Chance"	27
	pt. "Reserve"	32¼
h/o George Smith	pt. "Desart"	52
	pt. "Round Bottom Plains"	100
Dorothy Sollers	"Forked Neck"	110
	"Hyam"	10
William Skinner	pt. "Scrap"	38
	pt. "Prestons Desire"	25
	pt. "Chance"	27
	pt. "Reserve"	32¼
	pt. "Border Enlarged"	77½
James Skinner	pt. "Border Enlarged"	77½
	pt. "Dodsons Desire"	25
	pt. "Chance"	27
	pt. "Reserve"	33¼
h/o Adderton Skinner (cnp)	"Blind Tom"	72
	"Tauneys Delight"	70
	pt. "Marys Green"	36
	"Addition"	60

	"Gore"	48
	"Tauneys Right"	150
	"Millers Folly"	250
	"Neglect"	25
Elizabeth Skinner	pt. "Tauneys Right"	150
	"Scrap"	62
	pt. "Reserve"	121
	pt. "Newington"	94
	pt. "Williams Purchase"	103
11:1765:23 ...		
h/o Samuel Sly	pt. "Morocco" – in corn	100
Alexander Somerwell	"Foxes Den"	50
	"Bartholomews Neck"	50
	pt. "Smiths Purchase"	238½
Joseph Strickland	pt. "Robinsons Rest"	50
William Sollers	pt. "Dorington"	182½
	"Bowdleys Chance"	34
Joshua Sedwick	pt. "Neighbourhood"	150
	"Adjoinder"	50
	pt. "Nortons Purchase"	83⅓
John Scott	pt. "Lordships Favour"	100
Joseph Skinner	pt. "Orchard"	50
	"Border Enlarged"	77½
	"Dodsons Desire"	25
	"Chance"	27
	"Reserve"	32½
Josias Sunderland	pt. "Swinfears Rest"	250
Josias Sunderland, Jr.	pt. "Upper Bennett"	50
h/o Richard Stallings	"Thack Corn"	236
	pt. "Robinsons Rest"	100
James Sewall	pt. "Dear Quarter"	62½
	pt. "Chance"	72½
	"Maidens Delight"	200
	pt. "Cops Hall"	80
John Standforth	pt. "Poor Land"	104
11:1765:24 ...		

h/o John Skinner	"Halls Hills"	877½
	"Sneaking Point"	50
	"Lingans Purchase"	94
	pt. "Hamiltons Park"	33
William Sandsberry	pt. "Archers Hays"	40
Joseph Smith, Jr.	pt. "Turners Pasture"	50
	pt. "Smiths Pasture"	100
	pt. "Archers Hays"	15½
William Smith	pt. "Smiths Chance"	50
	pt. "Sumers Place"	50
	pt. "Mordyke"	50
Mordecai Smith	pt. "Smiths Chance"	100
	pt. "Sumers Place"	50
	pt. "Welch Pool"	72½
	pt. "Calender"	77
Joseph Smith	"Mordyke"	50
w/o John Stone	pt. "Defence"	65
John Stallings	pt. "Upper Bennett"	25
Ellis Slater	pt. "Laureys Reserve"	100
Stephen Stamp	pt. "Red Hall"	125
Mary Smith (PG)	"Good Prospect"	50
	"Lands Land"	192
	"Small Reward"	111
	"Addition"	28
Clement Smith	pt. "Halls Craft"	486
11:1765:25 ...		
Nicholas Swamstead	pt. "Lordships Favour"	100
Thomas Stallings	pt. "Swinfears Rest"	64½
h/o Col. John Smith (cnp)	pt. "Halls Craft"	665
	pt. "Batchelors Quarter"	250
	"Soldiers Fortune"	200
	pt. "Ordinary"	75
	pt. "Grantham"	20
	1½ lots in Lower Marlbro	1½
	pt. "Dowdswells Manor"	400
	pt. "Ordinary"	80½

	"Hazard"	18
Stockett Sunderland	pt. "Laureys Chance or Resurvey"	100
John Davis Scarth	pt. "Robinsons Rest"	50
Benjamin Sedwick	pt. "Bulmores Branch" a/s "Right"	475
	pt. "Elton Head Manor"	200
Jonathan Slater	pt. "Halls Revenge"	28
	1 lot in Lower Marlbro	1
	"Sampsons Dividend"	168
	pt. "Manington"	25
	"Neglect"	50
Stephen Stewart	pt. "Illingsworths Fortune"	200
Jacob Tucker	"Tuckers Thickett"	200
	pt. "Chance"	50
h/o Philip Thomas	"Majors Choice"	500
Joseph Talbutt, Jr.	pt. "Expectation"	100
11:1765:26 ...		
h/o John Tannehill	pt. "Calender"	123
	"Friendship"	150
	"Cooper"	150
Joseph Talbutt	pt. "Freemans Chance"	123
	pt. "Tillington"	150
	"Batchelors Fortune"	200
John Talbutt	pt. "Expectation"	50
Catharine Thornbury	pt. "Dunkirk"	50
Edward Talbutt	pt. "Tillington"	415½
Gideon Turner	"Bowdleys Chance"	91
Thomas Talbutt	pt. "Expectation"	100
Benjamin Tasker, Esq.	"Hard Travell"	300
h/o Miles Tauney	"Berry"	600
	"Long Point"	100
	"Wooden Point"	25
	pt. "Letchworth"	50
	pt. "Angle"	3
John Tucker	pt. "Neighbourhood"	82½
Joseph Vanswearingan	pt. "Neighbourhood"	26
	pt. "Prevent Danger"	100

William Vermilion	"Creeds Chance"	64
11:1765:27 ...		
Joseph Wilson	"Tamott"	300
	pt. "Fosters Purchase"	150
	pt. "Robinson"	136
	pt. "Addition Spittle"	8
	pt. "Peahens Nest"	40
	pt. "Cedar Branch"	50
	"Letchworths Cyprus"	200
	pt. "Bowen" – for h/o (N) King	230
	pt. "Arnolds Purchase"	100
	pt. "Brookes Adventure"	150
	pt. "Cedar Branch"	75
	"Stones Lott"	50
	pt. "Arnolds Purchase"	50
h/o Joseph Wilson, Jr.	pt. "Lower Bennett"	400
	"Mackalls Desire"	78
h/o John Ward	"Goldsons Inheritance"	150
	"Velchees Rest"	50
John Wood	pt. "Magruder"	150
Aaron Williams, Jr.	pt. "Friendship Rectified"	200
	pt. "Swinfins Adventure"	50
Dr. Aaron Williams	"Williams's Hardship"	250
	"Williams's Rest"	50
	"Little Field"	25
	pt. "Friendship Rectified"	150
	pt. "Swinfins Adventure"	100
James Weems, Jr.	"Success, Tauneys Ease, & Stockly"	200
h/o Joseph Wilkinson	pt. "Godsgrace"	120
	pt. "Stockley"	70
John Waters	pt. "Stockley"	419
	pt. "Gunterton"	40
	"Mirtle Point"	7
11:1765:28 ...		
James Weems (cnp)	pt. "Magruder"	410
	"Hogs Haunt"	50

	"Mauldens Luck"	25
	pt. "Busseys Orchard"	400
	pt. "Inland"	1
	"Meadows Preserved"	46
	pt. "Birks Chance"	150
	"Bigger for Crumpton"	1055
	"Parkers Fortune" a/s "Chance"	263
	pt. "Godsgrace"	100
	pt. "Morrocco, Caterton Lott, & Barbers Delight"	294
	1 lot in Hunting Town	1
	pt. "Cuckolds Miss"	60
	pt. "Youngs Fortune"	60
	pt. "Youngs Attempt"	62
	pt. "Youngs Desire"	25
	"Pinmar Muse"	50
	pt. "Reserve"	50
	pt. "Trouble"	10
John Willing	pt. "Taylors Joy"	128
	"Jarusalem"	108
	pt. "Rich Bottom"	25
Francis Woolf, Jr.	pt. "Theobald Manor"	50
	pt. "Grays Chance"	50
h/o William Wilmott	pt. "Arnolds Purchase"	50
Richard Ward	pt. "Swinfins Rest"	116
James Weems s/o David	"Bingan"	200
	"Green House"	155
	"Chews Purchase"	145
	"Grantham"	45
	"Marshalls Addition"	70
Basil Williamson	"Lingans Adventure"	310
11:1765:29 ...		
Edward Wood	pt. "Woods Adventure"	150
	"Titmarsh"	100
	pt. "Poor Land"	11
Jonah Winfield	pt. "Lands Land"	112
	pt. "Johnsons Farme"	100

Thomas Wells	pt. "Grantham Hall"	155
	"Arthurs Hall"	44
Rev. James Williamson	"Den"	725
	"Foxes Nettles"	20
	pt. "Batchelors Quarter"	420
h/o Roger Wheeler	pt. "Henry Chew"	237
	"Coxcomb"	150
	"Coxhead"	50
	pt. "Newington"	109
	"Smiths Conveyance"	60
John Wilkinson	pt. "Henry Chew"	400
Thomas Wilson	pt. "St. Edmunds"	163
	pt. "Neglect"	16½
Leonard Wood	pt. "Woods Adventure"	100
Edward Wilson	"Dear Quarter"	25
	pt. "Robinsons Rest"	150
Hilleary Wilson	pt. "Robinson"	200
John Weems	pt. "Dowdswell"	600
	pt. "Chance"	25
11:1765:30 ...		
William White	pt. "Smiths Joy"	100
Philemon Young	pt. "Henry Chew"	175
	1 lot in Lower Marlbro	1
	pt. "Youngs Desire"	50
Parker Young	"Hope Yard"	150
	"Punch"	150
	pt. "Youngs Desire"	25
	pt. "Hoppers Neck"	275
	pt. "Hoppers Neck" [!]	275
John Yoe	pt. "Rattle Snake Hills"	100
	pt. "Inland"	100
	"Hutchins's Chance"	50
	pt. "Orchard"	40
h/o Benjamin Johns (cnp)	"Anglica"	600
	pt. "Mears"	200
	"Whittles Rest"	336

	pt. "Devise"	75
	"Chance"	50
	"Parkers Clift"	180
	pt. "Inland"	2
	"Johns's Addition"	112
	"Letchworths Chance"	275
	"Fuller"	300
Joseph Isaac	"Plumb Point"	400
	pt. "Lordships Favour"	205
	"Purchase"	100
William Ireland	pt. "Bridge"	100
	"Georges Desire"	50
	"Addition"	43
	"Angle"	87
	pt. "Peahens Nest"	35
	pt. "Island Plains"	32
	"Lyons Creek"	300
William Johnson s/o George	pt. "Redd Hall"	100
11:1765:<unnumbered>	**Recapitulation**	
	Certification	
11:1765:<unnumbered>	**<blank>**	

11:1766:\<unnumbered\> Index – A & B		Acres
11:1766:1 ...		
Eleanor Alton	pt. "Hardestys Choice"	50
h/o David Arnold	pt. "Henry Chew"	290
	pt. "Abbington"	350
	pt. "Hardesty Choice"	130
w/o Samuel Austin	pt. "Coxes Choice"	140
	pt. "Farme"	20
h/o Michael Askew	pt. "Lawreys Chance"	118
James Alnutt	pt. "Trumans Chance"	153
William Alnutt	pt. "Trumans Chance"	156
	pt. "Agreement"	100
Samuel Austin	pt. "Coxes Choice"	117
Roger Brooke	pt. "Brooke Place Mannor"	1096
John & Isaac Baker	"Devils Wood Yard"	150
Jacob Bowen	pt. "Elton Head Manner"	300
John Beveridge	"Dearbought"	21
John Benion	pt. "Desart"	198
Abraham Bowen	pt. "Dividing Branch"	169½
David Bowen	pt. "Dividing Branch"	189
Isaac Bowen	pt. "Dividing Branch"	190
Roger Brooke s/o Roger	"White Marsh"	68
h/o James Brooke	pt. "Brooke's Adventure"	350
	pt. "Cedar Branch"	75
Jesse Bourn	pt. "Eltonhead Mannor"	1167
11:1766:2 ...		
Charles Bowen	pt. "Neighbourhood"	74
Basil Bowen	pt. "Forge"	50
Henry Broome	pt. "Austins Choice"	65
	pt. "Howard & Letchworth"	200
	pt. "Broad Point"	10
	pt. "Austins Addition"	23
William Blackburn	pt. "Black Pasture"	50
h/o James Bowen	pt. "Dividing Branch"	215
h/o Abraham Barnes	"Fishers Orchard"	255
	"Bran Fry"	100

Roger Brooke, Jr.	pt. "Bowen"	75
	"Knowles Branch"	98
	"Tauney's Addition"	125
	"Stones Hills"	50
Edward Blackburn	"Readley"	100
Thomas Broome	"Rick Neck"	52
	"Marys Widowhood"	30
	pt. "Youngs Attempt"	100
	"Hap at a Venture"	50
	pt. "Horse Range"	125
	"Addition to Island Neck"	30
John Broome	pt. "Island Neck"	500
	"Stones Bays"	200
	"Adventure"	82½
	"Broad Point"	140
	pt. "Austins Addition"	23
Ann Bond	"Middle Fuller"	200
	"Lower Fuller"	200
	"Lower Bennett"	250
Isabella Barton	pt. "Upper Bennett"	50
11:1766:3 ...		
w/o John Bickett	"Selbys Clifts"	200
	pt. "Mears"	200
	pt. "Gunterton"	250
	pt. "Hardesty"	50
	"Poppy Gray"	40
h/o Richard Blake	pt. "Upper Bennett"	557
	pt. "St. Edmonds"	200
	pt. "Lordships Favour"	192
	pt. "Neglect"	50
Jesse Bowen	"Lambeth"	94
Mary Bond	pt. "Hodsdown"	275
	"Micham"	243
	pt. "Brooke Partition"	104
	"Lawreys Chance"	135

Richard Bond	pt. "Lawreys Chance"	50
	"Small Land"	6¾
	"Small Reward"	111
Samuel Chew	"Letchworths Chance"	550
	pt. "Upper Bennett"	456
	"Lane & Gore"	51½
Joseph Chilton	"Terra in Aque"	4
Philip Lloyd Chew	"Popping Jay"	540
Bennett Chew	"Chews Fortune"	49
Josias Crosby	pt. "Archers Hays"	30
	pt. "Goughs Purchase"	60
Michael Catterton	pt. "Lingans Purchase"	125
Richard Chew	"Stallings Lott"	150
	pt. "Robinsons Rest"	250
Henry Cambden	"Highland"	200
	"Chance"	70
11:1766:4 ...		
John Chesley	pt. "Batchelors Quarter"	420
Michael Culpepper	"Venture"	16
Young Cox	pt. "Little Land"	17
	pt. "Coxes Inclosure"	65
	pt. "Cops Hall"	25
	pt. "Coxes Freehold"	120
	pt. "Merry Greenwood"	163
	"Musqueto Point"	46
	pt. "Good Luck"	10
	"Turnors Chance"	50
John Clare	pt. "Elton Head Manor"	157
	pt. "Lowreys Chance"	130
Calvert County School	"Security"	87
	pt. "Orchard"	100
h/o Charles Claggett	"Blink Horn"	300
	pt. "Foxes Road"	42
	pt. "Allens Neck" – Recekah Hungerford	36
h/o Edward Cole	"Brooke Bottle"	230
Calvert County	pt. "Inland"	3

Rev. George Cook	pt. "Prestons Clifts"	239
	pt. "Gore"	100
Isaac Clare	"Horse Path"	200
	pt. "Elton Head Manor"	143
	"Concord"	161
	"Addition to Horse Path"	40
John Culpepper	"Woolfs Quarter"	40
Thomas Crutchley	"Addition"	50
Benjamin Dixon	"Middle Sex"	100
	"Addition to Middlesex"	95
	"Foxes Walks"	5
11:1766:5 ...		
h/o William Dorumple	"Hap at a Venture"	150
	"Foxes Road"	158
James Duke	"Brooke Place"	171
Samuel Dare	pt. "Angle"	140
	pt. "Gideon & Clevelys Right"	336
	pt. "Smiths Purchase"	119⅓
Benjamin Duke	pt. "Rich Levels"	247
	pt. "Inland"	1
	pt. "Brooke Place Manor"	300
	pt. "Howard & Letchworth"	303
Joseph Dawkins	pt. "Friendship" a/s "Copartnership Rectified" – Rebekah Hungerford, William Dawkins paid	31¼
	"Dicks Cabbin" – Rebekah Hungerford, William Dawkins paid	50
	pt. "Taylors Joy" – Rebekah Hungerford, William Dawkins paid	114
h/o James Dodson	"Huckleberry Hills"	50
	"Littleworth"	21
John Dossey	pt. "Mary Green"	63
	pt. "Dear Quarter"	62½
	pt. "Bennetts Desire"	10
	pt. "Robinsons Rest"	66⅔
Robert Day	pt. "No Name"	150
Benjamin Day	"Frampton"	50
	"Brandon"	57

Nathaniel Dare	pt. "Gideon & Clevelys Right"	160
William Dawkins	"Mary Dukes Doom"	100
James Dawkins	"Josephs Place"	200
11:1766:6 ...		
Mary Dawkins	"Josephs Reserve"	196
Susanah Dare	pt. "Gideon & Clevelys Right"	472
Philip Dossey	pt. "Youngs Mount"	59
	pt. "Youngs Fortune"	40
	"School House" tbc B. Mackall s/o John	100
	resurvey of several tracts	312
	"Tauneys Addition"	132
	"Brigantines Adventure" tbc B. Mackall s/o John	24
w/o William Day	pt. "No Name"	100
Clevely Dare	"Gideon & Clevelys Right"	1199
	pt. "Prestons Clifts"	100
Ellis Dixon	"Hogskin Clifts"	100
Thomas Denton	"Island Neck"	99
	"Puddington"	50
John Dare	pt. "Gideon & Clevelys Right"	100
John Dowell	pt. "Swinfears Rest"	50
	pt. "Lingans Purchase"	100
Richard Deale	pt. "Newington"	200
	pt. "Timberwell"	74
James Deale	pt. "Swinfears Rest"	64½
Daniel Dossey	pt. "Garden"	67
Philip Dossey, Jr.	pt. "Robinsons Rest"	150
11:1766:7 ...		
Francis Dossey	pt. "Bennetts Desire"	50
Jacob Deal	pt. "Upper Bennett"	75
James Dossey	pt. "Garden"	100
	pt. "Robinsons Rest"	64
William Dare	pt. "Swinfins Rest"	250
Thomas Clevely Dare	pt. "Agreement"	150
	"Bite the Biter"	112
Alexander Deale	pt. "Newington"	46
	"Islington"	25

Philip Dowell	pt. "Lingans Purchase"	116
John Dew	pt. "Archers Hays"	43½
James Dossey, Jr.	pt. "Youngs Mount"	100
John Samuel Dossey	pt. "Youngs Attempt"	100
Richard Everist	pt. "Highland"	100
h/o Benjamin Elt	pt. "Elton Head Mannor"	336
Richard Everist, Jr.	pt. "Rocky Neck" – for h/o (N) Pardo	50
	"Foxes Walks" – for h/o (N) Pardo	70
Isaac Essex	pt. "Woolf Trap"	55
11:1766:8 ...		
Robert Ethrington	pt. "Comsey"	92½
Barnaby Eagan	pt. "Brooke Place Mannor"	400
h/o George Fowler	pt. "Tillington"	45½
h/o Thomas Freeman	pt. "Rock Hold"	135
James Frasor	"Hills Hall"	100
Joseph Freeman	"Arnolds Purchase"	50
Col. William Fitzhugh	pt. "Elton Head Mannor"	2500
	pt. "Miles End"	399½
	pt. "Miles Run"	150
	"Hattons Cave"	70
	"Staffords Freehold"	70
	"Round Ponds"	100
	"Leach" or "Smiths Hills"	100
	"Gore"	70
Henry Fryor	pt. "Arnolds Purchase"	50
Robert Freeland	"Mackalls Force"	647
	pt. "Trumans Chance"	232
	"Dosseys Folly"	70
	"Burks Purchase"	50
	pt. "Dear Quarter"	100
Sarah Freeland	pt. "Parkers Clifts"	50
	"Good Luck"	150
Jacob Freeland	pt. "Letchworths Chance"	179
	"Neglect"	125
John Furguson (cnp)	pt. "Griffiths & Govers Pasture"	40
	pt. "Skinners Chance"	30

	pt. "Turners Place"	126
11:1766:9 ...		
Alexander Frasor	"Sterlings Chance"	40
	"Sterlings Nest"	550
Jacob French	pt. "Danvin"	125
Francis Freeland	pt. "Letchworth Chance"	409½
Richard Gibson	pt. "Swinfins Rest"	72
h/o John Griffith	pt. "Welch Pool"	143¾
	pt. "Skinners Chance"	90
John Gibson	pt. "Spittle"	20
	"Additional Spittle"	50
	pt. "Spittle"	70
	"Additional Spittle"	22
John Gardnor	pt. "Johnsons Lott"	100
h/o Samuel Gover	pt. "Aldermason"	150
	"Govers Expectation"	89
	pt. "Welch Pool"	2
Charles Grahame	pt. "Halls Craft"	521
	"Howard"	42
	"Bell"	68
	"Blackwall"	38
	pt. "Hardesty"	180
Joseph Galloway	pt. "Spittle"	20
	"Additional Spittle"	28
Richard Gibson, Jr.	pt. "Lordships Favour"	50
Lewis Griffith	pt. "Watch Pool"	215
	pt. "Anchors Hays"	231
	"Lewis's Slipe & Dews Purchase"	26
	"Long Land"	63
	"All Points"	24
James Gibson	pt. "Additional Spittle"	88
	pt. "Newington"	22
11:1766:10 ...		
h/o Robert Gover (cnp)	pt. "Archors Hays"	190
	"Goughs Purchase" a/s "Goughs Pasture"	50
	"Govers Addition"	167

	"Govers Meadows"	59
	pt. "Dunkirk"	150
	pt. "Exchange"	66
John Griffin	pt. "Robinson"	60
Edward Gantt	pt. "Ordinary"	606
	"Kingsberry March"	130
	"Craft"	90
	pt. "Nortons Purchase"	166⅔
John Gray (Patuxent)	"Marsh Land & Burk Head"	345
	"Hazard"	42
	"Reserve"	50
	pt. "Brooke Adventure"	100
	pt. "Tonottle" a/s "Tuxbury"	100
	"Stinnetts Ramble"	35
Howerton Games	pt. "Johnsons Lott"	50
	"Hazard"	25
Robert Gardner	pt. "Johnsons Lott"	200
	"Woolfs Hole"	50
Samuel Gray	"Norwood"	200
	"Theobush Manning"	50
	pt. "Austins Chance"	91
John Graves	"Stephens Plains"	50
	"Graves's Rehobeth"	111
Edward Gardnor	"Chatham"	80
	pt. "Dorington"	115
	"Short Neck"	76
11:1766:11 ...		
Benjamin Gardenor	pt. "Round Pond Plains"	100
h/o James Truman Greenfield	pt. "Aldermason"	150
	"Addition"	56½
Mary Graves	"Hap Hazard"	135
	"Batchelors Hall"	300
	"Timber Neck"	50
	"Clares Littleworth"	43
Esther Gray (cnp)	"Fishing Creek"	165
	"Chaplin"	100

	"East Fishing Creek"	50
	"Nutts Clifts"	150
	"East Chaplin"	100
h/o Job Hunt	pt. "Upper Bennett"	195
	pt. "Robinson"	13
	pt. "Lordships Favour"	9
James Heigh	pt. "Beakley"	300
	"Forsters Purchase"	150
	pt. "Roberts Chance"	34
	"James's Chance"	40
	"Samuels Addition"	15
	"James's Addition"	21
	"Clarks Hills"	19
	"Little Land"	11
	"Heighs Addition"	15
	"Brooke Place"	300
Thomas Hollingshead	pt. "Kents Freehold"	250
Dr. John Hamilton	"Branford"	150
	pt. "Hardestys Choice"	150
	pt. "Henry Chew"	75
	"Little Gandry"	42
	"Grantham"	200
	"Sams Addition"	78
William Harrison	pt. "Brookes Discovery"	200
	pt. "Islington" – William Hickman	282
Henry Hardesty	pt. "Den"	37
	pt. "Nicholls Chance"	55
11:1766:12 ...		
Joseph Hardesty	pt. "Den"	37½
	pt. "Nichollds Chance"	55
	"Nelsons Reserve"	22
William Hardesty	pt. "Lordships Favour"	75
William Hickman	pt. "Newington"	220
	pt. "Islington"	260
John Hance (cnp)	pt. "Newington"	9
	"Johns Neglect"	128

	"Illingsworths Fortune"	65
Henry House	pt. "Refuse"	50
	"Jensbeys Lott"	46
	"Purchase"	23
Thomas Hunt	pt. "Lordships Favour"	50
William Harrison, Jr.	pt. "Lawreys Reserve"	75
	"Brooke Discovery"	126
	pt. "Coxes Freehold"	128
Henry Harrison	pt. "Swinfins Rest"	100
Thomas Holland	pt. "St. James's Enland"	1138
	pt. "Alexander Pope"	38
George Hall	pt. "Chance"	25
h/o Jacob Hooper	pt. "Taylors Joy"	258
William Harris	pt. "Durvain"	200
	pt. "Illingsworths Fortune"	100
	pt. "Littleworth"	150
	pt. "Tillington"	73
	pt. "Letchworths Chance"	225
Susanah Hoxton	"Homesham"	117
11:1766:13 ...		
Ann Holland	pt. "Abbington"	150
Newman Harvey	pt. "Turnors Place"	126
Benjamin Hance	"Parkers Clifts"	100
	pt. "Warington"	175
	pt. "Agreement"	50
	"Busseys Garden"	175
	pt. "Illington"	250
	"Sewells Purchase"	30
	"Hance Lane"	20
	pt. "Newington"	3
	"Purchase"	154
	"Warings Chance"	56
	pt. "Cedar Branch"	240
	resurvey of several tracts	119½
Benjamin Harris	pt. "Expectation"	100
William Harris, Jr.	"Addition"	100

James Henley	"Smuggs Folly"	80
Joseph Hance	"Warbleton"	404
	pt. "Stockley" a/s resurvey of several tracts	100
David Hellen s/o John	pt. "Elton Head Manor"	200
	"Friendship"	100
	"Jermin Quarter Enlarged"	143
William Hudson	pt. "Arnolds Purchase"	100
James Hellen	pt. "Truswell"	150
Samuel Hance	pt. "Theobush Manning"	189
Walter Hellen	pt. "Hoopers Neck"	275
Robert Jenkins Henry	pt. "St. James's"	300
Thomas Hellen	pt. "Waring"	121
	pt. "Boudleys Chance"	75
	"Busseys Lott"	75
	"Hellens Lott"	12
11:1766:14 ...		
Dr. Leonard Hollyday	"Buzzard Island"	700
	"Addition"	51
	pt. "Arnolds Purchase"	50
Edmund Hungerford	"Hodskins Neck"	100
	"Stephens Land"	100
	"Purchase"	24
	pt. "Desart'"	100
Philip Hunt	pt. "Lordships Favour"	100
Richard Hellen	"Trustwell"	150
	"Melton Lott"	100
	"Persie"	100
	"Harrow on the Hill"	80
	pt. "Rich Levells"	20
h/o Benjamin Johns (cnp)	"Angelica"	600
	pt. "Mears"	200
	"Whittles Rest"	336
	pt. "Desire"	75
	"Chance"	50
	"Parkers Clifts"	180
	pt. "Inland"	2

	"Johnsons Addition"	112
	"Fuller"	300
Joseph Isaac	"Plumb Point"	400
	pt. "Lordships Favour"	205
	"Purchase"	100
William Ireland	pt. "Bridge"	100
	"Georges Desire"	50
	"Addition"	43
	"Angle"	87
	pt. "Pehens Nest"	35
	pt. "Island Plans"	32
	"Lyons Creek"	300
William Johnson s/o George	pt. "Red Hall"	100
h/o Richard Johns	pt. "Billingslys Farme"	136
	"Purchase"	100
	pt. "Youngs Desire"	12
William Ireland, Jr.	"Halls Hills"	650
11:1766:15 ...		
Mary Ireland	pt. "Elton Head Mannor"	200
	"Irelands Hope"	50
	pt. "Prestons Clifts"	108
	pt. "Angle"	88
	pt. "No Name"	100
	"Mill Marsh"	63
John Ireland	pt. "Tillington"	189
	"Woolfs Trap"	45
Thomas Johnson	"Brew House"	260
John Johnson	"Elizabeth"	200
	pt. "Gift"	70
	pt. "Prestons Clifts"	314
William Johnson s/o Jere	pt. "Exchange"	50
Dr. Edward Johnson	"Preston"	200
	"Moffatts Mount"	200
	"Woods Adventure"	50
	"Hays Marsh"	18
	pt. "Poor Land"	185

h/o John Kent	pt. "Rock Hold"	160
James Kirshaw	pt. "Prevent Danger"	100
John Kirshaw	pt. "Prevent Danger"	50
Francis Kirshaw	pt. "Sharpes Outlett"	100
Joseph Kent	pt. "Timberwell"	326
h/o James Leach	"Leaches Freehold"	125
John Lawrence	"Lawreys Addition"	145
	pt. "Islington"	50
William Lyles	pt. "Red Hall"	150
	pt. "Slipe"	8
	pt. "Turners Pasture"	170
h/o Lewis Lewin	pt. "Red Hall"	37½
11:1766:16 ...		
Mary Lyles	pt. "Swinfins Rest" – Henry Harrison	50
John Laveal	"Whittles Rest"	210
Robert Lyles	pt. "Red Hall"	100
Sarah Land	pt. "Homesham"	233
Samuel Lyles	pt. "Lawreys Chance"	50
Jeremiah Maulding	pt. "Parkers Clifts"	250
Thomas Marshall, Jr.	"Coxes Folly"	50
	pt. "Farme"	19
Thomas Marshall 3rd	pt. "Coxes Choice"	50
	pt. "Coxes Choice"	93
Thomas Manning	pt. "Theobald Manor"	112
	pt. "Gunsbey"	168
William Monnett	"Williams Purchase"	206
w/o William McDowell	pt. "Coles Clifts"	50
h/o James Mackall	"Cage"	250
	"Busseys Lott"	100
	"Mackalls Desire"	10
h/o Thomas Morgan	pt. "Desire"	79
	pt. "Grays Chance"	350
	"Fellowship"	160
John Mackall (cnp)	pt. "Morgan"	60
	pt. "Littleworth" – James Morsell	60
	pt. "Mary Green" – James Morsell	55

	"Horse Range"	180
	"Claggetts Desire"	376
	"Desart"	350
James Morsell	"Rattle Snake Hills"	120
	"Chance"	70
	"Labour in Vain" – Henry Gray	100
11:1766:17 ...		
Rousby Miller	pt. "Orchard"	253
Ann Mills	pt. "Wolton"	25
	pt. "Catch"	50
h/o Barbara Mackall	"Brooke Partition"	200
	pt. "Hallowing Point"	200
	pt. "Chance"	75
	pt. "Coursey"	46½
Benjamin Mackall	"Copartnership"	182
	"Chance"	232
	pt. "Hallowing Point"	200
	"Semores Neck"	382
	pt. "Horse Range"	165
	pt. "Sharpes Outlett"	100
	"Thorough Bridge"	250
	"Brooke Choice"	146
	pt. "Dividing Branch"	179
	pt. "Trouble"	27
	pt. "Morocco" – in corn	50
	"Jarusalem"	124
	"Addition to Sharpes Outlett"	112
	pt. "Read"	46½
	pt. "Read & Magruder"	92½
	pt. "Swintons Adventure"	25
Walter Murry (cnp)	pt. "Parkers Clifts"	100
	"Foxes Road"	100
	"Woolfs Quarter"	300
	"Smiths Hogpen"	319
	pt. "St. Leonards" – in corn	175
	"Taylors Disposal"	270

	pt. "Stone Hills"	25
	"Purchase"	22
John Norfolk	"Kidds Levells"	84
	pt. "Irelands Plains"	27
	pt. "Ridge"	100
	pt. "Refuse"	100
	"Refuge"	14
James Norfolk	pt. "Pehens Nest"	50
11:1766:18 ...		
James John Mackall	pt. "Lower Bennett"	500
	pt. "Theobush"	100
	"Corn Hill"	350
	pt. "Alexanders Hope"	200
	pt. "Grays Chance"	200
	pt. "Bone Road"	89
	"Gunsby"	38
	"Cold Harbour"	100
	pt. "Brooke Place"	432
	pt. "Stonesbay"	225
	"Piney Point"	50
	"Exchange"	350
	pt. "Lawreys Rest"	295
	"Lawreys Point" pt. "Lawreys Rest"	100
	"Little Worth"	77
	"Cold Harbour"	200
	pt. "Angle"	350
	"Foxes Walks"	40
	"Bramhall"	500
	"Neglect"	30
	pt. "Godsgrace"	617
	"Meads"	166
	pt. "Evans Land"	200
	pt. "Coles Clifts"	150
	pt. "Prestons Clifts"	63
Margarett Parran late Rawlings (cnp)	"Bethens Loss"	50
	pt. "Elton Head Mannor"	300

	"Cumpton"	75
	"Rawlings Purchase"	60
	"Dearbought"	200
Elizabeth Prindowell	pt. "Parkers Clifts"	100
	pt. "Roberts Addition"	5
	pt. "Roberts Chance"	5½
	pt. "Beakley"	66⅔
Leonard Prindowell	pt. "Roberts Addition"	10
	pt. "Chance"	11
	pt. "Beakley"	133⅓
Mary Parker	"Clay Hammond"	380
	"Wilsons Commons"	29
John Peters	pt. "Upper Bennett"	50
	pt. "Kents Freehold"	50
	pt. "Lordships Favour"	100
	pt. "Danvin & Clares Hundred"	280
11:1766:19 ...		
William Patterson	pt. "Stones Bay"	75
	pt. "Evans Land"	65
Alexander Parran	"Point Patience"	360
	"Addition"	19
h/o Hutcheson Parker	pt. "St. Leonards" – in corn	175
	"Bulmores Branch"	50
	pt. "Stones Hills"	25
Young Parran	pt. "Desart"	349
	"Preston"	400
	pt. "Winfields Resurvey"	207
	"Prestons Neglect"	200
	pt. "Burmingham"	25
	pt. "Parrans Park"	150
	pt. "Morgan"	45
	"Brooke Chance"	100
	pt. "Inland"	2
	"Discovery"	99
Samuel Parran (cnp)	pt. "Winfields Resurvey"	207
	pt. "Burmingham"	25

	pt. "Morgan"	45
	pt. land without name	100
	pt. "Parrans Park"	150
John Robertson (Halls Creek)	pt. "Johnsons Farm"	150
	pt. "Turners Place"	100
	pt. "Griffiths & Govers Pasture"	20
Thomas Rhodes	"Black Robin"	38
Daniel Ross	pt. "Robinsons Rest"	200
Samuel Robinson	"Emmersons Addition"	20
	pt. "Halls Hills"	85
	"Broughton Aspley"	73
John Robertson	pt. "Magruder"	175
Daniel Rawlings	pt. "Eltonhead Manor"	200
11:1766:20 ...		
Thomas Reynolds (cnp)	pt. "Robinson"	191
	pt. "St. Edmonds"	150
	pt. "Robinsons Rest"	368
	pt. "Good Luck"	100
	"Adjoinder" a/s "Adjunction"	10
	pt. "Brooke Discovery"	64
	"Crouders Lott"	60
	"Reserve"	300
	"Foxes Chance"	72
	"Rich Hill"	5½
	"Foxes Home"	30
	"Sterlings Perch"	300
	pt. "Lordships Favour"	285
	pt. "Neglect"	60
	pt. "Coxes Inclosure"	70
	pt. "Foxes Freehold"	142
	"Troublesome"	150
	"Bennetts Refuge"	33
	pt. "Hopewell"	36
	pt. "Abbington Manor"	769
	"Angle Lane"	37
	"Stallings Lott"	31

	pt. "Meadows"	132
	"Thomas & Williams Chance"	107
	pt. "Thatchcomb"	114
	pt. "Lingons Purchase"	8
	pt. "Brooke Neck"	150
	"Stallings Swamp"	10
	pt. "Spittle"	90
	pt. "Hogsdown"	25
	"Meadows"	54
	"Hopewell"	58
	"Bite"	5
	pt. "Robinsons Rest"	150
h/o John Somervell	pt. "Gore"	200
	"Goldens Folly"	75
James Somervell	"Tobys Quarter"	100
	"Rocky Neck"	50
	pt. "Allens Neck"	164
	"Narrow Neck & Gore"	18
	"Swamp"	67
h/o Maryland Skinner	pt. "Newington"	94
	pt. "Millers Folly"	250
John Simmonds	pt. "Rich Bottom"	25
	"Short Hills"	40
h/o George Smith	pt. "Desart"	52
	pt. "Round Bottom Plains"	100
11:1766:21 ...		
h/o Leonard Skinner	"Borders"	77½
	pt. "Dobsons Desire"	25
	pt. "Chance"	27
	pt. "Reserve"	32¼
Dorothy Sollers	"Forked Neck"	110
	"Hyam"	10
William Skinner (cnp)	pt. "Scrap"	38
	pt. "Prestons Desire"	25
	pt. "Chance"	27
	pt. "Reserve"	32¼

	pt. "Border Enlarged"	77½
James Skinner	pt. "Border Enlarged"	77½
	pt. "Dotsons Desire"	25
	pt. "Chance"	27
	pt. "Reserve"	33¼
Truman Skinner	pt. "Blind Tom"	40
	"Addition"	60
	"Tauneys Right"	150
h/o Adderton Skinner	pt. "Blind Tom"	32
	"Tauneys Delight"	70
	pt. "Mary Green"	36
	"Gore"	48
	"Millers Folly"	250
	"Neglect"	25
Elizabeth Skinner	pt. "Tauneys Right"	150
	"Scrap"	62
	pt. "Reserve"	121
	pt. "Newington"	94
h/o Samuel Sly	pt. "Morrocco" – in corn	100
Alexander Somervell	"Foxes Den"	50
	"Bartholomews Neck"	50
	pt. "Smiths Purchase"	238½
Joseph Strickland	pt. "Robinsons Rest"	50
William Sollers	pt. "Dorington"	182½
	"Boudleys Chance"	34
11:1766:22 ...		
Joshua Sedwick	pt. "Neighbourhood"	150
	"Adjoinder"	50
	pt. "Mortons Purchase"	83⅓
Joseph Skinner	pt. "Orchard"	50
	"Border Enlarged"	77½
	"Dotsons Desire"	25
	"Chance"	27
	"Reserve"	32¼
Josias Sunderland	pt. "Swinfins Rest"	250
Josias Sunderland, Jr.	pt. "Upper Bennett"	50

h/o Richard Stallings	"Thachcom"	236
	pt. "Robinsons Rest"	100
James Sewall	pt. "Dear Quarter"	62½
	pt. "Chance"	72½
	"Maidens Delight"	200
	pt. "Cope Hall"	80
John Standforth	pt. "Poor Land"	104
h/o John Skinner	"Halls Hills"	877½
	"Sneaking Point"	50
	"Lingans Purchase"	94
	pt. "Hamiltons Park"	33
William Sandsbury	pt. "Archers Hays"	40
Joseph Smith, Jr.	pt. "Turners Pasture"	50
	pt. "Smiths Pasture"	100
	pt. "Archers Hays"	15½
William Smith	pt. "Smiths Chance"	50
	pt. "Turners Place"	50
	pt. "Mordyke"	50
Mordecai Smith	pt. "Smiths Chance"	100
	pt. "Welch Pool"	72½
	pt. "Turners Place"	50
	pt. "Callinder"	77
Joseph Smith	"Mordyke"	50
11:1766:23 ...		
w/o John Stone	pt. "Defence"	65
John Stallings	pt. "Upper Bennett"	25
Ellis Slater	pt. "Lawreys Reserve"	100
Stephen Stamp	pt. "Red Hall"	125
Mary Smith (PG)	"Good Prospect"	50
	"Lands Land"	192
	"Addition"	28
Benjamin Skinner	<n/g>	<n/g>
Clement Smith	pt. "Halls Craft"	486
Nicholas Swamsted	pt. "Lordships Favour"	100
Thomas Stallings	pt. "Swinfears Rest"	64½

h/o John Smith	pt. "Halls Craft" – P. T. Blake	665
	pt. "Batchellors Quarter"	250
	"Soldiers Fortune"	200
	pt. "Ordinary"	75
	pt. "Grantham"	20
	1½ lots in Lower Marlbro	1½
	pt. "Dowdswell Manor"	400
	pt. "Ordinary"	80½
	"Hazard" – Dr. Hamilton	18
Stockett Sunderland	pt. "Lawreys Chance or Resurvey"	100
John Davis Scarth	pt. "Robinsons Rest"	50
Benjamin Sedwick	pt. "Bulmores Branch" a/s "Right"	475
	pt. "Eltonhead Manor"	200
Stephen Stewart	pt. "Illingsworths Fortune"	200
11:1766:24 ...		
Jonathan Slater	pt. "Halls Revenge"	28
	1 lot in Lower Marlbro	1
	"Sampsons Dividend"	158
	pt. "Mannington"	25
	"Neglect"	50
Jacob Tucker	"Tuckers Thicksett"	200
	pt. "Chance"	50
h/o Philip Thomas	"Majors Choice"	500
Joseph Talbott, Jr.	pt. "Expectation"	100
h/o John Tanyhill	pt. "Calender"	123
	pt. "Friendship"	150
	"Cooper"	150
Joseph Talbutt	pt. "Freemans Chance"	123
	pt. "Tillington"	150
	"Batchelors Fortune"	200
John Talbutt	pt. "Expectation"	50
Catharine Thornby	pt. "Dunkirk"	50
Edward Talbutt	pt. "Tillington"	415½
Gideon Turnor	"Bowdleys Chance"	91
Thomas Talbott	pt. "Expectation"	100
Benjamin Tasker, Esq.	"Hard Travell"	300

h/o Miles Tauney	"Berry"	600
	"Long Point"	100
	"Wooden Point"	25
	pt. "Letchworth"	50
	pt. "Angle"	3
John Tucker	pt. "Neighbourhood"	82½
Joseph Vanswearingan	pt. "Neighbourhood"	26
	"Prevent Danger"	100
11:1766:25 ...		
William Vermilion	"Creeds Chance"	64
Joseph Wilson	"Tamot"	300
	pt. "Forsters Purchase"	150
	pt. "Robinson"	136
	pt. "Addition to Spittle"	8
	pt. "Peahens Nest"	40
	pt. "Cedar Branch"	50
	"Letchworths Cyprus"	200
	pt. "Bowen" – for h/o (N) King	230
	pt. "Arnolds Purchase"	100
	pt. "Brookes Adventure"	150
	pt. "Cedar Branch"	75
	"Stones Lott"	50
	pt. "Arnolds Purchase"	50
h/o Joseph Wilson, Jr.	pt. "Lower Bennett"	400
	"Mackalls Desire"	78
h/o John Ward	"Goldsons Inheritance"	150
	"Velchee's Rest"	50
John Wood	pt. "Magruder" – Eleanor Sly	150
Aaron Williams, Jr.	pt. "Friendship Rectified"	200
	pt. "Swinfins Adventure"	50
Hilleary Wilson	pt. "Robinson"	200
Dr. Aaron Williams	"Williams's Hardship"	250
	"Williams's Rest"	50
	"Little Fields"	25
	pt. "Friendship Rectified"	150
	pt. "Swinfins Adventure"	100

James Weems, Jr.	"Success, Tauneys Ease, & Stokeley"	200
h/o Joseph Wilkinson	pt. "Godsgrace"	120
	pt. "Stokeley"	70
John Waters	pt. "Stokley"	419
	pt. "Gunterton"	40
	"Murtle Point"	7
John Willing	pt. "Taylors Joy"	128
	"Jarusalem"	108
	pt. "Rich Bottom"	25
Francis Woolf, Jr.	pt. "Theobald Manor"	50
	pt. "Grays Chance"	50
11:1766:26 ...		
Richard Ward	pt. "Swinfins Rest"	116
James Weems	pt. "Magruder"	410
	"Hogs Haunt"	50
	"Mauldins Luck"	25
	pt. "Busseys Orchard"	400
	pt. "Inland"	1
	"Meadows Preserved"	46
	pt. "Bucks Chance"	150
	"Parkers Fortune" a/s "Chance"	263
	"Bigger for Crumpton"	1055
	pt. "Godsgrace"	100
	pt. "Morrocco, Catterton Lott, & Barbers Delight"	294
	1 lot in Huntingtown	1
	pt. "Cuckoldds Miss"	60
	"Youngs Desire"	25
	pt. "Youngs Fortune"	60
	pt. "Youngs Attempt"	62
	"Pinman Mare"	50
	pt. "Reserve"	50
	pt. "Trouble"	10
	pt. "Magruder"	40
James Weems s/o David (cnp)	"Bingan"	200
	"Green House"	155
	"Chews Purchase"	145

	"Grantham"	45
	"Marshall Addition"	70
Basil Williamson	"Lingans Adventure"	310
Edward Wood	pt. "Woods Adventure"	150
	"Titmarsh"	100
	pt. "Poor Land"	11
Jonah Winfield	pt. "Lands Land"	112
	pt. "Johnsons Farme"	100
Thomas Wells	pt. "Grantham Hall"	155
	"Arthers Hall"	44
Rev. James Williamson	"Den"	726
	"Foxes Nettles"	20
	pt. "Batchelors Quarter"	420
h/o Roger Wheeler	pt. "Henry Chew"	23½
	"Coxcomb"	150
	"Coxhead"	50
	pt. "Newington"	19
	"Smiths Conveyance"	60
11:1766:27 ...		
John Wilkinson	pt. "Henry Chew"	400
Thomas Wilson	pt. "St. Edmonds"	163
	pt. "Neglect"	16½
Leonard Wood	pt. "Woods Adventure"	100
Edward Wilson	"Dear Quarter"	25
	pt. "Robinsons Rest"	150
John Weems	pt. "Dowdswell"	600
	pt. "Chance"	25
William White	pt. "Smiths Joy"	100
Philemon Young	pt. "Henry Chew"	175
	1 lot in Lower Marlbro	1
	pt. "Youngs Desire"	50
Parker Young	"Hop Yard"	150
	"Punch"	150
	pt. "Youngs Desire"	25
	pt. "Hoopers Neck"	275

John Yoe	pt. "Rattle Snake Hills"	100
	pt. "Inland"	100
	"Hutchesons Chance"	50
	pt. "Orchard"	40
Ann Griffith	pt. "Grays Chance"	50
John Scott	pt. "His Lordship's Favour"	100
Mary Smith	"Smell Reward"	111
11:1766:<unnumbered>	**<blank>**	

11:1767:1 ...		Acres
Eleanor Alton	pt. "Hardesty's Choice"	50
h/o David Arnold	pt. "Henry Chew"	290
	pt. "Abington"	350
	pt. "Hardesty's Choice"	130
w/o Samuel Austin	pt. "Cox's Choice"	140
	pt. "Farm"	20
h/o Michael Askew	pt. "Lawry's Chance"	118
James Alnutt	pt. "Trueman's Chance"	153
William Alnutt	pt. "Trueman's Chance"	156
	pt. "Agreement"	100
Samuel Austin	pt. "Cox's Choice"	117
Roger Brooke	pt. "Brooke Place Manor"	1096
John & Isaac Baker	"Devils Woodyard"	150
Jacob Bowen	pt. "Elton Head Manor"	300
John Beveridge	"Dearbought"	21
John Binion (Richard Ireland)	pt. "Desart"	198
Abraham Bowen	pt. "Dividing Branch"	169½
David Bowen	pt. "Dividing Branch"	189
Isaac Bowen	pt. "Dividing Branch"	190
Roger Brooke s/o Roger	"White Marsh" – James Fraizer	68
h/o James Brooke	pt. "Brooke's Adventure"	350
	"<t> Branch"	75
11:1767:2 ...		
Charles Bowen	pt. "Neighbourhood"	74
Basil Bowen	pt. "Forge" – Ezra Freeman	50
Henry Broome	pt. "Austin's Chance"	65
	pt. "Howard & Letchworth"	200
	pt. "Broad Point"	10
	pt. "Austin's Addition"	23
William Blackburn	pt. "Black Pasture"	50
h/o James Bowen	pt. "Dividing Branch"	210
h/o Abraham Barnes	"Fisher's Orchard"	255
	"Bran Fry"	100
Roger Brooke, Jr. (cnp)	pt. "Bowen"	70
	"Knowles Branch"	98

	"Tawney's Addition"	123
	"Stone's Hills"	50
Edward Blackburn	"Readly" – Thomas Blackburn	100
Thomas Broome	"Rich Neck"	52
	"Mary's Widowhood"	30
	pt. 'Young's Attempt" tbc Jos. Wilson, Sr.	100
	"Hap at a Venture" – tbc Jos. Wilson, Sr.	50
	pt. "Horse Range" tbc Jos. Wilson, Sr.	125
	"Addition to Island Neck"	30
John Broome	pt. "Island Neck"	500
	"Stone's Bay"	200
	"Adventure"	82½
	"Broad Point"	140
	pt. "Austin's Addition"	30
Ann Bond	"Middle Fuller"	200
	"Lower Fuller"	200
	"Lower Bennett"	250
Isabella Barton	pt. "Upper Bennett"	50
w/o John Beckett	"Selby's Cliffs"	200
	pt. "Mears"	200
	pt. "Gunterton"	250
	pt. "Hardesty"	50
	"Poppy Gray"	40
Jesse Bowen	"Lamberth"	96
h/o Richard Blake	<t>	<t>
11:1767:3 ...		
Mary Bond	pt. "Hodsdown"	275
	"Micham"	243
	pt. "Brooke Partition"	104
	"Lawry's Chance"	135
Richard Bond	pt. "Lawry's Chance"	50
	"Small Land"	6¾
	"Small Reward"	111
Samuel Chew	"Letchworth's Chance"	550
	pt. "Upper Bennett"	456
	"Lane & Gore"	51½

Joseph Chilton	"Terra in Aqua"	4
Philip Lloyd Chew	"Popping Jay" – Samuel Chew	540
Bennett Chew	"Chew's Fortune"	49
Josias Crosby	pt. "Archers Hays"	30
	pt. "Goughs Purchase"	60
Michael Catterton	pt. "Lingans Purchase"	125
Richard Chew	"Stallings Lott"	150
	pt. "Robinson's Rest"	250
Henry Camden	"Highland"	200
	"Chance"	70
John Chesly	pt. "Batchelors Quarter"	420
Michael Culpepper	"Venture"	16
Young Cox	pt. "Little Land"	17
	pt. "Coxes Inclosure"	65
	pt. "Cops Hall"	25
	pt. "Coxes Freehold"	120
	pt. "Merry Greenwood"	163
	"Musqueto Point" – Edward Johnson	46
	pt. "Good Luck"	10
	"Turnor's Chance" – Edward Johnson	50
	"Hatchet"	25
John Clare	pt. "Eltonhead Manor" – Mary Clare	157
	pt. "Lawry's Chance" – Betty Clare	130
Calvert County School	"Security"	87
	pt. "Orchard"	100
h/o Charles Clagget	"Blinkhorn"	300
	pt. "Foxes Road"	42
	pt. "Allens Neck"	36
h/o <t> Cole	"<t> Battle" – Roger Brooke, Jr.	230
11:1767:4 ...		
Rev. George Cook	pt. "Preston Clifts" – Francis Lauder	239
	pt. "Gore" – Francis Lauder	100
Isaac Clare	"Horse Path"	200
	pt. "Elton Head Manor"	143
	"Concord"	161
	"Addition to Horse Path"	40

Thomas Crutchley	"Addition"	50
John Culpepper	"Wolfs Quarter"	40
Benjamin Dixon	"Middlesex"	100
	"Addition to Middlesex"	95
	"Foxes Walks"	5
h/o William Dorumple	"Hap at a Venture"	150
	"Foxes Road"	158
James Duke	"Brooke Place"	171
Samuel Dare	pt. "Angle"	140
	pt. "Gideon & Cleverly Right"	336
	pt. "Smith's Purchase"	119⅓
Benjamin Duke	pt. "Rich Levels"	247
	pt. "Inland"	1
	pt. "Brooke Place Manor"	300
	pt. "Howard & Letchworth"	303
Joseph Dawkins	pt. "Friendship" a/s "Copartnership Rectified"	31¼
	"Dick's Cabbin"	50
	pt. "Taylor's Joy"	114
h/o James Dodson	"Huckleberry Hills"	50
	"Littleworth"	21
John Dossey	pt. "Marys Green"	63
	pt. "Dear Quarter"	62½
	pt. "Bennetts Desire"	10
	pt. "Robinson's Rest"	66⅔
Robert Day	pt. "No Name"	150
Benjamin Day	"Frampton"	50
	"Brandon"	57
Nathaniel Dare	pt. "Gideon & Cleverly's Right" – Samuel Dare	160
William Dawkins	"Mary Duke's Doom"	100
James Dawkins	"<t> Place"	<t>
11:1767:5 ...		
Susanna Dare	pt. "Gideon & Cleverly's Right"	472

Philip Dossey	pt. "Young's Mount" – James Dossey, Jr.	59
	pt. "Youngs Fortune" – James Dossey, Jr.	40
	"Schoolhouse" – Benjamin Mackall s/o John	100
	resurvey of several tracts: • John Mackall s/o John – 104 a. • James Mackall – 104 a.	312
	"Tawneys Addition": • John Mackall s/o John – 44 a. • James Mackall s/o John – 44 a.	132
	"Brigantine's Adventure" – Benjamin Mackall s/o John	24
w/o William Day	pt. "No Name"	100
Cleverly Dare	"Gideon & Cleverly's Right"	1199
	pt. "Preston Clifts"	100
Ellis Dixon	"Hogskins Cliffs"	100
Thomas Denton	"Island Neck"	99
	"Puddington"	50
John Dare	pt. "Gideon & Cleverly's Right"	100
John Dowell	pt. "Swinfears Rest"	50
	pt. "Lingan's Purchase"	100
Richard Deale	pt. "Newington"	200
	pt. "Timberwell"	74
James Deale	pt. "Swinfears Rest"	64½
Daniel Dossey	pt. "Garden"	67
Philip Dossey, Jr.	pt. "Robinsons's Rest"	150
Francis Dossey	pt. "Bennetts Desire"	50
Jacob Deale	pt. "Upper Bennett"	75
James Dossey	pt. "Garden"	100
	pt. "Robinson's Rest"	64
William Dare	pt. "Swinfins Rest"	250
Thomas Cleverly Dare	pt. "Agreement"	150
	"Bite the Biter"	112
Alexander Deale	<t>	46
	<t>	25
11:1767:6 ...		
John Dew	pt. "Archers Hays"	43½
James Dossey, Jr.	pt. "Youngs Mount"	100

John Samuel Dossey	pt. "Youngs Attempt"	100
Richard Everist	pt. "Highland" – Anes Henry Scott (50 a.)	100
h/o Benjamin Elt	pt. "Eltonhead Manor"	336
Richard Everist, Jr. for h/o (N) Pardo	pt. "Rocky Neck" – John Pardo	50
	"Foxes Walk" – John Pardo	70
Isaac Essex	pt. "Wolf Trap"	55
Robert Ethrington	pt. "Comsey"	92½
Barnaby Eagan	pt. "Brooke Place Manor"	400
h/o George Fowler	pt. "Tillington"	45½
h/o Thomas Freeman	pt. "Rockhold"	135
James Fraizer	"Hills Hall"	100
Joseph Freeman	"Arnolds Purchase"	50
Col. William Fitzhugh	pt. "Eltonhead Manor"	2500
	pt. "Miles End"	399½
	pt. "Miles Run"	150
	"Hatton's Cave"	70
	"Stafford's Freehold"	70
	"Round Ponds"	100
	"Leach" or "Smith's Hills"	100
	"Gore"	70
Henry Fryer	pt. "Arnold's Purchase" – John Brooke	50
Robert Freeland	"Mackalls Force" – Frisby Freeland (323½ a.)	647
	pt. "Truemans Chance"	232
	"Dossey's Folly"	70
	"Burks Purchase"	50
	pt. "Dear Quarter"	100
Sarah Freeland	pt. "Parker's Clifts" – James Sewall	50
	"Good Luck" – James Sewall	150
Jacob Freeland	pt. "Letchworth's Chance"	<t>
	"Neglect"	<t>
<t>	<t>	<t>
11:1767:7 ...		
Alexander Fraizer	"Sterling's Chance"	40
	"Sterlings Nest"	550
Jacob French	pt. "Danvin"	125
Francis Freeland	pt. "Letchworth's Chance"	409½

Richard Gibson	pt. "Swinfins Rest"	72
h/o John Griffith	pt. "Welch Pool"	143¾
	pt. "Skinners Chance"	90
John Gibson	pt. "Spittle"	20
	"Additional Spittle"	50
	pt. "Spittle"	70
	"Additional Spittle"	22
John Gardner	pt. "Johnson's Lott"	100
h/o Samuel Gover	pt. "Aldemason" – Ben Kid Wilson & Perscile Gover	150
	"Govers Expectation" – Ben Kid Wilson & Perscile Gover	89
	pt. "Welch Pool" – Ben Kid Wilson & Perscile Gover	2
Charles Graham	pt. "Halls Craft"	521
	"Howard"	42
	"Bell"	68
	"Blackwall"	38
	pt. "Hardesty"	180
Joseph Galloway	"Spittle"	20
	"Additional Spittle"	28
Richard Gibson	pt. "Lordship's Favour"	50
Lewis Griffith	pt. "Welch Pool"	215
	pt. "Archers Hays"	231
	"Lewis Slipe & Dews Purchase"	26
	"Long Lane" – William Lyles (32 a.)	63
	"Allpoints"	24
James Gibson	pt. "Additional Spittle"	88
	pt. "Newington"	22
h/o Robert Gover	pt. "Archers Hays"	190
	"Goughs Purchase" a/s "Gough's Pasture"	50
	"Govers Addition"	167
	"Govers Meadows"	59
	pt. "Dunkirk"	150
	pt. "Exchange"	66

11:1767:7 [!]   ...

Edward Gantt	pt. "Ordinary"	606
	"Kinsburys Marsh"	130
	"Craft"	90
Thomas Gray	pt. "Wolton"	75
William Gray s/o Thomas	"Grays Addition" – from Thomas Gray	109
John Gray (Patuxent)	"Marsh Land & Burkhead"	345
	"Hazard"	42
	pt. "Brooke Adventure"	100
	pt. "Tonottle" a/s "Tuxbury"	100
William Gray	"Reserve" – from John Gray (Patuxent)	50
	"Stennetts Ramble" – from John Gray (Patuxent)	35
Howerton Games	pt. "Johnson's Lott"	50
	"Hazard"	25
Robert Gardner	pt. "Johnson's Lott" – John Gardner (100 a.)	200
	"Wolf's Hole"	50
Samuel Gray	"Norwood"	200
	"Theobush Manning"	50
	pt. "Austin's Chance"	91
John Greeves	"Stephen's Plains"	50
	"Greeves's Rehobeth"	111
Edward Gardner	"Chatham" or "Chilton"	80
	pt. "Dorington" or pt. "Forked Neck"	115
	"Shortneck"	76
Benjamin Gardiner	pt. "Round Pond Plains"	100
h/o James T. Greenfield	pt. "Aldermason"	150
	"Addition"	56½
Mary Graves	"Hap Hazard" – John Dawkins s/o James (90 a.)	135
	"Batchelor's Hall"	300
	"Timber Neck"	50
	"Clares Littleworth"	43
Esther Gray	"Fishing Creek"	165
	"Chaplain"	100
	"East Fishing Creek"	50
	"Nutts Clifts"	150
	"East Chaplain"	100

h/o Job Hunt	pt. "Upper Bennett"	195
	pt. "Robinson"	13
	pt. "Lordship's Favour"	<t>
11:1767:8 ...		
James Heigh	pt. "Beakly"	300
	"Foster's Purchase"	150
	pt. "Robert's Chance"	34
	"James's Chance"	40
	"Samuel's Addition"	15
	"James's Addition"	21
	"Clark's Hills"	19
	"Little Land"	11
	"Heigh's Addition"	15
	"Brooke Place" – Thomas Holdsworth Heighe	300
John Hamilton	"Branford"	150
	pt. "Hardesty's Choice"	150
	pt. "Henry Chew"	75
	"Little Ganery"	42
	"Grantham"	200
	"Sam's Addition"	78
	"Hazard" – from h/o Col. John Smith	18½
William Harrison	pt. "Brooke's Discovery"	200
Henry Hardesty	pt. "Den"	37
	pt. "Nicholls Chance"	55
Joseph Hardesty	pt. "Den"	37½
	pt. "Nicholl's Chance"	55
	"Nelson's Reserve"	22
William Hardesty	pt. "Lordship's Favour"	75
William Hickman	pt. "Newington"	220
	pt. "Islington"	260
	pt. "Islington" – from William Harrison	282
h/o John Hance	pt. "Newington"	9
	"John's Neglect"	128
	pt. "Illingsworth's Fortune"	65
Henry Howes (cnp)	pt. "Refuse"	50
	"Jensby's Lott"	46

	"Purchase"	23
Thomas Hunt	pt. "Lordship's Favor"	50
William Harrison, Jr.	pt. "Laurie's Reserve"	75
	"Brooke's Discovery"	126
	pt. "Cox's Freehold"	128
Henry Harrison	pt. "Swinfin's Rest"	100
	pt. "Swinfin's Rest" – from Mary Lyles	50
Thomas Holland	"<t> Enlargd"	1138
	"<t> Hope"	38
11:1767:9 ...		
h/o Jacob Hooper	pt. "Taylor's Joy"	258
William Harris	pt. "Durain"	200
	pt. "Illingsworth's Fortune"	100
	pt. "Littleworth" – disclaim 73 a.	150
	pt. "Tillington"	73
	pt. "Letchworth's Chance"	275
Susanna Hoxton	pt. "Homesham"	117
Ann Holland	pt. "Abington"	150
Newman Harvey	pt. "Turner's Place"	126
Benjamin Hance	"Parkers Clifts"	100
	pt. "Warington"	175
	pt. "Agreement"	50
	"Bussey's Garden"	175
	pt. "Illington"	250
	"Hance Lane"	20
	pt. "Newington"	3
	"Purchase"	154
	"Waring's Chance"	56
	resurvey of several tracts	119½
Benjamin Harris	pt. "Expectation"	100
William Harris, Jr.	"Addition"	1000
James Henley	"Smuggs Folly"	80
Joseph Hance	"Warbleton"	404
	pt. "Stockley" a/s resurvey of several tracts	100
David Hellen s/o John (cnp)	pt. "Eltonhead Manor"	200
	"Friendship" – Joseph Dawkins (25 a.)	100

	"Jermin Quarter Enlarg'd"	143
James Hellen	pt. "Truswell"	150
Walter Hellen	pt. "Hooper's Neck"	275
Samuel Hance	pt. "Theobush Manning"	189
h/o Robert Jenkins Henry	pt. "Saint James's"	300
Edmund Hellen	pt. "Waring" – from Thomas Hellen	121
	pt. "Boudley's Chance" – from Thomas Hellen	75
	"Bussey's Lott" – from Thomas Hellen	75
	"Hellen's Lott" – from Thomas Hellen	12
Dr. Leonard Holliday	"Buzzard Island"	700
	"Addition"	<t>
	pt. "Arnold's Purchase"	<t>
11:1767:10 ...		
Edmund Hungerford	"Hogskin Neck"	100
	"Stephen's Land"	100
	"Purchase"	24
	pt. "Desart"	100
Richard Hellen	pt. "Truswell"	150
	"Milton Lott"	100
	"Persia"	100
	"Harrow on the Hill"	80
	pt. "Rich Levells"	20
David Hellen s/o Richard	"Gully" – lies in an elder survey	63½
h/o Benjamin Johns (cnp)	"Angelica" – • Kensey Johns – 200 a. • Benjamin Johns – 400 a.	600
	pt. "Mears" – Kensey Johns	200
	"Whittle's Rest" – Richard Johns	336
	pt. "Devise" – Richard Johns	75
	"Chance" – Richard Johns	50
	"Parker's Clifts" – Richard Johns	180
	pt. "Inland" – • Kensey Johns – 1 a. • Benjamin Johns – 1 a.	2
	"Johns's Addition" – Benjamin Johns	112

	"Fuller" – • Jacob Freeland – 100 a. • Robert Freeland – 200 a.	300
h/o Joseph Isaac	"Plumb Point"	400
	pt. "Lordship's Favor"	205
	"Purchase"	100
Col. William Ireland	pt. "Bridge"	100
	"George's Desire"	50
	"Addition"	43
	"Angle"	87
	pt. "Peahen's Nest"	35
	pt. "Island Plains"	32
	"Lyon's Creek"	300
William Johnson s/o George	pt. "Redd Hall"	100
h/o Richard Johns	pt. "Billingsley's Farme"	136
	"Purchase"	100
	pt. "Young's Desire"	12
William Ireland s/o Thomas	"Hall's Hills"	550
Mary Ireland	pt. "Eltonhead Manor"	200
	pt. "Preston's Clifts"	108
	pt. "Angle"	88
	pt. "No Name"	100
	"Mill Marsh"	63
John Ireland	pt. "Tillington"	189
	"Wolf's Trap"	45
Thomas Johnson	"Brewhouse"	200
John Johnson	<t>	200
	<t>	70
	<t>	314
11:1767:11 ...		
Dr. Edward Johnson	"Preston"	200
	"Moffatts Mount" – old rent	200
	"Woods Adventure"	50
	"Hays Marsh"	18
	pt. "Poor Land"	185
Richard Ireland	"Ireland's Hope" – from Mary Ireland	50

h/o John Kent	pt. "Rockhold"	160
James Kirshaw	pt. "Prevent Danger"	100
John Kirshaw	pt. "Prevent Danger"	50
Francis Kirshaw	pt. "Sharpes Outlett"	100
	pt. "Concord"	63
Joseph Kent	pt. "Timberwell"	326
h/o James Leach	"Leach's Freehold"	125
John Lawrence	"Lawrie's Addition"	145
	pt. "Islington"	50
William Lyles	pt. "Redd Hall"	150
	pt. "Stripe"	8
	pt. "Turner's Pasture"	170
h/o Lewis Lewin	pt. "Redd Hall"	37½
John Laveal	"Whittle's Rest" – disclaim 50 a.	210
Robert Lyles	pt. "Red Hall"	100
Sarah Lane	pt. "Homesham"	233
Samuel Lyles	pt. "Lawrie's Chance"	50
Jeremiah Maulden	pt. "Parker's Clifts"	250
w/o Thomas Marshall	"Coxe's Folly"	50
	pt. "Farme"	19
Thomas Marshall 3rd	pt. "Coxes Choice"	50
	pt. "Coxes Choice"	93
Thomas Manning	pt. "Theobald Manor"	112
	pt. "Gunsby"	168
William Monnitt	"William's Purchase"	<t>
11:1767:12 ...		
h/o James Mackall	"Cage"	250
	"Bussey's Lott"	100
	"Mackall's Desire"	10
h/o Thomas Morgan	pt. "Devise"	79
	pt. "Gray's Chance"	350
	"Fellowship"	160
John Mackall	pt. "Morgan" – disclaimed	60
	"Horse Range"	180
	"Clagget's Desire"	376
	"Desert" – he says only 300 a. per patent	350

James Morsell	"Rattle Snake Hills"	120
	"Chance"	70
	pt. "Littleworth" – from John Mackall	60
	pt. "Mary Green" – from John Mackall	55
Rousby Miller	pt. "Orchard"	253
Ann Mills	pt. "Wolten"	25
	pt. "Catch"	50
h/o Barbara Mackall	"Brooke Partition"	200
Benjamin Mackall	pt. "Hallowing Point" – from h/o Barbara Mackall	200
	pt. "Chance" – from h/o Barbara Mackall	75
	pt. "Coursey" – from h/o Barbara Mackall	46½
	"Copartnership"	182
	"Chance"	232
	pt. "Hallowing Point"	200
	"Seamor's Neck"	382
	pt. "Horse Range"	165
	pt. "Sharpe's Outlett"	100
	"Thorough Bridge"	250
	"Brooke Choice"	146
	pt. "Dividing Branch"	179
	pt. "Trouble"	27
	pt. "Morocco" – in corn	50
	"Addition to Sharpe's Outlett"	112
	pt. "Read"	46½
	pt. "Read & Magruder"	92½
Walter Murray	pt. "Parker's Clifts" – for h/o (N) Smith	100
	"Foxes Road" – for h/o (N) Smith	100
	"Wolfs Quarter" – for h/o (N) Smith	300
	"Smiths Hog Pen" – for h/o (N) Smith	319
	pt. "St. Leonards" – in corn; for h/o (N) Smith	175
	"Taylor's Disposal" – for h/o (N) Smith	270
	pt. "Stone's Hills" – for h/o (N) Smith	25
	"Purchase" – for h/o (N) Smith	22
John Norfolk (cnp)	"Kidd's Levels"	84
	pt. "Irelands Plains"	27
	pt. "Ridge"	100

	pt. "Refuse"	100
	\<t>	14
\<t>	\<t>	\<t>
11:1767:13 ...		
James John Mackall	pt. "Lower Bennett"	500
	pt. "Theobush Manor"	100
	"Cornhill"	350
	pt. "Alexanders Hope"	200
	pt. "Grays Chance"	200
	pt. "Bone Road"	89
	"Gunsby"	38
	"Cold Harbor"	100
	pt. "Brooke Place"	432
	pt. "Stone's Bay"	225
	"Piney Point"	50
	"Exchange"	350
	"Laurie's Point" pt. "Lawries Rest"	100
	"Littleworth"	77
	"Cold Carbey"	200
	pt. "Angle"	350
	pt. "Laurie's Rest"	295
	"Foxes Walks"	40
	"Bram Hall"	500
	"Neglect"	30
	pt. "Godsgrace"	617
	"Meads"	166
	pt. "Evans's Land"	200
	pt. "Cole's Clifts"	150
	pt. "Prestons Clifts"	63
	"Cedar Branch" – from Benjamin Hance	240
	"Sewall's Purchase" – from Benjamin Hance	30
Margaret Parran	"Bathen's Loss"	50
	pt. "Eltonhead Manor" – John Rawlings	300
	"Cumpton"	75
	"Rawlings's Purchase"	60
	"Dearbought"	200

Elizabeth Prindowell	pt. "Parker's Clifts"	100
	pt. "Roberts's Addition"	5
	pt. "Roberts Chance"	5½
	pt. "Beakly"	66⅔
Leonard Prindowell	pt. "Robert's Addition"	10
	pt. "Robert's Chance"	11
	pt. "Beakly"	133⅔
Mary Parker	"Clay Hammond"	380
	"Wilson's Commons"	29
John Peters	pt. "Upper Bennett" – Samuel Chew	50
	pt. "Kent's Freehold"	50
	pt. "Lordship's Favor"	100
	pt. "Danvin & Clares Hundred"	280
William Patterson	pt. "Stone's Bay"	75
	pt. "Evans's Land"	65
h/o Alexander Parran	"Point Patience"	360
	"Addition"	19
h/o Hutcheson Parker	pt. "St. Leonards" – in corn	175
	"Bulmores Branch"	50
	pt. "Stone's Hills"	25
Samuel Parran	pt. "Winfields Resurvey"	<t>
	<t>	<t>
11:1767:14 ...		
Young Parran	pt. "Desart"	349
	"Preston"	400
	pt. "Winfields Resurvey"	207
	"Preston's Neglect"	200
	pt. "Bermingham"	25
	pt. "Parran's Park"	150
	pt. "Morgan"	45
	"Brooke Plains"	100
	pt. "Inland"	2
	pt. "Discovery"	99
John Robinson (Halls Creek)	pt. "Johnson's Farm"	150
	pt. "Turner's Place"	100
	pt. "Griffiths & Gover's Pasture"	20

Thomas Rhodes	"Black Robin"	38
Daniel Ross	pt. "Robinsons Rest"	200
Thomas Reynolds	pt. "Robinson"	191
	pt. "St. Edmunds"	150
	pt. "Robinsons Rest"	368
	pt. "Good Luck"	100
	"Adjoinder" a/s "Adjunction"	10
	pt. "Brookes Discovery"	64
	"Crouders Lott"	60
	"Reserve"	300
	"Foxes Chance"	72
	"Rich Hill"	5½
	"Foxes Home"	30
	"Sterling's Perch"	300
	pt. "Lordship's Favor"	275
	pt. "Neglect"	60
	pt. "Coxes Inclosure"	70
	pt. "Foxes Freehold"	142
	"Troublesome"	150
	"Bennetts Refuge"	33
	pt. "Hopewell"	36
	pt. "Abington Manor"	769
	"Angle Lane"	37
	"Stallings Lott"	31
	pt. "Meadows"	132
	"Thomas & William's Chance"	101
	pt. "Thatchcomb"	114
	pt. "Lingan's Purchase"	8
	pt. "Brooke's Neck"	150
	"Stallings Swamp"	10
	pt. "Spittle" – Richard Bond	90
	pt. "Hogdsdown" – Richard Bond	25
	"Meadows"	54
	"Hopewell"	58
	"Bite"	5
	pt. "Robinson's Rest"	150

Samuel Robertson	"Emmertons Addition"	20
	pt. "Hall's Hills"	85
	pt. "Broughton Ashley"	73
John Robinson	pt. "Magruder" – Thomas Goslin Hutchings	175
Daniel Rawlings	pt. "Eltonhead Manor"	200
James Somervill	\<t>	100
	\<t>	\<t>
11:1767:15 ...		
h/o Maryland Skinner	pt. "Newington"	94
	pt. "Millers Folly"	250
John Simmonds	pt. "Rich Bottom"	25
	pt. "Short Hills"	40
h/o Leonard Skinner	"Borders"	77½
	pt. "Dodson's Desire"	25
	pt. "Chance"	27
	pt. "Reserve"	32¼
h/o George Smith	pt. "Desart"	52
	pt. "Round Bottom Plains"	100
Dorothy Sollers	"Forked Neck"	110
	"Hyam"	10
William Skinner	pt. "Scrap"	38
	pt. "Preston's Desire"	25
	pt. "Chance"	27
	pt. "Reserve"	32¼
	pt. "Broder Enlarg'd"	77½
James Skinner	pt. "Border Enlarg'd"	77½
	pt. "Dodson's Desire"	25
	pt. "Chance"	27
	pt. "Reserve"	33½
Trueman Skinner	pt. "Blind Tom"	40
	"Addition"	60
	"Tauney's Right"	150
h/o Adderton Skinner (cnp)	pt. "Blind Tom"	32
	"Tawney's Delight"	70
	pt. "Mary Green"	36
	"Gore"	36

	pt. "Miller's Folly"	48
	"Neglect"	25
Elizabeth Skinner	pt. "Tawney's Right"	150
	pt. "Scrap"	62
	pt. "Reserve"	121
	pt. "Newington"	94
William Sly	pt. "Morocco" – in corn; from h/o Samuel Sly	100
Alexander Somerveill	"Foxes Den"	50
	"Bartholomew's Neck"	50
	pt. "Smiths Purchase"	238½
	pt. "Gore" – from John Somervill	100
	"Golden Folly" – from John Somervill	75
Joseph Strickland	pt. "Robinson's Rest"	50
William Sollers	pt. "Dorington"	182½
	"Bowdly's Chance"	34
Joseph Skinner	pt. "Orchard"	<t>
	<t>	<t>
11:1767:16 ...		
Joshua Sedwick	pt. "Neighbourhood"	150
	"Adjoinder"	50
	pt. "Norton's Purchase"	83¼
Josias Sunderland	pt. "Swinfins Rest"	250
Josias Sunderland, Jr.	pt. "Upper Bennett"	50
h/o Richard Stallings	"Tatchcomb"	236
	pt. "Robinson's Rest"	100
James Sewall	pt. "Deer Quarter"	62½
	pt. "Chance"	72½
	"Maiden's Delight"	200
	pt. "Cops Hall"	80
John Standforth	pt. "Poor Land"	104
h/o John Skinner	pt. "Hall's Hills"	877½
	"Sneaking Point"	50
	pt. "Lingan's Purchase"	94
	pt. "Hamilton's Park"	33
William Sansbury	pt. "Archer's Hays"	40

Joseph Smith, Jr.	pt. "Turner's Pasture"	50
	pt. "Smiths Pasture"	100
	pt. "Archer's Hays"	15½
William Smith	pt. "Smith's Chance"	50
	pt. "Turner's Place"	50
	pt. "Mordyke"	50
Mordecai Smith	pt. "Smith's Chance"	100
	pt. "Welchpool"	72½
	pt. "Turner's Place"	50
	pt. "Calender"	77
Joseph Smith	pt. "Mordyke"	50
w/o John Stone	pt. "Defence"	65
John Stallings	pt. "Upper Bennett"	25
Ellis Slater	pt. "Lawrie's Reserve"	100
Stephen Stamp	pt. "Red Hall"	125
Clement Smith	pt. "Hall's Craft"	486
Nicholas Swamstead	pt. "Lordship's Favour"	100
Thomas Stallings	pt. "Swinfin's Rest"	64½
11:1767:17 ...		
h/o Col. John Smith	pt. "Hall's Craft"	665
	pt. "Batchelors Quarter"	250
	"Soldier's Fortune"	200
	pt. "Ordinary"	75
	pt. "Grantham"	20
	1½ lots in Lower Marlborough	1½
	pt. "Dowdeswell Manor"	400
	pt. "Ordinary"	80½
Benjamin Sedwick	pt. "Bulmore's Branch" a/s "Right"	475
	pt. "Eltonhead Manor"	200
Johnathan Slater	pt. "Halls Revenge"	28
	1 lot in Lower Marlbro	1
	"Sampsons Dividend" – Thomas Cleverly Dare	158
	pt. "Mannington" – Thomas Cleverly Dare	25
	"Neglect" – Thomas Cleverly Dare	50
Stephen Steward	pt. "Illingsworth's Fortune"	200

Jacob Tucker	"Tucker's Thickett"	200
	pt. "Chance"	50
Eleanor Sly	pt. "Magruder"	150
h/o Philip Thomas	"Major's Choice"	500
Joseph Talbutt, Jr.	pt. "Expectation"	100
John Tannehill	pt. "Calender"	123
	"Friendship"	150
	"Cooper"	150
Joseph Talbutt	pt. "Freeman's Choice"	123
	pt. "Tillington"	150
	"Batchelor's Fortune"	200
John Talbutt	pt. "Expectation"	50
Catharine Thornbury	pt. "Dunkirk" – Col. Ireland	50
Edward Talbutt	pt. "Tillington"	415½
John Turner	pt. "Bowdley's Chance" – from Gideon Turner	91
Thomas Talbutt	pt. "Expectation"	100
Benjamin Tasker, Esq.	"Hard Travell"	300
John Tucker	<t>	<t>
11:1767:18 ...		
Joseph Vanswearingan	pt. "Neighbourhood" – John Kinbugrin holds the land	26
	"Prevent Danger" – John Kinbugrin holds the land	100
George Wheeler	"Berry" – for h/o Miles Tauney	600
	"Long Point" – for h/o Miles Tauney	100
	"Wooden Point" – for h/o Miles Tauney	25
	pt. "Letchworth" – for h/o Miles Tauney	50
	pt. "Angle" – for h/o Miles Tauney	3
Joseph Wilson (cnp)	"Tarnott"	300
	pt. "Foster's Purchase"	150
	pt. "Robinson"	136
	pt. "Addition to Spittle"	8
	pt. "Peahen's Nest"	40
	pt. "Cedar Branch"	50
	"Letchworth's Cyprus"	200
	pt. "Bowen" – for h/o (N) King	230
	pt. "Arnolds Purchase"	100

	pt. "Brookes Adventure"	150
	pt. "Cedar Branch"	75
	"Stone's Lott"	50
	pt. "Arnolds Purchase"	50
h/o Joseph Wilson, Jr.	pt. "Lower Bennett" – James Duke (211 a.)	400
	"Mackall's Desire" – James Duke	78
John Ward	"Velchee's Rest"	50
Samuel Ward	"Goldson's Inheritance" – from h/o John Ward	150
Aaron Williams, Jr.	pt. "Friendship Rectified"	200
	pt. "Swinfins Adventure"	50
	pt. "Young's Desire" – from Phil. Young	50
Hilleary Wilson	pt. "Robinson"	200
Dr. Aaron Williams	pt. "Williams's Hardship"	175
	"Williams's Rest"	50
	"Littlefield"	25
	pt. "Friendship Rectified"	25
	pt. "Swinfin's Rest"	50
James Weems, Jr.	"Success, Tauney's Ease, & Stockley"	200
	"Partnership"	75
h/o Joseph Wilkinson	pt. "Godsgrace"	120
	pt. "Stockley"	70
John Waters	pt. "Stockley"	419
	pt. "Gunterton"	40
	"Mirtle Point"	7
John Willing	pt. "Taylor's Joy"	128
	"Jerusalem"	108
	"<t> Bottom"	25
	<t>	<t>
11:1767:19 ...		
Richard Ward	pt. "Swinfin's Rest"	116
James Weems (cnp)	pt. "Magruder"	410
	"Hogs Haunt"	50
	"Maulden's Luck"	25
	pt. "Bussey's Orchard"	400
	pt. "Inland"	1
	"Meadows Preserved"	46

	pt. "Buck's Chance"	150
	1 lot in Hunting Town	1
	pt. "Cuckold's Miss"	60
	"Young's Desire"	25
	pt. "Young's Fortune"	60
	pt. "Young's Attempt"	62
	"Penmarmure"	50
	pt. "Reserve"	50
	pt. "Trouble" – lies in elder survey	10
	pt. "Magruder"	40
James Weems s/o David	"Ringan"	200
	"Green House"	155
	"Chews Purchase"	145
	"Grantham"	45
	"Marshall's Addition"	70
Basil Williamson	"Lingan's Adventure"	310
Edward Wood	pt. "Woods Adventure"	150
	"Titmarsh"	100
	pt. "Poor Land"	11
Jonah Winfield	pt. "Lands Land"	112
	pt. "Johnson's Farme"	100
Thomas Wells	pt. "Grantham Hall"	155
	"Arthur's Hall"	44
Rev. James Williamson	"Den"	726
	"Foxes Nettles"	20
	pt. "Batchelor's Quarter"	420
h/o Roger Wheeler	pt. "Henry Chew"	237
	"Coxcomb"	150
	"Coxhead"	50
	pt. "Newington"	109
	"Smith's Conveyance"	60
John Wilkinson	pt. "Henry Chew"	400
Thomas Wilson	pt. "St. Edmunds"	163
	pt. "Neglect"	16½
Leonard Wood	pt. "Woods Adventure"	100

Edward Wilson	"Deer Quarter"	25
	pt. "Robinson's Rest"	150
<t> Weems	<t>	<t>
11:1767:20 ...		
William Winnull	pt. "Norton's Purchase" – from Thomas Gray	166⅔
William Hunton Wood	pt. "Arnolds Purchase" – from William Hudson	100
Francis Whittington	pt. "Halls Hills" – from William Ireland	100
Francis Williams	pt. "Inland" – from John Yoe	100
	"Hutchins's Chance" – from John Yoe	50
	pt. "Orchard" – from John Yoe	40
Ithamor Williams	pt. "Swinfins Rest" – from Dr. Aaron Williams	50
	pt. "Williams's Hardship" – from Dr. Aaron Williams	75
	pt. "Friendship Rectified" – from Dr. Aaron Williams	125
Philemon Young	pt. "Henry Chew"	175
	1 lot in Lower Marlbro	1
Parker Young	"Hopyard"	150
	"Punch"	150
	pt. "Young's Desire"	25
	pt. "Hooper's Neck"	275
Mary Yoe	pt. "Rattle Snake Hills" – from John Yoe	100
Thomas Crumpton	"Jerusalem" – from Benjamin Mackall	124
	pt. "Swinfin's Adventure" – from Benjamin Mackall	25
	"Parker's Fortune" a/s "Chance" – from James Weems	263
	"Bigger" – from James Weems	1055
	pt. "Godsgrace" – from James Weems	100
	pt. "Morocco, Catterton's Lott, & Barber's Delight"	294
Henry Gray	"Labour in Vain" – from James Moncle	100
Mary Smith (PG)	"Good Prospect"	50
	"Lands Land"	192
	"Addition"	28
John Scott (PG)	pt. "His Lordships Favor"	100
Mary Smith	"Small Reward"	111

11:1767:<unnumbered>	Recapitulation
	Certification: by John Thomas (Quaker)
11:1767:<unnumbered>	Certification (continued)
11:1767:<unnumbered>	<blank>

11:1768:1 ...		Acres
Eleanor Alton	pt. "Hardesty's Choice" – now John Alton	50
h/o David Arnold	pt. "Henry Chew"	290
	pt. "Abington"	350
	pt. "Hardestys Choice"	130
w/o Samuel Austin	pt. "Coxes Chance"	140
	pt. "Farme"	20
Ann Askew	pt. "Lawrey's Chance"	118
James Alnutt	pt. "Trueman's Chance"	153
William Alnutt	pt. "Trueman's Chance"	156
	pt. "Agreement"	100
Samuel Austin	pt. "Coxes Chance"	117
Roger Brooke	pt. "Brooke Place Manor"	1096
John & Isaac Baker	"Devils Woodyard"	150
Jacob Bourn	pt. "Eltonhead Manor"	300
John Beveridge	"Dear Bought"	21
Abraham Bowen	pt. "Dividing Branch"	169½
David Bowen	pt. "Dividing Branch"	189
Isaac Bowen	pt. "Dividing Branch"	190
11:1768:2 ...		
John Brooke	pt. "Brooke's Adventure" – from h/o Js. Brooke	116⅓
	pt. "Cedar Branch" – from h/o Js. Brooke	25
	pt. "Arnolds Purchase" – from Henry Fryer	50
Jesse Bourn	pt. "Eltonhead Manor"	1167
Henry Broome	pt. "Austins Chance"	65
	pt. "Howard & Letchworth"	200
	pt. "Broad Point"	10
	pt. "Austins Addition"	23
William Blackburn	pt. "Black Pasture"	50
James Bowen	pt. "Dividing Branch" – from h/o Js. Bowen	105
Thomas Bowen	pt. "Dividing Branch" – from h/o J. Bowen	105
Col. Abraham Barnes (SM)	"Fisher's Orchard"	255
	"Bran Fry"	100
Roger Brooke, Jr. (cnp)	pt. "Bowen"	70
	"Knowles's Branch"	98
	"Tawneys Addition"	123

	"Stones Hills" tbc Raphael Tawney	50
	"Brooke Battle" – from h/o Edward Cole	230
	pt. "Brookes Adventure" – from h/o James Brooke	233⅓
	pt. "Cedar Branch" – from h/o James Brooke	50
Thomas Blackburn	"Readly"	100
Thomas Broome	"Rich Neck"	52
	"Mary's Widowhood"	30
	"Addition to Island Neck"	30
John Broome	pt. "Island Neck"	500
	pt. "Stone's Bay"	200
	"Adventure"	82½
	"Broad Point"	140
	pt. "Austin's Addition"	23
11:1768:3 ...		
Ann Bond	"Middle Fuller"	200
	"Lower Fuller"	200
	pt. "Lower Bennett"	250
Isabella Barton	pt. "Upper Bennett"	50
w/o John Beckett	"Selby's Clifts"	200
	pt. "Meair"	200
	pt. "Gunterton"	250
	pt. "Hardesty"	50
	"Poppy Gray"	40
Jesse Bowen	"Lambeth"	94
h/o Richard Blake	pt. "Upper Bennett"	557
	pt. "St. Edmunds"	200
	pt. "Lordship's Favor"	192
	pt. "Neglect"	50
Mary Bond	pt. "Hogsdown"	275
	"Micham"	243
	pt. "Brooke Partition"	104
	"Lawrey's Chance"	135
Richard Bond (cnp)	pt. "Lawrey's Chance"	50
	"Small Land"	6¾
	"Small Reward"	111
	pt. "Spittle" – from Thomas Reynolds	90

	pt. "Hogsdown" – from Thomas Reynolds	25
Samuel Chew	pt. "Letchworth's Chance"	550
	pt. "Upper Bennett"	456
	"Lane & Gore"	51½
	pt. "Upper Bennett" – from John Peters	50
Joseph Chilton	"Tenua in Ague" a/s "Terra in Aqua"	4
Samuel Chew (AA)	"Popping Gay" – from P. L. Chew	540
Bennett Chew	"Chew's Fortune"	49
Josias Crosby	pt. "Archer's Hays"	30
	pt. "Gough's Purchase"	60
11:1768:4 ...		
Michael Caterton	pt. "Lingans Purchase"	125
Richard Chew	"Stallings Lott" – not to be found	150
	pt. "Robinson's Rest" – not to be found	250
Henry Camden	"Highland"	200
	"Chance"	70
Elizabeth Chesly w/o John	pt. "Batchelor's Quarter"	420
Michael Culpepper	"Venture"	16
Young Cox	pt. "Little Land"	17
	pt. "Cox's Inclosure"	65
	pt. "Cop's Hall"	25
	pt. "Cox's Freehold"	120
	pt. "Merry Green Wood"	163
	pt. "Good Luck"	10
	"Hatchet"	25
Betty Clare	pt. "Lawry's Chance" – from John Clare	130
Mary Clare	pt. "Eltonhead Manor" – from John Clare	157
Calvert County School	"Security"	87
	pt. "Orchard"	100
h/o Charles Claggett	"Blink Horn" tbc Joseph Dawkins	300
	pt. "Fox's Road" tbc Joseph Dawkins	42
	pt. "Allen's Neck" tbc Rebecca Hungerford	36
Calvert County	pt. "Inland"	3
Isaac Clare (cnp)	"Horse Path"	200
	pt. "Eltonhead Manor"	143
	"Concord"	161

	"Addition to Horsepath"	40
John Culpepper	"Wolf's Quarter"	40
Thomas Crutchley	"Addition"	50
h/o Benjamin Dixon	"Addition to Middlesex"	95
	"Foxes Walks"	5
11:1768:5 ...		
Andrew Duke	"Middlesex" – from Benjamin Dixon	100
h/o William Dorumple	"Hap at a Venture"	150
	pt. "Fox's Road"	158
James Duke	pt. "Brooke Place"	171
	pt. "Lower Bennett" – from h/o Jos. Wilson, Jr.	211
	"Mackall's Desire" – from h/o Jos. Wilson, Jr.	78
Samuel Dare	pt. "Angle"	140
	pt. "Cleverly & Gideon's Right" – should be 342 a.	336
	pt. "Smith's Purchase"	119⅓
	pt. "Gideon & Cleverly's Right" – from Nathan Dare	160
Benjamin Duke	pt. "Rich Levells"	247
	pt. "Inland"	1
	pt. "Brooke Place Manor"	300
	pt. "Howard & Letchworth"	303
Joseph Dawkins	pt. "Partnership" a/s "Copartnership Rectified" tbc Rebecca Hungerford	31¼
	"Dick's Cabbin"	50
	pt. "Taylor's Joy" tbc Rebecca Hungerford	114
	pt. "Friendship" – from D. Hellen s/o John	25
h/o James Dodson	"Huckleberry Hills"	50
	"Littleworth"	21
John Dossey	pt. "Mary Green"	63
	pt. "Dear Quarter"	62½
	pt. "Bennetts Desire"	10
	pt. "Robinson's Rest"	66⅔
Robert Day	pt. "No Name"	150
Benjamin Day	"Framton"	50
	"Brandon"	57
William Dawkins	"Mary's Dukedom"	100

James Dawkins	"Joseph's Place"	200
Mary Dawkins	"Joseph's Reserve" tbc Joseph Dawkins	196
Susanna Dare	pt. "Gideon's & Cleverly's Right"	472
11:1768:6 ...		
Philip Dossey	pt. resurvey of several tracts	104
	pt. "Tauney's Addition"	44
William Day	pt. "No Name"	100
Cleverly Dare	pt. "Gideon & Cleverly's Right"	1199
	pt. "Preston's Clifts"	100
Ellis Dixon	"Hogskin Cliffts"	100
Thomas Denton	"Island Neck"	99
John Dare	pt. "Gideon & Cleverlys Right"	100
John Dowell	pt. "Swinfin's Rest"	50
	pt. "Lingan's Purchase"	100
Richard Deale	pt. "Newington"	200
	pt. "Timberwell"	74
James Deale	pt. "Swinfin's Rest"	64¼
Daniel Dossey	pt. "Garden"	67
Philip Dossey, Jr.	pt. "Robinson's Rest"	150
Francis Dossey	pt. "Bennetts Desire"	50
Jacob Deale	pt. "Upper Bennett"	75
James Dossey	pt. "Garden"	100
	pt. "Robinson's Rest"	64
William Dare	pt. "Swinfin's Rest"	250
Thomas Cleverly Dare	pt. "Agreement"	150
	"Bite the Biter"	112
	"Sampson's Dividend" – from Jonathan Slater; should be only 150 a.	158
	pt. "Mannington" – from Jonathan Slater	25
	"Neglect" – from Jonathan Slater	50
Philip Dowell	pt. "Lingan's Purchase"	116
11:1768:7 ...		
Alexander Deale	pt. "Newington"	46
	pt. "Islington"	25
John Dew	pt. "Archer's Hays"	43½

James Dossey, Jr.	pt. "Young's Mount"	100
	pt. "Young's Mount" – from P. Dossey	59
	pt. "Youngs Fortune" – from P. Dossey	40
Richard Everist	pt. "Highland"	50
h/o Benjamin Elt	pt. "Eltonhead Manor" tbc Ann Elt	336
Isaac Essex	pt. "Wolf Trap"	55
Robert Ethrington	pt. "Comsey"	92½
Barnaby Eagan	pt. "Brooke Place Manor"	400
George Fowler	pt. "Tillington"	45½
Ezra Freeman	pt. "Forge" – from Basil Bowen	50
Thomas Freeman	pt. "Rockhold"	135
James Fraizer	"Hill's Hall"	100
	"White Marsh" – from Roger Brooke s/o Roger	68
Joseph Freeman	pt. "Arnolds Purchase"	50
Col. William Fitzhugh	pt. "Eltonhead Manor"	2500
	pt. "Mile's End"	399½
	pt. "Mile's Run"	150
	"Hatton's Cave"	70
	"Stafford's Freehold"	70
	"Round Ponds"	100
	"Leach" or "Smith's Hills"	100
	"Gore"	70
Jacob Freeland	pt. "Letchworth's Chance"	179
	"Neglect"	125
	pt. "Fuller" – from h/o Benjamin Johns	100
11:1768:8 ...		
Robert Freeland	pt. "Mackall's Force" tbc Peregrine Freeland	323½
	pt. "Trueman's Chance"	232
	"Dosseys Folly"	70
	"Burk's Purchase"	50
	pt. "Dear Quarter"	100
	pt. "Fuller" – from h/o Benjamin Johns	200
Frisby Freeland	pt. "Mackall's Force"	323½
John Ferguson	pt. "Griffiths & Gover's Pasture"	40
	pt. "Skinner's Chance"	30
	pt. "Turner's Place"	126

Alexander Fraizer	"Sterlings Chance"	40
	"Sterlings Nest"	550
Jacob French	pt. "Danvin"	125
Francis Freeland	pt. "Letchworth's Chance" – should be 306 a. & tbc Gabriel Child	409½
Richard Gibson	pt. "Swinfin's Rest"	72
	pt. "Lordship's Favour" – from R. Gibson, Jr.	50
h/o John Griffith	pt. "Welch Poole"	143¾
	pt. "Skinner's Chance"	90
John Gibson	pt. "Spittle"	90
	pt. "Additional Spittle"	72
John Gardner	pt. "Johnson's Lott"	100
Charles Grahame, Esq.	pt. "Hall's Craft"	521
	"Howard"	42
	"Bell"	68
	"Blackwall"	38
	pt. "Hardesty"	180
Joseph Galloway	pt. "Spittle"	20
	pt. "Additional Spittle"	28
Lewis Griffiths	pt. "Welch Poole" tbc John Tannehill (86 a.)	215
	pt. "Archer's Hays"	231
	"Lewis's Slipe & Dews Purchase"	26
	"Long Lane"	31
	"All Points"	24
11:1768:9 ...		
James Gibson	pt. "Additional Spittle"	85
	pt. "Newington"	22
h/o Robert Gover	pt. "Archer's Hays"	490
	"Goughs Purchase" a/s "Goughs Pasture"	50
	"Gover's Addition"	167
	"Gover's Meadow"	59
	pt. "Dunkirk"	150
	pt. "Exchange"	66
John Griffin	pt. "Robinson"	60
Edward Gantt (cnp)	pt. "Ordinary"	606
	"Kingsbury Marsh"	130

	"Craft"	90
Thomas Gray	pt. "Wolton"	75
William Gray s/o Thomas	"Grays Addition"	109
John Gray (Patuxent)	"Marsh Land & Burkhead"	345
	"Hazard"	42
	pt. "Brooke's Adventure"	100
	pt. "Jonottle" a/s "Tuxbury"	100
William Gray	"Reserve"	50
	"Stennetts Ramble"	35
Howerton Games	pt. "Johnson's Lott"	50
	"Hazard"	25
Robert Gardiner	pt. "Johnson's Lott"	100
	"Wolf's Hole"	50
John Gardiner	pt. "Johnson's Lott" – from Robert Gardiner	100
Samuel Gray	"Norwood"	200
	"Theobush Manning"	50
	pt. "Austins Chance"	91
John Graves	"Stevens Plains"	50
	"Greeves's Rehobeth"	111
11:1768:10 ...		
Edward Gardner	"Chilton" or "Chatham"	80
	pt. "Forked Neck" or "Dorington" – should be 50 a.	115
	"Short Neck"	76
Benjamin Gardiner	pt. "Round Pond Plains"	100
h/o James T. Greenfield	pt. "Aldermason"	150
	"Addition"	56½
Mary Graves	pt. "Hap Hazard"	45
	"Batchelor's Hall"	300
	"Timber Neck"	50
	"Clare's Littleworth"	43
Esther Gray	"Fishing Creek"	165
	"Chaplain"	100
	"East Fishing Creek"	50
	"Nutt's Clifts"	150
	"East Chaplain"	100

h/o Job Hunt	pt. "Upper Bennett"	195
	pt. "Robinson" tbc Hillary Willson	13
	pt. "Lordship's Favor" tbc Hillary Willson	9
Thomas Hollingshead	pt. "Kent's Freehold"	250
James Heighe	pt. "Beakley"	300
	"Foster's Purchase"	150
	pt. "Robert's Chance"	34
	"James's Chance"	40
	"Samuel's Addition"	15
	"James's Addition"	21
	"Clarke's Hills"	19
	"Little Land"	11
	"Heighe's Addition"	15
Thomas Holdsworth Heighe	pt. "Brooke Place" – from James Heighe	300
James Dawkins s/o James	pt. "Hap Hazard" – from Mary Graves	90
William Harrison	pt. "Brooke's Discovery"	200
Joseph Hardesty	pt. "Den"	37½
	pt. "Nichols's Chance"	55
	"Nelson's Reserve"	22
11:1768:11 ...		
h/o Dr. John Hamilton	"Branford" tbc Dr. John Hamilton Smith	150
	pt. "Hardestys Choice" tbc Dr. John Hamilton Smith	150
	pt. "Henry Chew" tbc Dr. John Hamilton Smith	75
	"Little Ganery"	42
	"Grantham" tbc Gavin Hamilton Smith	200
	"Sam's Addition" tbc Gavin Hamilton Smith	78
	"Hazard" – from h/o Col. John Smith; tbc Gavin Hamilton Smith	18½
Henry Hardesty	pt. "Den"	37
	pt. "Nichols's Chance"	55
William Hardesty	pt. "Lordship's Favour"	75
William Hickman	pt. "Newington"	220
	pt. "Islington"	260
	pt. "Islington" – from W. Harrison	282

h/o John Hance	pt. "Newington"	9
	"John's Neglect"	128
	pt. "Illingsworth's Fortune"	65
Henry Howes	pt. "Refuse"	50
	"Jensby's Lott"	46
	"Purchase"	23
Thomas Hunt	pt. "Lordship's Favor"	50
William Harrison, Jr.	pt. "Lawrey's Reserve"	75
	pt. "Brooke's Discovery"	126
	pt. "Cox's Freehold"	128
Henry Harrison	pt. "Swinfen's Rest"	100
	pt. "Swinfen's Rest" – from Mary Lyles	50
Thomas Holland	pt. "St. James's Enlargd"	1138
	pt. "Alexander's Hope"	38
George Hall	pt. "Chance"	25
Abraham Hooper	pt. "Taylor's Joy"	258
Susanna Hoxton	pt. "Homesham" tbc Walter Hoxton	117
Ann Holland	pt. "Abington"	150
11:1768:12 ...		
William Harris	pt. "Durain"	200
	pt. "Illingsworth's Fortune"	100
	pt. "Littleworth"	150
	pt. "Tillington"	73
	pt. "Letchworth's Chance"	275
Newman Harvey	pt. "Turner's Place"	126
Benjamin Hance	"Parker's Clifts"	100
	pt. "Warington"	175
	pt. "Agreement"	50
	pt. "Bussey's Garden"	175
	pt. "Illington"	250
	"Hance Lane"	20
	pt. "Newington"	3
	"Purchase"	154
	"Waring's Chance"	56
	resurvey of several tracts	119½
Benjamin Harris	pt. "Expectation"	100

William Harris, Jr.	"Addition"	100
James Henley	"Smuggs Folly"	80
Joseph Hance	"Wabbleton"	404
	pt. "Stockley" a/s resurvey of several tracts	100
David Hellen s/o John	pt. "Eltonhead Manor"	200
	pt. "Friendship"	75
	"Jermyn Quarter Enlarged"	143
James Hellen	pt. "Truswell"	150
Samuel Hance	pt. "Theobush Manning"	189
Walter Hallen	pt. "Hooper's Neck"	275
h/o Robert Jenkins Henry	pt. "St. James's" tbc John Makall (St. Leonards)	300
Edmund Hellen	pt. "Waring"	121
	pt. "Bowdley's Chance"	75
	"Bussey's Lott"	75
	"Hellen's Lott"	12
Dr. Leonard Holliday	"Buzzard Island"	700
	"Addition"	51
	pt. "Arnolds Purchase"	50
11:1768:13 ...		
Edmund Hungerford	"Hogskin Neck"	100
	pt. "Stephens Land"	100
	"Purchase"	24
	pt. "Desart"	100
Philip Hunt	pt. "Lordship's Favour"	100
Richard Hellen	pt. "Trustwell"	150
	"Milton's Lott"	100
	"Persia"	100
	"Harrow on the Hill"	80
	pt. "Rich Levell"	20
David Hellen s/o Richard	"Gully" – lies in elder surveys	63½
Thomas Goslin Huchins	pt. "Magruder" – from John Robinson	175
Kensey Johns (AA)	pt. "Angelica" – from h/o Benjamin Johns	200
	pt. "Mears" – from h/o Benjamin Johns	200
	pt. "Inland" – from h/o Benjamin Johns	1
Benjamin Johns (cnp)	pt. "Angelica" – from h/o Benjamin Johns	400
	"Johns's Addition" – from h/o Benjamin Johns	112

	pt. "Inland" – from h/o Benjamin Johns	1
Richard Johns	"Whittle's Rest" – from h/o Benjamin Johns	336
	pt. "Devise" – from h/o Benjamin Johns	75
	"Chance" – from h/o Benjamin Johns	50
	"Parker's Clifts" – from h/o Benjamin Johns	180
h/o Joseph Isaac	"Plumb Point"	400
	pt. "Lordship's Favor"	205
	"Purchase"	100
Col. William Ireland	pt. "Bridge"	100
	"George's Desire"	50
	"Addition"	43
	"Angle"	87
	pt. "Peahen's Nest"	35
	pt. "Irland Plains"	32
	"Lyon's Creek"	300
	"Dunkirk" – from Catherine Thornbury	50
William Johnson s/o George	pt. "Redd Hall"	100
h/o Richard Johns	pt. "Billingsley's Farm" tbc Abraham Bowen	136
	"Purchase"	100
	pt. "Young's Desire"	12
William Ireland s/o Thomas	pt. "Hall's Hills"	550
11:1768:14 ...		
Mary Ireland	pt. "Eltonhead Manor"	200
	pt. "Preston's Clifts"	108
	pt. "Angle"	88
	pt. "No Name"	100
	"Mill Marsh"	63
John Ireland	pt. "Tillington"	189
	"Wolf Trap"	45
Thomas Johnson	"Brewhouse"	260
John Johnson	"Elizabeth"	200
	pt. "Gift"	70
	pt. "Preston's Clifts"	314
William Johnson s/o Jere	pt. "Exchange"	150
Dr. Edward Johnson (cnp)	"Preston"	200
	"Moffatts Mount"	200

	"Woods Adventure"	50
	"Hays Harsh"	18
	pt. "Poor Land"	185
	"Musqueto Point" – from Young Cox	46
	"Turner's Chance" – from Young Cox	50
Richard Ireland	"Irelands Hope" – from Mary Ireland	50
	pt. "Desart" – from John Binion	198
h/o John Kent	pt. "Rockhold"	160
James Kirshaw	pt. "Prevent Danger"	100
John Kirshaw	pt. "Prevent Danger"	50
Francis Kirshaw	pt. "Sharpe's Outlett"	100
	pt. "Concord"	63
Joseph Kent	pt. "Timberwell"	326
	pt. "Additional Spittle" – from J. Gibson	50
Rev. Francis Lauder	pt. "Preston's Clifts" – from George Cooke	239
	pt. "Gore" – from George Cooke	100
h/o James Leach	"Leaches Freehold"	125
John Lawrence	pt. "Laury's Addition"	145
	pt. "Islington"	50
h/o Lewis Lewin	pt. "Redd Hall"	37½
11:1768:15 ...		
William Lyles	pt. "Red Hall"	150
	pt. "Stripe"	8
	pt. "Turner's Pasture"	170
	pt. "Long Lane" – from Leonard Griffiths	32
John Laveal	pt. "Whittles Rest"	210
Robert Lyles	pt. "Red Hall"	100
Sarah Lane	pt. "Homesham"	233
Samuel Lyles	pt. "Lawreys Chance"	50
Jeremiah Maulden	pt. "Parker's Clifts"	250
John Mackall s/o John	pt. resurvey of several tracts – from P. Dossey	104
	pt. "Tauney's Addition" – from P. Dossey	44
James Mackall s/o John	pt. resurvey of several tracts – from P. Dossey	104
	pt. "Tauney's Addition" – from P. Dossey	44
Benjamin Mackall s/o John	"Schoolhouse" – from P. Dossey	100
	"Brigantine's Adventure" – from P. Dossey	24

Eliza Marshall w/o Thomas, Jr.	"Cox's Folly"	50
	pt. "Farm"	19
Thomas Marshall 3rd	pt. "Cox's Choice"	50
	pt. "Cox's Choice"	93
John Manning	pt. "Theobalds Manor"	112
	pt. "Gunsby"	168
William Monnett	"Williams Purchase"	206
Jane Macdowell	pt. "Cole's Clifts"	50
h/o James Mackall	"Cage"	250
	"Bussey's Lott"	100
	"Mackall's Desire"	10
h/o Thomas Morgan	pt. "Desire"	79
	pt. "Gray's Chance"	350
	"Fellowship"	160
John Mackall (St. Leonards)	pt. "Morgan"	60
	"Horse Range"	180
	"Clagget's Desire"	376
	"Desert"	350
11:1768:16 ...		
James Morsell	"Rattle Snake Hills"	120
	"Chance"	70
	pt. "Littleworth"	60
	pt. "Mary Green"	55
Rousby Miller	pt. "Orchard"	253
Ann Mills	pt. "Wolton"	25
	pt. "Catch"	50
h/o Barbara Mackall	"Brooke Partition"	200
Benjamin Mackall (Holland Point) (cnp)	"Copartnership"	182
	"Chance"	232
	pt. "Hallowing Point"	200
	"Seamor's Neck"	382
	pt. "Horse Range"	165
	pt. "Sharpe's Outlett"	100
	"Thorough Bridge"	250
	"Brooke Choice"	146
	pt. "Dividing Branch"	179

	pt. "Trouble"	27
	pt. "Morrocco" – in corn	50
	"Addition to Sharpe's Outlett"	112
	pt. "Read"	46½
	pt. "Read & Magruder"	92½
	pt. "Hallowing Point" – from h/o Barbara Mackall	200
	pt. "Chance" – from h/o Barbara Mackall	75
	pt. "Coursey" – from h/o Barbara Mackall	46½
James John Mackall	pt. "Lower Bennett"	500
	pt. "Theobush Manor"	100
	"Corn Hill"	350
	pt. "Alexander's Hope"	200
	pt. "Gray's Chance"	200
	pt. "Bone Road"	89
	"Grunsbey"	38
	"Cold Harbour"	100
	pt. "Brooke Place"	432
	pt. "Stones Bay"	225
	"Piney Point"	50
	"Exchange"	350
	"Laurey's Point" & pt. "Lawrey's Rest"	100
	"Littleworth"	77
	"Cold Cowbey"	200
	pt. "Angle"	350
	pt. "Lawrey's Rest"	295
	"Foxes Walks"	40
	"Bram Hall"	500
	"Neglect"	30
	pt. "Godsgrace"	617
	"Meads"	166
	pt. "Evans's Land"	200
	pt. "Cole's Clifts"	150
	pt. "Preston's Clifts"	63
	"Cedar Branch" – from B. Hance	30
	pt. "Sewall's Purchase" – from B. Hance	30

11:1768:17 ...

Walter Murray for h/o (N) Smith	pt. "Parker's Clifts" tbc Walter Smith	100
	"Fox's Road" tbc Walter Smith	100
	"Wolf's Quarter" tbc Walter Smith	300
	"Smith's Hogpen" tbc Walter Smith	319
	pt. "St. Leonards" tbc Walter Smith – in corn	175
	"Taylor's Disposal" tbc Walter Smith	270
	pt. "Stone's Hills" tbc Walter Smith	25
	"Purchase" tbc Walter Smith	22
John Norfolk	"Kidd's Levels"	84
	pt. "Island's Plains"	27
	pt. "Ridge"	100
	pt. "Refuse"	100
	"Refuge"	14
James Norfolk	pt. "Peahen's Nest"	50
John Pardo	pt. "Rocky Neck" – from Richard Everist, Jr.	50
	"Foxe's Walks" – from Richard Everist, Jr.	70
Margaret Parran	"Bathen's Loss"	50
	"Cumpton"	75
	"Rawlings's Purchase"	60
	"Dear Bought"	200
Elizabeth Prindowell	pt. "Parker's Clifts"	100
	pt. "Robert's Addition"	5
	pt. "Robert's Chance"	5½
	pt. "Beakly"	66⅔
Leonard Prindowell	pt. "Robert's Addition"	10
	pt. "Chance"	11
	pt. "Beakley"	133⅓
Mary Parker	"Clay Hammond"	380
	"Wilson's Commons"	29
h/o John Peters	pt. "Kent's Freehold"	50
	pt. "Lordship's Favour"	100
	pt. "Danvin & Clares Hundred" tbc • Robert Peters – 142 a. • Richard Ward – 138 a.	280
William Patterson	pt. "Stones Bay"	75
	pt. "Evans's Land"	65

h/o Alexander Parran	"Point Patience"	360
	"Addition"	19
h/o Hutcheson Parker	pt. "St. Leonards" – in corn	175
	"Bulmores Branch"	50
	pt. "Stone's Hills"	25
11:1768:18 ...		
Young Parran	pt. "Desart"	349
	"Preston"	400
	pt. "Winfields Resurvey"	207
	"Preston's Neglect"	200
	pt. "Bermingham"	25
	pt. "Parran's Park"	150
	pt. "Morgan"	45
	"Brooke Plains"	100
	pt. "Inland"	2
	"Discovery"	99
Samuel Parran	pt. "Winfields Resurvey"	207
	pt. "Bermingham"	25
	pt. "Morgan"	45
	pt. land without name	100
	pt. "Parran's Park"	150
John Peters	pt. "Johnson's Farm" – from John Robinson (Halls Creek)	150
	pt. "Turner's Place" – from John Robinson (Halls Creek) • Stephen Stamp – 33⅓ a.	100
	pt. "Griffith's & Gover's Pasture" – from John Robinson (Halls Creek)	20
John Rawlings	pt. "Eltonhead Manor" – from Mr. Parran	300
Thomas Rhodes	"Black Robin"	38
Daniel Ross	pt. "Robinson's Rest"	200
Thomas Reynolds (cnp)	pt. "Robinson"	191
	pt. "St. Edmunds"	150
	pt. "Robinson's Rest"	368
	pt. "Good Luck"	100
	"Adjoinder" a/s "Adjunction"	10
	pt. "Brookes Discovery"	64

	"Crouder's Lott"	60
	"Reserve"	300
	"Foxes Chance"	72
	"Rich Bitt"	5½
	"Foxes Home"	30
	"Sterling's Perch"	300
	pt. "Lordship's Favor"	285
	pt. "Neglect"	60
	pt. "Coxes Inclosure"	70
	pt. "Coxes Freehold"	142
	"Troublesome"	150
	"Bennetts Refuge"	33
	pt. "Hopewell"	36
	pt. "Abington Manor"	769
	"Angle Lane"	37
	"Stallings's Lott"	31
	pt. "Meadows"	132
	"Thomas & Williams Chance"	101
	pt. "Thatchcomb"	114
	pt. "Lingan's Purchase"	8
	pt. "Brooke Neck"	150
	"Stallings's Swamp"	10
	"Meadows"	54
	"Hopewell"	58
	"Bite"	5
	pt. "Robinson's Rest"	150
11:1768:19 ...		
Samuel Robertson	"Emmertons Addition"	20
	pt. "Halls Hills"	85
	pt. "Broughton Ashly"	73
Daniel Rawlings	pt. "Eltonhead Manor"	200
Henry Scott	pt. "Highland" – from Richard Everist	50
James Somervill (cnp)	"Toby's Quarter"	100
	"Rocky Neck"	50
	pt. "Allen's Neck"	164
	"Narrow Neck & Gore"	18

	"Swamp"	67
	pt. "Gore" – from J. Somervill	100
h/o Maryland Skinner	pt. "Newington"	94
	pt. "Millers Folly"	250
John Simmonds	pt. "Rich Bottom"	25
	"Short Hills"	40
h/o Leonard Skinner	"Borders"	77½
	pt. "Dodson's Desire"	25
	pt. "Chance"	27
	pt. "Reserve"	32¼
h/o George Smith	pt. "Desart"	52
	pt. "Round Bottom Plains"	100
Dorothy Sollers	"Forked Neck"	110
	"Hyam"	10
William Skinner	pt. "Scrap"	38
	pt. "Preston's Desire"	25
	pt. "Chance"	27
	pt. "Reserve"	32¼
	pt. "Border Enlarg'd"	77½
James Skinner	pt. "Border Enlarged"	77½
	pt. "Dodson's Desire"	25
	pt. "Chance"	27
	pt. "Reserve"	33¼
Trueman Skinner	pt. "Blind Tom" tbc Robert Skinner	40
	"Addition" tbc Robert Skinner	60
	"Tauney's Right" tbc Robert Skinner	150
Elizabeth Skinner	pt. "Tauney's Right"	150
	pt. "Scrap"	62
	pt. "Reserve"	121
	pt. "Newington"	94
11:1768:20 ...		
h/o Adderton Skinner (cnp)	pt. "Blind Tom"	32
	"Tauney's Delight"	70
	pt. "Mary Green"	36
	"Gore"	48
	"Millers Folly"	250

	"Neglect"	25
William Sly	pt. "Morocco" – in corn	100
Alexander Somervell	"Fox's Den"	50
	"Bartholomew's Neck"	50
	pt. "Smith's Purchase"	238½
	pt. "Gore"	100
	"Golden's Folly"	75
Joseph Strickland	pt. "Robinson's Rest"	50
William Sollers	pt. "Dorington"	182½
	"Bowdley's Chance"	34
Joshua Sedwick	pt. "Neighbourhood"	150
	"Adjoinder"	50
	pt. "Morton's Purchase"	83⅛
Joseph Skinner	pt. "Orchard"	50
	pt. "Border Enlarged"	77½
	pt. "Dodson's Desire"	25
	pt. "Chance"	27
	"Reserve"	32¼
Josias Sunderland	pt. "Swinfin's Rest"	250
Josias Sunderland, Jr.	pt. "Upper Bennett" tbc his widow	50
h/o Richard Stallings	pt. "Thatchcomb"	236
	pt. "Robinson's Rest"	100
James Sewall	pt. "Dear Quarter"	62½
	pt. "Chance"	72½
	"Maiden's Delight"	200
	pt. "Cop's Hall"	80
	pt. "Parker's Clifts" – from Sarah Freeland	50
	"Good Luck" – from Sarah Freeland	150
John Standforth	pt. "Poor Land"	104
h/o John Skinner	pt. "Halls Hills"	877½
	"Sneaking Point"	50
	"Lingan's Purchase"	94
	pt. "Hamilton's Park"	33
11:1768:21 ...		
William Sansbury	pt. "Archers Hays"	40

h/o Joseph Smith, Jr.	pt. "Turner's Pasture"	50
	pt. "Smith's Pasture"	100
	pt. "Mordyke"	15½
h/o William Smith	pt. "Smith's Chance"	50
	pt. "Turner's Place"	50
	pt. "Mordyke"	50
Mordecai Smith	pt. "Smith's Chance"	100
	pt. "Welch Poole"	72½
	pt. "Turner's Place"	50
	pt. "Calender"	77
Joseph Smith	pt. "Mordyke"	50
w/o John Stone	pt. "Defence"	65
John Stallings	pt. "Upper Bennett"	25
Ellis Slater	pt. "Lawrey's Reserve"	100
Stephen Stamp	pt. "Red Hall"	125
Clement Smith	pt. "Hall's Craft" tbc: • Partrick Smith – 265 a.	486
Nicholas Swamstead	pt. "Lordship's Favour"	100
Thomas Stallings	pt. "Swinfins Rest"	64½
h/o Col. John Smith	pt. "Hall's Craft"	665
	pt. "Batchelors Quarter" tbc Alexander Ham. Smith	250
	"Soldiers Fortune" tbc Philemon Smith	200
	pt. "Ordinary" tbc Philemon Smith	75
	pt. "Grantham" tbc Gavin Smith	20
	1½ lots in Lower Marlbro tbc Dr. John H. Smith	1½
	pt. "Dowdeswell Manor" tbc Dr. John H. Smith	400
	pt. "Ordinary" tbc Dr. John H. Smith	80½
Stockett Sunderland	pt. "Laurey's Chance or Resurvey"	100
John Davis Scarth	pt. "Robinson's Rest"	50
Benjamin Sedwick	pt. "Bulmores Branch" a/s "Right"	475
Jonathan Slater	pt. "Hall's Revenge"	28
	1 lot in Lower Marlbro	1
Stephen Steward (AA)	pt. "Illingsworth's Fortune"	200
Mary Smith (PG)	"Good Prospect"	50
	"Lands Land"	192
	"Addition"	28

Eleanor Sly	pt. "Magruder"	150
11:1768:22 ...		
John Scott	pt. "Lordship's Favour"	100
Marga Smith	"Small Reward" – twice charged, before to Richard Bond	111
Jacob Tucker	"Tucker's Thickett"	200
	pt. "Chance"	50
h/o Philip Thomas	"Major's Choice"	500
Joseph Talbutt, Jr.	pt. "Expectation"	100
John Tannehill – pt. "Cooper" & pt. "Friendship" tbc:	pt. "Calender"	123
• Ann Tannehill – 173 a.	"Friendship"	150
• Lewis Griffith – 86 a.	"Cooper"	150
Joseph Talbutt	pt. "Freeman's Chance"	123
	pt. "Tillington"	150
	"Batchelor's Fortune"	200
John Talbutt	pt. "Expectation"	50
Edward Talbutt	pt. "Tillington"	415½
John Turner	"Bowdley's Chance"	91
Thomas Talbott	pt. "Expectation"	100
h/o Benjamin Tasker, Esq.	"Hard Travell"	300
John Tucker	pt. "Neighbourhood"	82½
William Vermilion	"Creeds Chance"	64
John Wilkinson	pt. "Young's Attempt" – from John Samuel Dossey	100
Ben Kid Wilson & Priscilla Gover	pt. "Aldermason" – from h/o Samuel Gover	150
	"Gover's Expectation" – from h/o Samuel Gover	89
	pt. "Welch Poole"	2
Joseph Wilson (cnp)	"Tamot"	300
	pt. "Foster's Purchase"	150
	pt. "Robinson"	136
	pt. "Additional Spittle"	8
	pt. "Peahen's Nest"	40
	pt. "Cedar Branch"	125
	"Letchworth's Cyprus"	200
	pt. "Bowen" – for h/o (N) King	230

	pt. "Arnold's Purchase" tbc John Brooke	100
	pt. "Brooke's Adventure"	150
	"Stones Lott"	50
	pt. "Arnolds Purchase"	50
Joseph Wilson, Jr.	pt. "Lower Bennett"	189
11:1768:23 ...		
George Wheeler	"Berry" – for h/o Miles Tawney	600
	"Long Point" – for h/o Miles Tawney	100
	"Wooden Point" – for h/o Miles Tawney	25
	pt. "Letchworth" – for h/o Miles Tawney	50
	pt. "Angle" – for h/o Miles Tawney	3
John Ward	"Velchee's Rest"	50
Samuel Ward	"Goldson's Inheritance"	150
Aaron Williams, Jr.	pt. "Friendship Rectified"	200
	pt. "Swinfins Adventure"	50
	pt. "Youngs Desire"	50
Hilleary Wilson	pt. "Robinson"	200
Aaron Williams, Sr.	pt. "William's Hardship"	175
	"Williams's Rest"	50
	"Littlefield"	25
	pt. "Friendship Rectified"	25
	pt. "Swinfin's Adventure" – should only be 25 a.	50
James Weems, Jr.	"Success, Tauney's Case, & Stockley"	200
	"Partnership"	75
h/o Joseph Wilkinson	pt. "Godsgrace"	120
	pt. "Stockley"	70
John Waters	pt. "Stockley"	419
	pt. "Gunterton"	40
	"Myrtle Point"	7
John Willing	pt. "Taylors Joy"	128
	"Jerusalem"	108
	pt. "Rich Bottom"	25
Francis Wolf, Jr.	pt. "Theobald Manor"	50
	pt. "Gray's Chance"	50
Richard Ward	pt. "Swinfin's Rest"	116

James Weems	pt. "Magruder"	450
	"Hogs Haunt"	50
	"Maulden's Luck"	25
	pt. "Bussey's Orchard"	400
	pt. "Inland"	1
	"Meadows Preserv'd"	46
	pt. "Burk's Chance"	150
	1 lot in Hunting Town	1
	pt. "Cuckolds Miss"	60
	"Youngs Desire"	25
	pt. "Youngs Fortune"	60
	pt. "Youngs Attempt"	62
	"Penmanmaure"	50
	pt. "Reserve"	50
	pt. "Trouble"	10
11:1768:23a ...		
owner	"Swinfields Rest" tbc: • Jo. Sunderland – 250 a. • William Dare – 250 a. • John Dowell – 50 a. • James Deal – 60½ a. • Richard Gibson – 72 a. • Richard Ward – 116 a. • Henry Harrison – 150 a. • Thomas Stallings – 64½ a.	1017
11:1768:24 ...		
James Weems s/o David	"Ringan"	200
	"Greenhouse"	155
	"Chew's Purchase"	145
	"Grantham"	45
	"Marshall's Addition"	70
Basil Williamson	"Lingan's Adventure"	310
Edward Wood	pt. "Woods Adventure"	150
	"Titmarsh"	100
	pt. "Poor Land"	11
Jonah Winfield	pt. "Lands Land"	112
	pt. "Johnson's Farme"	100

Thomas Wells	pt. "Grantham Hall"	155
	"Arthur's Hall"	44
h/o James Williamson	"Den"	726
	"Fox's Nettles"	20
	pt. "Batchelor's Quarter"	420
h/o Roger Wheeler	pt. "Henry Chew"	237
	"Coxcomb"	150
	"Coxhead"	50
	pt. "Newington"	109
	"Smith's Conveyance"	60
John Wilkinson	pt. "Henry Chew"	400
Thomas Wilson	pt. "St. Edmunds"	163
	pt. "Neglect"	16½
Leonard Wood	pt. "Woods Adventure"	100
Edward Wilson	"Dear Quarter"	25
	pt. "Robinson's Rest"	150
John Weems	pt. "Dowdeswell"	600
	pt. "Chance"	25
William White	pt. "Smith's Joy"	100
William Winnull	pt. "Norton's Purchase"	166⅔
William Hunton Wood	pt. "Arnolds Purchase"	100
Francis Whittington	pt. "Hall's Hills"	100
Francis Williams	pt. "Inland"	100
	"Hutchings's Chance"	50
	pt. "Orchard"	40
11:1768:25 ...		
Ithamor Williams	pt. "Swinfin's Adventure"	50
	pt. "William's Hardship"	75
	pt. "Friendship Rectified"	125
Philemon Young	pt. "Henry Chew"	175
	1 lot in Lower Marlbro	1
Parker Young	"Hopyard"	150
	"Punch"	150
	pt. "Youngs Desire"	25
	pt. "Hooper's Neck"	275
Mary Yoe	pt. "Rattle Snake Hills"	100

James Kent Byrn	pt. "Neighbourhood"	26
	pt. "Prevent Danger"	100
Thomas Crumpton	"Jerusalem"	124
	pt. "Swinfin's Adventure"	25
	"Parker's Fortune" a/s "Chance"	263
	"Bigger"	1055
	pt. "Godsgrace"	100
	pt. "Morocco, Catterton's Lott, & Barbers Delight"	294
Edmund Clare	pt. "Eltonhead Manor" – from Benjamin Sedwick	200
Henry Gray	"Labour in Vain" – from James Morsell	100
Joseph Wilson (brought from f. 22)	pt. "Young's Attemp" – from Thomas Broome	100
	pt. "Hap at a Venture" – from Thomas Broome	50
	pt. "Horse Range" – from Thomas Broome	125
11:1768:<unnumbered>	Certification	
11:1768:<unnumbered>	Recapitulation	

12:1769:1 ...		Acres
John Alton	pt. "Hardesty's Choice" – from Eleanor Alton	50
h/o David Arnold	pt. "Henry Chew"	290
	pt. "Abington"	350
	pt. "Hardesty's Choice"	130
w/o Samuel Austin	pt. "Coxe's Chance"	140
	pt. "Farme"	20
Ann Askew	pt. "Lawrey's Chance"	118
James Alnutt	pt. "Trueman's Chance"	153
William Alnutt	pt. "Trueman's Chance"	156
	pt. "Agreement"	100
Samuel Austin	pt. "Coxe's Chance"	117
Roger Brooke	pt. "Brooke Place Manor"	1096
John & Isaac Baker	"Devils Woodyard"	150
Jacob Bourn	pt. "Eltonhead Manor"	300
John Beveridge	"Dear Bought"	21
Abraham Bowen	pt. "Dividing Branch"	169½
	pt. "Billingsley's Farm" – from h/o Richard Johns	136
David Bowen	pt. "Dividing Branch"	189
Isaac Bowen	pt. "Dividing Branch"	190
John Brooke	pt. "Brookes Adventure"	116⅔
	pt. "Cedar Branch"	25
	pt. "Arnolds Purchase"	50
	pt. "Arnolds Purchase" – from Joseph Wilson	100
12:1769:2 ...		
Jesse Bourne	pt. "Eltonhead Manor"	1167
Jacob Bowen	pt. "Neighbourhood"	74
Henry Broome	pt. "Austin's Chance"	65
	pt. "Howard & Letchworth"	200
	pt. "Broad Point"	10
	pt. "Austin's Addition"	23
William Blackburn	pt. "Back Pasture"	50
James Bowen	pt. "Dividing Branch"	105
Thomas Bowen	pt. "Dividing Branch"	105
Col. Abraham Barnes (SM)	"Fishers Orchard"	255
	"Bran Fry"	100

Roger Brooke, Jr.	pt. "Bowen"	70
	"Knowles Branch"	98
	"Tauneys Addition"	123
	"Brooke Battle"	230
	pt. "Brooke's Adventure"	233⅔
	pt. "Cedar Branch"	50
Thomas Blackburn	"Readby"	100
Thomas Broome	"Rich Neck"	52
	"Marys Widowhood"	30
	"Addition to Island Neck"	30
John Broome	pt. "Island Neck"	500
	pt. "Stones Bay"	200
	"Adventure"	82½
	"Broad Point"	140
	pt. "Austin's Addition"	23
Ann Bond	"Middle Fuller"	200
	"Lower Fuller"	200
	pt. "Lower Bennett"	250
12:1769:3 ...		
Isabella Barton	pt. "Upper Bennett"	50
w/o John Beckett – George Gantt on Debt Book 1775	"Selby's Clifts"	200
	pt. "Mears"	200
	pt. "Gunterton"	250
	pt. "Hardesty"	50
	"Poppy Gray"	40
Jesse Bowen	"Lambeth"	94
h/o Richard Blake	pt. "Upper Bennett"	557
	pt. "St. Edmunds"	200
	pt. "Lordships's Favour"	192
	pt. "Neglect"	50
Mary Bond	pt. "Hogsdown"	275
	"Micham"	243
	pt. "Brooke Partition"	104
	pt. "Lawrey's Chance" tbc William Dare in 1770	135
Richard Bond (cnp)	pt. "Lawreys Chance"	50
	"Small Land"	6¾

	"Small Reward"	111
	pt. "Spittle"	90
	pt. "Hogsdown"	25
James Kent Byrn	pt. "Neighbourhood"	26
	pt. "Prevent Danger"	100
Thomas Crumpton	"Jerusalem"	124
	pt. "Swinfin's Adventure"	25
	"Parkers Fortune" a/s "Chance"	263
	"Bigger"	1055
	pt. "Godsgrace"	100
	pt. "Morocco, Cattertons Lot, & Barbers Delight"	294
Edmund Clare	pt. "Eltonhead Manor"	200
Gabriel Child	pt. "Letchworth's Chance" – from Fra. Freeland	336
Bennett Chew	"Chew's Fortune"	49
12:1769:4 ...		
Samuel Chew	pt. "Letchworths Chance"	550
	pt. "Upper Bennett"	506
	"Lane & Gore"	51½
h/o Joseph Chilton	"Terra in Agua"	4
Samuel Chew (AA)	"Popping Gay"	540
Josias Crosby	pt. "Archers Hays"	30
	pt. "Goughs Purchase"	60
Michael Caterton	pt. "Lingans Purchase"	125
~~h/o Richard Chew~~	~~"Stallings Lot"~~	~~150~~
	~~pt. "Robinsons Rest"~~	~~250~~
Henry Camden	"Highland"	200
	"Chance"	70
Elizabeth Chesley w/o John	pt. "Batchelors Quarter"	420
Michael Culpepper	"Venture"	16
Young Cox	pt. "Little Land"	17
	pt. "Cox's Inclosure"	65
	pt. "Cops Hall"	25
	pt. "Cox's Freehold"	120
	pt. "Merry Green Wood"	163
	pt. "Good Luck"	10
	"Hatchet"	25

Betty Clare	pt. "Lawrys Chance"	130
Mary Clare	pt. "Eltonhead Manor"	157
Calvert County School	"Security"	87
	pt. "Orchard"	100
Calvert County	pt. "Inland"	3
12:1769:5 ...		
Isaac Clare	"Horse Path"	200
	pt. "Eltonhead Manor"	143
	"Concord"	161
	"Addition to Horsepath"	40
John Culppepper	"Wolfs Quarter"	40
Thomas Crutchley	"Addition"	50
John Cox	pt. "Smiths Lott"	33⅛
	pt. "Johnsons Farme, Good Prospect, & Lands Land"	87½
Joseph Dawkins	"Dicks Cabbin"	50
	pt. "Friendship"	25
	"Blinkhorn" – from h/o Charles Clagget	300
	"Foxes Road" – from h/o Charles Clagget	42
	"Joseph's Reserve" – from Mary Dawkins	196
h/o Benjamin Dixon – Henry Dixon on Debt Book 1770	"Addition to Middlesex"	95
	"Fox's Walks"	5
Andrew Duke	"Middlesex"	100
h/o William Dorumple	"Hap at a Venture"	150
	pt. "Fox's Road"	158
James Duke	pt. "Brooke Place"	171
	pt. "Lower Bennett"	211
	"Mackall's Desire"	78
Samuel Dare	pt. "Angle"	140
	pt. "Gideon & Cleverlys Right"	342
	pt. "Smiths Purchase"	119⅔
	pt. "Gideon's & Cleverlys Right"	160
Benjamin Duke	pt. "Rich Levells"	247
	pt. "Inland"	1
	pt. "Brooke Place Manor"	300
	pt. "Howard & Letchworth"	303

h/o James Dodson	"Huckleberry Hills"	50
	"Littleworth"	21
12:1769:6 ...		
John Dossey	pt. "Mary Green"	63
	pt. "Dear Quarter"	62½
	pt. "Bennetts Desire"	10
	pt. "Robinson's Rest"	66⅔
Robert Day	pt. "No Name"	150
Benjamin Day	"Brandon"	57
	"Frampton"	50
William Dawkins	"Marys Dukedom"	100
James Dawkins	"Josephs Place"	200
Susanna Dare	pt. "Gideon & Cleverlys Right" tbc Nathaniel Dare (315 a.) in Debt Book 1770	472
Philip Dossey	pt. resurvey of several tracts	104
	pt. "Tauneys Addition"	44
William Day	pt. "No Name"	100
Cleverly Dare	pt. "Gideon & Cleverlys Right" tbc: • Andrew Duke – 19 a. in Debt Book 1770 • William Powell – 5½ a. in Debt Book 1770	1199
	pt. "Prestons Clifts"	100
Ellis Dixon	"Hogskin Clifts"	100
Thomas Denton	pt. "Island Neck"	99
John Dare	pt. "Gideon & Cleverly's Right"	100
John Dowell	pt. "Swinfen's Rest"	50
	pt. "Lingans Purchase"	100
Richard Deale	pt. "Newingham"	200
	pt. "Timberwell"	74
James Dossey – John Dossey s/o John on Debt Book 1770	pt. "Garden"	100
	pt. "Robinson's Rest"	64
12:1769:7 ...		
James Deale	pt. "Swinfens Rest"	64½
Daniel Dossey	pt. "Garden"	67
Philip Dossey, Jr.	pt. "Robinsons Rest"	150
Francis Dossey	pt. "Bennett's Desire"	50
Jacob Deale	pt. "Upper Bennett"	75

William Dare	pt. "Swinfex's Rest"	250
Thomas Cleverly Dare	pt. "Agreement"	150
	"Bite the Biter"	112
	"Sampsons Dividend"	150
	pt. "Mannington"	25
	"Neglect"	50
Philip Dowell	pt. "Lingans Purchase"	116
Alexander Deale	pt. "Newington"	46
	pt. "Islington"	25
John Dew	pt. "Archers Hays"	43½
James Dossey, Jr.	pt. "Youngs Mount"	159
	pt. "Youngs Fortune"	40
Richard Everist	pt. "Highland"	50
Ann Elt	pt. "Eltonhead Manor"	336
Isaac Essex	pt. "Wolf Trap"	55
Robert Ethrington	pt. "Comsey"	92½
Barnaby Eagan	pt. "Brooke Place Manor"	400
12:1769:8 ...		
h/o George Fowler	pt. "Tillington"	45½
Thomas Freeman	pt. "Rockhold"	135
James Fraizer	"Hills Hall"	100
	"White Marsh"	68
Joseph Freeman	pt. "Arnolds Purchase"	50
Col. William Fitzhugh	pt. "Eltonhead Manor"	2500
	pt. "Mile's End"	399½
	pt. "Miles Run"	150
	"Hattons Case"	70
	"Staffords Freehold"	70
	"Round Ponds"	100
	"Leach" or "Smiths Hills"	100
	"Gore"	70
Jacob Freeland	pt. "Letchworths Chance"	179
	"Neglect"	125
	pt. "Fuller"	100
Robert Freeland (cnp)	pt. "Truemans Chance"	232
	"Dosseys Folly"	70

	"Burks Purchase"	50
	pt. "Rear Quarter"	100
	pt. "Fuller"	200
Peregrine Freeland	pt. "Mackalls Force" – from Robert Freeland	323½
Frisby Freeland	pt. "Mackalls Force"	323½
John Ferguson	pt. "Griffiths & Govers Pasture"	40
	pt. "Skinners Chance"	30
	pt. "Turners Place"	126
Alexander Fraizer	"Sterlings Chance"	40
	"Sterlings Rest"	550
Jacob French	pt. "Danvin"	125
12:1769:9 ...		
Richard Gibson	pt. "Swinfens Rest"	72
	pt. "Lordships Favor"	50
h/o John Griffith	pt. "Welch Poole"	143¾
	pt. "Skinners Chance"	90
John Gibson	pt. "Spittle"	90
	pt. "Additional Spittle"	22
John Gardiner	pt. "Johnsons Lott"	100
Charles Grahame	pt. "Halls Craft"	521
	"Howard"	42
	"Bell"	68
	"Blackwall"	38
	pt. "Hardesty"	180
Joseph Galloway	pt. "Spittle"	20
	pt. "Additional Spittle"	28
Lewis Griffiths	pt. "Welchpoole"	135
	pt. "Archers Hays"	231
	"Lewis's Slipe & Dews Purchase"	26
	"Long Lane"	31
	"All Points"	24
	pt. "Cooper" – from John Taneyhill	86
James Gibson	pt. "Additional Spittle"	88
	pt. "Newington"	22
h/o Robert Gover (cnp)	pt. "Archers Hays"	190
	"Goughs Purchase" a/s "Goughs Pasture"	50

	"Govers Addition"	167
	"Govers Meadows"	59
	pt. "Dunkirk"	150
	pt. "Exchange"	66
John Griffin	pt. "Robinson"	60
Edward Gantt	pt. "Ordinary"	606
	"Kingsburys Marsh"	130
	"Craft"	90
12:1769:10 ...		
Thomas Gray	pt. "Wolton"	75
William Gray s/o Thomas	"Grays Addition"	109
John Gray (Patuxent)	"Marshland & Bushhead"	345
	"Hazard"	42
	pt. "Brooke Adventure"	100
	"Jonattle" a/s "Tuxberry"	100
	"Toddy"	138
William Gray	"Reserve"	50
	"Stennetts Ramble"	35
Howerton Games	pt. "Johnson's Lott"	50
	"Hazard"	25
Robert Gardiner	pt. "Johnsons Lott"	100
	"Wolf's Hole"	50
John Gardiner	pt. "Johnsons Lot"	100
Samuel Gray	"Norwood"	200
	"Theobush Manning"	50
	pt. "Austin's Chance"	91
John Graves	"Stevens Plains" tbc: • John Ivey – 25 a. in Debt Book 1770 • Driver Greves – 25 a. in Debt Book 1770	50
	"Greeves Rehobeth" tbc Driver Greves (only 80 a.) in Debt Book 1770	111
Edward Gardner	"Chilton" or "Chetham"	80
	pt. "Forked Neck" or "Dorington"	50
	"Short Neck"	76
Benjamin Gardiner	pt. "Round Pond Plains"	100
h/o James T. Greenfield	pt. "Aldermason"	150
	"Addition"	56½

Henry Gray	"Labour in Vain"	100
12:1769:11 ...		
Mary Graves	pt. "Hap Hazard"	45
	"Batchelors Hall"	300
	"Timber Neck"	50
	"Clares Littleworth"	43
Esther Gray	"Fishing Creek"	165
	"Chaplain"	100
	"East Fishing Creek"	50
	"Nutts Clifts"	150
	"East Chaplain"	100
h/o Job Hunt	pt. "Upper Bennett"	195
Thomas Hollingshead	pt. "Kents Freehold"	250
James Heighe	pt. "Beakley"	300
	"Forsters Purchase"	150
	pt. "Roberts Chance"	34
	"James's Chance"	40
	"Samuels Addition"	15
	"James's Addition"	21
	"Clarks Hills"	19
	"Little Land"	11
	"Heighe's Addition"	15
Thomas Holdsworth Heighe	pt. "Brooke Place"	300
James Dawkins s/o James	pt. "Hap Hazard" – from Mary Graves	90
William Harrison	pt. "Brookes Discovery"	200
Joseph Hardesty	pt. "Den"	37½
	pt. "Nichols's Chance"	55
	"Nelsons Reserve"	22
William Hickman	pt. "Newington"	220
	pt. "Islington"	542
Thomas Hunt	pt. "Lordships Favour"	50
12:1769:12 ...		
h/o John Hance	pt. "Newington"	9
	"Johns Neglect"	128
	pt. "Illingsworths Fortune"	65

Henry Howes	pt. "Refuse"	50
	"Jensbys Lott"	46
	"Purchase"	23
Henry Hardesty	pt. "Den"	37
	pt. "Nichols's Chance"	55
William Hardesty	pt. "Lordships Favour"	75
William Harrison, Jr.	pt. "Lawreys Reserve" tbc William Harrison in Debt Book 1770	75
	pt. "Brookes Discovery" tbc William Harrison in Debt Book 1770	126
	pt. "Cox's Freehold" tbc William Harrison in Debt Book 1770	128
Henry Harrison	pt. "Swinfens Rest"	150
Thomas Holland	pt. "St. James's Enlarged"	1138
	pt. "Alexanders Hope"	38
George Hall	pt. "Chance"	25
Abraham Hooper	pt. "Taylors Joy" – resurveyed & found to contain 343 a. in Debt Book 1770	258
Walter Hoxton (CH)	pt. "Homesham" – from Susanna Hoxton	117
Ann Holland	pt. "Abington"	150
William Harris	pt. "Durain"	200
	pt. "Illingsworths Fortune"	100
	pt. "Littleworth"	150
	pt. "Tillingham"	73
	pt. "Letchworths Chance"	275
Dr. Leonard Holliday	"Buzzard Island"	700
	"Addition"	51
	pt. "Arnolds Purchase"	50
12:1769:13 ...		
Newman Harvey	pt. "Turners Place"	126
Benjamin Hance (cnp)	"Parkers Clifts"	100
	pt. "Warrington"	175
	pt. "Agreement"	50
	"Busseys Garden"	175
	pt. "Illington"	250
	"Hance Lane"	20
	pt. "Newington"	3

	"Purchase"	154
	"Warings Chance"	56
	resurvey of several tracts	119½
Benjamin Harris	pt. "Expectation"	100
William Harris, Jr.	"Addition"	100
James Henley	"Smugg's Folly"	80
Joseph Hance	"Wabbleton"	404
	pt. "Stockley" a/s resurvey of several tracts tbc Kensey Hance in Debt Book 1770	100
David Hellen s/o John	pt. "Eltonhead Manor" tbc John Hungerford in Debt Book 1770	200
	pt. "Friendship" tbc Hannah Hungerford in Debt Book 1770	75
	"Jermyn Quarter Enlarged" tbc John Hungerford in Debt Book 1770	143
James Hellen	pt. "Truswell"	150
Samuel Hance	pt. "Theobush Manning"	189
Walter Hellen	pt. "Hoopers Neck"	275
Edmund Hellen	pt. "Waring"	121
	pt. "Bowdleys Chance"	75
	"Busseys Lott"	75
	"Hellens Lot"	12
Edmund Hungerford	"Hogskin Neck"	100
	pt. "Stephen's Land"	100
	"Purchase"	24
	pt. "Desart"	100
12:1769:14 ...		
Philip Hunt	pt. "Lordships Favour"	100
Richard Hellen	pt. "Truswell"	150
	"Miltons Lott"	100
	"Persia"	100
	"Harrow on the Hill"	80
	pt. "Rich Levell"	20
David Hellen s/o Richard	"Gully" – lies in elder surveys	63½
Thomas Gosling Hutchins	pt. "Magruder"	175
Rebecca Hungerford (cnp)	pt. "Friendship" – from Jos. Dawkins	31¼
	pt. "Taylors Joy" – from Jos. Dawkins	114

	pt. "Allens Neck" – from h/o Charles Clagget	36
Kensey Johns (AA)	pt. "Angelica"	200
	pt. "Mears"	200
	pt. "Inland"	1
Benjamin Johns	pt. "Angelica"	400
	pt. "Johns's Addition"	112
	pt. "Inland"	1
Richard Johns	"Whittles Rest" tbc Benjamin Harris (148 a.) in Debt Book 1770	336
	pt. "Devise"	75
	"Chance" tbc Isaac Simmons in Debt Book 1770	50
	pt. "Parkers Clifts" tbc Benjamin Harris (50 a.) in Debt Book 1770	180
h/o Joseph Isaac	"Plum Point"	400
	pt. "Lordships Favour"	205
	"Purchase"	100
Col. William Ireland	pt. "Bridge"	100
	"George's Desire"	50
	"Addition"	43
	"Angle"	87
	pt. "Peahens Nest"	35
	pt. "Island Plains"	32
	"Lyons Creek"	300
	pt. "Dunkirk"	50
William Johnson s/o George	pt. "Redd Hall"	100
12:1769:15 ...		
h/o Richard Johns	"Purchase"	100
	pt. "Youngs Desire"	12
William Ireland s/o Thomas	pt. "Halls Hills"	550
Mary Ireland	pt. "Eltonhead Manor"	200
	pt. "Preston's Clifts"	108
	pt. "Angle"	88
	pt. "No Name"	100
	"Mill Marsh"	63
John Ireland	pt. "Tillington"	189
	"Wolf Trap"	45

Thomas Johnson	"Brewhouse"	260
John Johnson	"Elizabeth"	200
	pt. "Gift"	70
	pt. "Preston's Clifts" tbc Thomas Johnson in Debt Book 1770	314
William Johnson s/o Jere	pt. "Exchange"	150
Dr. Edward Johnson	"Preston"	200
	"Moffatts Mount" – overcharged	200
	"Wood's Adventure"	50
	"Hays Marsh"	18
	pt. "Poor Land"	185
	"Musqueto Point"	46
	"Turner's Chance"	50
Richard Ireland	"Ireland's Hope"	50
	pt. "Desart"	198
h/o John Kent	pt. "Rockhold"	160
James Kirshaw	pt. "Prevent Danger"	100
John Kirshaw	pt. "Prevent Danger"	50
Francis Kirshaw	pt. "Sharpe's Outlett"	100
	pt. "Concord"	63
h/o James Leach	"Leach's Freehold" tbc Jos. Ireland in Debt Book 1770	125
12:1769:16 ...		
Joseph Kent	pt. "Timberwell"	326
	pt. "Additional Spittle"	50
Rev. Francis Lauder	pt. "Preston's Clifts"	239
	pt. "Gore"	50
John Lawrence	pt. "Lawrey's Addition"	145
	pt. "Islington"	50
h/o Lewis Lewin	pt. "Red Hall"	37½
William Lyles	pt. "Red Hall"	150
	pt. "Stripe"	8
	pt. "Turners Pasture"	170
	pt. "Long Lane"	32
John Laveal	pt. "Whittle's Rest"	210
Robert Lyles	pt. "Red Hall"	100

Sarah Lane w/o Samuel (AA)	pt. "Homesham" tbc Capt. Richard Lane & Benjamin Lane in Debt Book 1770	233
Samuel Lyles	pt. "Lawrey's Chance"	50
Jeremiah Maulden	pt. "Parker's Clifts"	250
John Mackall s/o John	pt. resurvey of several tracts	104
	pt. "Tauney's Addition"	44
James Mackall s/o John	pt. resurvey of several tracts	104
	pt. "Tauney's Addition"	44
Benjamin Mackall s/o John	"Schoolhouse"	100
	"Brigantine Adventure"	24
Elizabeth Marshall w/o Thomas	"Cox's Folly"	50
	pt. "Farm"	19
Thomas Marshall 3rd	pt. "Cox's Choice"	143
John Manning	pt. "Theobald's Manor"	112
	pt. "Gunsby"	168
William Monnett	"Williams's Purchase"	206
12:1769:17 ...		
Jane Macdowell	pt. "Coles Clifts"	50
h/o James Mackall	"Cage"	250
	"Bussey's Lot"	100
	"Mackalls Desire"	10
h/o Thomas Morgan	pt. "Desire"	79
	pt. "Grays Chance"	350
	"Fellowship"	160
John Mackall (St. Leonards)	pt. "Morgan"	60
	pt. "Horse Range"	180
	"Claggets Desire"	376
	"Desert"	350
	pt. "St. James's" – from Robert Jenkins Henry	300
Benjamin Mackall (Holland Point) (cnp)	"Copartnership"	182
	pt. "Chance"	232
	pt. "Hallowing Point"	200
	"Seamour Neck"	382
	pt. "Horse Range"	165
	pt. "Sharpe's Outlett"	100
	"Thoroughbridge"	250

	"Brooke Choice"	146
	pt. "Dividing Branch"	179
	pt. "Trouble"	27
	pt. "Morocco" – in corn	50
	"Addition to Sharp's Outlett"	112
	pt. "Read"	46½
	pt. "Read & Magruder"	92½
	pt. "Hallowing Point"	200
	pt. "Chance"	75
	pt. "Coursey"	46½
h/o Barbara Mackall	pt. "Brooke Partition"	200
James Morsell	pt. "Rattle Snake Hills"	120
	"Chance"	70
	pt. "Littleworth"	60
	pt. "Mary Green"	55
Rousby Miller	pt. "Orchard"	253
Ann Mills	pt. "Wolton"	25
	pt. "Catch"	50
12:1769:18 ...		
James John Mackall (cnp)	pt. "Lower Bennett"	500
	pt. "Theobush Manor"	100
	"Corn Hill"	350
	pt. "Alexanders Hope"	200
	pt. "Grays Chance"	200
	pt. "Bone Road"	89
	pt. "Gunsbey"	38
	"Cold Harbour"	100
	pt. "Brooke Place"	432
	pt. "Stones Bay"	225
	"Piney Point"	50
	"Exchange"	350
	"Lawreys Point" & pt. "Lawreys Rest"	100
	"Littleworth"	77
	"Cold Carbey"	200
	pt. "Angle"	350
	pt. "Lawreys Rest"	295

	"Fox's Walks"	40
	"Bramhall"	500
	"Neglect"	30
	pt. "Godgrace"	617
	"Meads"	166
	pt. "Evans's Land"	200
	pt. "Coles Clifts"	150
	pt. "Prestons Clifts"	63
	"Cedar Branch"	240
	pt. "Sewalls Purchase"	30
	"Bramells Addition"	33
	"Angel" or "Angle"	87
John Norfolk	"Kidds Levells"	84
	pt. "Island Plains"	27
	pt. "Ridge"	100
	pt. "Refuse"	100
	"Refuge"	14
James Norfolk	pt. "Peahens Nest"	50
John Pardo	pt. "Rocky Neck"	50
	pt. "Foxes Walks"	70
Margaret Parran	"Bathen's Loss" tbc Daniel Rawlings in Debt Book 1770	50
	"Cumpton" tbc John Rawlings in Debt Book 1770	75
	"Rawlings's Purchase" tbc John Rawlings in Debt Book 1770	60
	"Dear Bought" tbc Daniel Rawlings in Debt Book 1770	200
Mary Parker	"Clay Hammond"	380
	"Wilson's Commons"	29
12:1769:19 ...		
Elizabeth Prindowell	pt. "Parkers Clifts"	100
	pt. "Roberts Addition"	5
	pt. "Roberts Chance"	5½
	pt. "Beakley"	66⅔
Leonard Prindowell	pt. "Roberts Addition"	10
	pt. "Roberts Chance"	11
	pt. "Beakley"	133⅓

h/o John Peters	pt. "Kents Freehold"	50
	pt. "Lordship's Favour"	100
	pt. "Danvin & Clares Hundred" – vid. Richard Ward	138
Robert Peters	pt. "Danvin & Clares Hundred" – from h/o John Peters	142
William Patterson	pt. "Stones Bay"	75
	pt. "Evans's Land"	65
h/o Alexander Parran	"Point Patience"	360
	"Addition"	19
h/o Hutcheson Parker	pt. "St. Leonards" – in corn	175
	"Bulmore's Branch"	50
	pt. "Stones Hills"	25
Young Parran, Esq.	pt. "Desart"	349
	"Preston"	400
	pt. "Winfields Resurvey"	207
	"Prestons Neglect"	200
	pt. "Bermingham"	25
	pt. "Parrans Park"	150
	pt. "Morgan"	45
	"Brooke Plains"	100
	pt. "Inland"	2
	"Discovery"	99
Samuel Parran	pt. "Winfield's Resurvey"	207
	pt. "Bermingham"	25
	pt. "Morgan"	45
	pt. land without name	100
	pt. "Parrans Park"	150
John Peters	pt. "Johnsons Farm"	150
	pt. "Turners Place"	66⅔
	pt. "Griffiths & Govers Pasture"	20
12:1769:20 ...		
John Rawlings	pt. "Eltonhead Manor"	300
Thomas Rhodes	"Black Robin"	38
Daniel Ross	pt. "Robinsons Rest"	200

Thomas Reynolds	pt. "Robinson"	191
	pt. "St. Edmunds"	150
	pt. "Robinsons Rest"	518
	pt. "Good Luck"	100
	"Adjoinder" a/s "Adjunction"	10
	pt. "Brookes Discovery"	64
	"Crouders Lott"	60
	"Reserve"	300
	"Fox's Chance"	72
	"Rich Bitt"	5½
	"Fox's Home"	30
	"Sterlings Perch"	300
	pt. "Lordships Favor"	285
	pt. "Neglect"	60
	pt. "Cox's Inclosure"	70
	pt. "Cox's Freehold"	142
	"Troublesome"	150
	"Bennetts Refuge"	33
	pt. "Hopewell"	94
	pt. "Abington Manor"	769
	"Angle's Lane"	37
	"Stallings's Lot"	31
	pt. "Meadows"	132
	"Thomas & William's Chance"	101
	pt. "Thatchcomb"	114
	pt. "Lingans Purchase"	8
	pt. "Brooke Neck"	150
	"Stallings's Swamp"	10
	"Meadows"	54
	"Bite"	5
Samuel Robertson	"Emmertons Addition"	20
	pt. "Halls Hills"	85
	pt. "Broughton Ashley"	73
Daniel Rawlings	pt. "Eltonhead Manor"	200
Henry Scott	pt. "Highland"	50

12:1769:21   ...

Dr. John Hamilton Smith	"Branford" – from Dr. John Hamilton	150
	pt. "Hardestys Choice" – from Dr. John Hamilton	150
	pt. "Henry Chew" – from Dr. John Hamilton	75
	1½ lots in Lower Marlbro – from h/o Col. John Smith	1½
	pt. "Dowdeswell Manor" – from h/o Col. John Smith	400
	pt. "Ordinary" – from h/o Col. John Smith	80½
Gavin Hamilton Smith	"Little Ganery" – from Dr. John Hamilton	42
	pt. "Grantham" – from Dr. John Hamilton	200
	"Sams Addition" – from Dr. John Hamilton	78
	"Hazard" – from Dr. John Hamilton	18½
	pt. "Grantham" – from h/o Col. John Smith	20
Philemon Smith	"Soldiers Fortune" – from h/o Col. John Smith	200
	pt. "Ordinary" – from h/o Col. John Smith	75
Alexander Hamilton Smith	pt. "Batchelors Quarter" – from h/o Col. John Smith	250
h/o Col. John Smith	pt. "Halls Craft" tbc: • Thomas Blake – 221⅔ a. in Debt Book 1770 • Rev. T. Claggett for h/o (N) Smith – 443⅓ in Debt Book 1770	665
Walter Smith	pt. "Parkers Clifts" – from Walter Murray	100
	"Fox's Road" – from Walter Murray	100
	"Wolf's Quarter" – from Walter Murray	300
	"Smiths Hog Pen" – from Walter Murray	319
	pt. "St. Leonards" – in corn; from Walter Murray	175
	"Taylors Disposal" – from Walter Murray	270
	pt. "Stones Hills" – from Walter Murray	25
	"Purchase" – from Walter Murray	22
James Somervill	"Toby's Quarter"	100
	"Rocky Neck"	50
	pt. "Allens Neck"	164
	"Narrow Neck & Gore"	18
	"Swamp"	67
	pt. "Gore"	100
h/o Maryland Skinner	pt. "Newington"	94
	pt. "Millers Folly"	250

John Simmonds	pt. "Rich Bottom"	25
	"Short Hills"	40
h/o Leonard Skinner	"Borders"	77½
	pt. "Dodsons Desire"	25
	pt. "Chance"	27
	pt. "Reserve"	32¼
12:1769:22 ...		
h/o George Smith	pt. "Desart"	52
	pt. "Round Bottom Plains"	100
Dorothy Sollers	"Forked Neck"	100
	"Hyam"	10
William Skinner	pt. "Scrap"	38
	pt. "Prestons Desire"	25
	pt. "Chance"	27
	pt. "Reserve"	32¼
	pt. "Border Enlarged"	77½
James Skinner	pt. "Border Enlarged"	77½
	pt. "Dodsons Desire"	25
	pt. "Chance"	27
	pt. "Reserve"	32¼
Robert Skinner	pt. "Blind Tom" – from Trueman Skinner	40
	"Addition" – from Trueman Skinner	60
	pt. "Tawneys Right" – from Trueman Skinner	150
Elizabeth Skinner	pt. "Tauneys Right"	150
	pt. "Scrape"	62
	pt. "Reserve"	121
	pt. "Newington"	94
h/o Adderton Skinner	pt. "Blind Tom"	32
	"Tauneys Delight"	70
	pt. "Mary Green"	36
	"Gore"	48
	pt. "Millers Folly"	250
	"Neglect"	25
William Sly	pt. "Morocco" – in corn	100
Alexander Somervill (cnp)	"Fox's Den"	50
	"Bartholomews Neck"	50

	pt. "Smiths Purchase"	238½
	pt. "Gore"	100
	"Goldens Folly"	75
Joseph Strickland	pt. "Robinsons Rest"	50
Josias Sunderland	pt. "Swinfen's Rest"	250
12:1769:23 ...		
William Sollers	pt. "Dorington"	182½
	pt. "Bowdleys Chance"	34
Joshua Sedwick	pt. "Neighbourhood"	150
	"Adjoinder"	50
	pt. "Nortons Purchase"	83⅓
Joseph Skinner	pt. "Orchard"	50
	pt. "Border Enlarged"	77½
	pt. "Dodsons Desire"	25
	pt. "Chance"	27
	"Reserve"	32¼
w/o Josias Sunderland, Jr.	pt. "Upper Bennett"	50
h/o Richard Stallings	pt. "Thatchcomb"	236
	pt. "Robinson's Rest" – overcharged	100
James Sewall	pt. "Dear Quarter"	62½
	pt. "Chance"	72½
	"Maidens Delight"	200
	pt. "Cops Hall"	80
	pt. "Parkers Clifts"	50
	"Good Luck"	150
John Standforth	pt. "Poor Land"	104
h/o John Skinner	pt. "Halls Hills"	877½
	"Sneaking Point"	50
	"Lingans Purchase"	94
	pt. "Hamiltons Park"	33
William Sansbury	pt. "Archers Hays"	40
h/o Joseph Smith, Jr.	pt. "Turners Pasture"	50
	pt. "Smiths Pasture"	100
	pt. "Mordyke"	15½
h/o William Smith (cnp)	pt. "Smiths Chance"	50
	pt. "Turners Place"	50

	pt. "Mordyke"	50
Mordecai Smith	pt. "Smith's Chance"	100
	pt. "Welch Poole"	72½
	pt. "Turners Place"	50
	pt. "Calender"	77
12:1769:24 ...		
Joseph Smith	pt. "Mordyke"	50
w/o John Stone	pt. "Defence"	65
John Stallings	pt. "Upper Bennett"	25
Ellis Slater	pt. "Laureys Reserve"	100
Stephen Stamp	pt. "Red Hall"	125
	pt. "Turner's Place" – from John Robinson	33⅓
	pt. "Turner's Place" – from Benjamin Skinner	111
Mary Smith	"Good Prospect"	50
	"Lands Land"	192
	"Addition"	28
	~~"Small Reward"~~	~~62½~~
Benjamin Skinner	<n/g>	<n/g>
Clement Smith	pt. "Halls Craft"	221
Patrick Smith	pt. "Halls Craft" – from Clement Smith	265
Nicholas Swamstead	pt. "Lordships Favor"	100
Thomas Stallings	pt. "Swinfens Rest"	64½
Stockett Sunderland	pt. "Laurey's Chance" or "Resurvey"	100
John Davis Scarth	pt. "Robinson's Rest"	50
Benjamin Sedwick	pt. "Bulmore's Branch" a/s "Right"	475
Jonathan Slater	pt. "Hall's Revenge"	28
	1 lot in Lower Marlbro	1
Stephen Steward (AA)	pt. "Illingsworths Fortune"	200
Eleanor Sly	pt. "Magruder"	150
12:1769:25 ...		
John Scott	pt. "Lordships Favor"	100
Raphael Tauney	"Stone's Hills" – from Roger Brooke, Jr.	50
Jacob Tucker	"Tucker's Thicket"	200
	pt. "Chance"	50
h/o Philip Thomas	"Major's Choice"	500
Joseph Talbutt, Jr.	pt. "Expectation"	100

John Tannehill	pt. "Calender"	123
	pt. "Cooper" & pt. "Friendship"	42
	pt. "Welch Poole" – from Lewis Griffiths	86
Ann Tannehill	pt. "Cooper" & pt. "Friendship" – from John Tannehill	173
Joseph Talbutt	pt. "Freemans Chance"	123
	pt. "Tillington"	150
	"Batchelers Fortune"	200
John Talbutt	pt. "Expectation"	50
Edward Talbutt	pt. "Tillington"	415½
John Turner	pt. "Bowdley's Chance"	91
Thomas Talbutt	pt. "Expectation"	100
h/o Benjamin Tasker, Esq.	"Hard Travel"	300
John Tucker	pt. "Neighbourhood"	82½
William Vermilion	"Creed's Chance"	64
John Wilkinson	pt. "Youngs Attempt"	100
Ben Kid Wilson & Priscilla Gover	pt. "Aldermason"	150
	"Govers Expectation"	89
	pt. "Welch Poole"	2
12:1769:26 ...		
George Wheeler	"Berry" – for h/o Miles Tauney	600
	"Long Point" – for h/o Miles Tauney	100
	"Wooden Point" – for h/o Miles Tauney	25
	pt. "Letchworth" – for h/o Miles Tauney	50
	pt. "Angle" – for h/o Miles Tauney	3
John Ward	"Velcher's Rest"	50
Samuel Ward	"Goldsons Inheritance"	150
Aaron Williams, Jr.	pt. "Friendship Rectified"	200
	pt. "Swinfens Adventure"	50
	pt. "Young's Desire"	50
Hilleary Wilson	pt. "Robinson"	200
	pt. "Robinson" – from h/o Job Hunt	13
	pt. "Lordships Favor" – from h/o Job Hunt	9
Aaron Williams, Sr. (cnp)	pt. "Williams's Hardship"	175
	"Williams's Rest"	50
	"Littlefield"	25

	pt. "Friendship Rectified"	25
	pt. "Swinfens Adventure"	25
James Weems, Jr.	"Success, Tauneys Ease, & Stockley"	200
	"Partnership"	75
h/o Joseph Wilkinson	pt. "Godsgrace"	120
	pt. "Stockley"	70
John Waters	pt. "Stockley"	419
	pt. "Gunterton"	40
	"Myrtle Point"	7
John Willing	pt. "Taylors Joy"	128
	"Jerusalem"	108
	pt. "Rich Bottom"	25
Francis Wolf, Jr.	pt. "Theobalds Manor"	50
	pt. "Grays Chance"	50
Richard Ward	pt. "Swinfens Rest"	116
	pt. "Danvin & Clares Hundred" – from h/o John Peters	138
12:1769:27 ...		
James Weems	pt. "Magruder"	450
	"Hogs Haunt"	50
	"Mauldens Luck"	25
	pt. "Busseys Orchard"	400
	pt. "Inland"	1
	pt. "Meadows Preserved"	46
	pt. "Bucks Chance"	150
	1 lot in Hunting Town	1
	pt. "Cuckolds Miss"	60
	pt. "Youngs Desire"	25
	pt. "Youngs Fortune"	60
	pt. "Youngs Attempt"	62
	"Penmanmure"	50
	pt. "Reserve"	50
	pt. "Trouble"	10
James Weems s/o David (cnp)	"Ringan"	200
	"Greenhouse"	155
	"Chews Purchase"	145

	pt. "Grantham"	45
	"Marshalls Addition"	70
Basil Williamson	pt. "Lingans Adventure"	310
Edward Wood	pt. "Woods Adventure"	150
	pt. "Titmarsh"	100
	pt. "Poor Land"	11
Jonah Winfield	pt. "Lands Land"	112
	pt. "Johnsons Farm"	100
Thomas Wells	pt. "Grantham Hall"	155
	"Arthur's Hall"	44
h/o James Williamson	"Den"	726
	"Foxes Nettle's"	20
	pt. "Batchelers Quarter"	420
h/o Roger Wheeler	pt. "Henry Chew"	237
	"Coxcomb"	150
	"Coxhead"	50
	pt. "Newington"	109
	"Smiths Conveyance"	60
12:1769:28 ...		
John Wilkinson	pt. "Henry Chew"	400
Thomas Wilson	pt. "St. Edmunds"	163
	pt. "Neglect"	16½
Leonard Wood	pt. "Woods Adventure"	100
Edward Wilson	"Dear Quarter"	25
	pt. "Robinson's Rest"	150
John Weems	pt. "Dowdeswell"	600
	pt. "Chance"	25
William White	pt. "Smiths Joy"	100
William Winnull	pt. "Nortons Purchase"	166⅔
William Hunton Wood	pt. "Arnolds Purchase"	100
Francis Whittington	pt. "Halls Hills"	100
Francis Williams	pt. "Inland"	100
	"Hutchings's Chance"	50
	pt. "Orchard"	40
Ithamor Williams (cnp)	pt. "Swinfens Adventure"	50
	pt. "Williams's Hardship"	75

	pt. "Friendship Rectified"	125
Joseph Wilson	"Tamot"	300
	pt. "Forsters Purchase"	150
	pt. "Robinson"	136
	pt. "Additional Spittle"	8
	pt. "Peahens Nest"	40
	pt. "Cedar Branch" tbc Richard Hellen s/o Richard in Debt Book 1770	125
	"Letchworths Cyprus"	200
	pt. "Bowen" – for h/o (N) King	230
	pt. "Brooke's Adventure"	150
	"Stones Lott"	50
	pt. "Arnolds Purchase"	50
	pt. "Youngs Attempt"	100
	pt. "Hap at a Venture"	50
	pt. "Horse Range"	125
12:1769:29 ...		
Philemon Young	pt. "Henry Chew"	175
	1 lot in Lower Marlbro	1
Joseph Wilson, Jr.	pt. "Lower Bennett"	189
Parker Young	"Hopyard"	150
	"Punch"	150
	pt. "Youngs Desire"	25
	pt. "Hoopers Neck"	275
Mary Yoe	pt. "Rattle Snake Hills"	100
Ezra Freeman	pt. "Forge"	50
Recapitulation		
12:1769:29a	**Sundry Errors & Overcharges**	
Gabriel Child	pt. "Letchworths Chance" – overcharge	336
Richard Chew	pt. "Robinsons Rest" – no such land	250
	"Stallings's Lott" – no such land	150
Samuel Davis	error	<n/g>
	"Gideon & Cleverly Right" – overcharge	342
Benjamin Duke	pt. "Brooke Place Manor" – overcharge	300
Thomas C. Dare	"Sampsons Divident" – overcharge	150
Thomas Hollingshead	"Kents Freehold" – overcharge	250

William Lyle	error	<n/g>
Edward Gardiner	pt. "Forked Neck" – overcharge	50
Dorothy Sollers	pt. "Forked Neck" – overcharge	100
John Brooke	pt. "Arnolds Purchase" – overcharge	100
Aaron Williams, Sr.	"Swinfens Adventure" – overcharge	25
Joseph Wilson	pt. "Robinson" – overcharge	136
Mary Smith	"Small Reward" – overcharge; also charged to Richard Bond	111
12:1769:<unnumbered>	**Certification**	

12:1770:1 ...		Acres
John Alton	pt. "Hardesty's Choice"	50
h/o David Arnold	pt. "Henry Chew"	290
	pt. "Abington"	350
	pt. "Hardesty's Choice"	130
w/o Samuel Austin	pt. "Cox's Chance"	140
	pt. "Farme"	20
Ann Askew	pt. "Laurey's Chance"	118
James Alnutt	pt. "Truemans Chance"	153
William Alnutt	pt. "Trueman's Chance"	156
	pt. "Agreement"	100
Samuel Austin	pt. "Cox's Chance"	117
Roger Brooke	pt. "Brooke Place Manor"	1096
John & Isaac Baker	"Devils Woodyard"	150
Jacob Bourn	pt. "Eltonhead Manor"	300
John Beveridge	"Dear Bought"	21
Abraham Bowen	pt. "Dividing Branch"	169½
	pt. "Billingsley's Farm"	136
David Bowen	pt. "Dividing Branch"	189
Isaac Bowen	pt. "Dividing Branch"	190
John Brooke	pt. "Brooke's Adventure"	116⅓
	pt. "Cedar Branch"	25
	pt. "Arnold's Purchase"	150
Jesse Bourne	pt. "Eltonhead Manour"	1167
12:1770:2 ...		
Jacob Bowen	pt. "Neighbourhood"	74
Henry Broome	pt. "Austin's Chance"	65
	pt. "Howard & Letchworth"	200
	pt. "Broad Point"	10
	pt. "Austin's Addition"	23
William Blackburn	pt. "Back Pasture"	50
James Bowen	pt. "Dividing Branch"	105
Thomas Bowen	pt. "Dividing Branch"	105
Col. Abraham Barnes	"Fishers Orchard"	255
	"Bran Fry"	100

h/o Roger Brooke, Jr.	pt. "Bowen"	70
	"Knowles's Branch"	98
	"Tauney's Addition"	123
	"Brooke Battle"	230
	pt. "Brookes Adventure"	233⅓
	pt. "Cedar Branch"	50
Thomas Blackburn	"Readby"	100
h/o Thomas Broome	"Rich Neck"	52
	"Mary's Widowhood"	30
	"Addition to Island Neck"	30
John Broome	pt. "Island Neck"	500
	pt. "Stone's Bay"	200
	"Adventure"	82½
	"Broad Point"	140
	pt. "Austin's Addition"	23
Ann Bond	"Middle Fuller"	200
	"Lower Fuller"	200
	pt. "Lower Bennett"	250
Isabella Barton	pt. "Upper Bennett"	50
Jesse Bowen	"Lambeth"	94
12:1770:3 **...**		
h/o Richard Blake	pt. "Upper Bennett"	557
	pt. "St. Edmunds"	200
	pt. "Lordship's Favour"	192
	pt. "Neglect"	50
Thomas Blake	pt. "Hall's Craft" – from h/o Col. Smith	221⅔
Mary Bond	pt. "Hogsdown"	275
	"Micham"	243
	pt. "Brooke Partition"	104
	pt. "Lawrey's Chance"	98¼
Richard Bond	pt. "Lawrey's Chance"	50
	"Small Land"	6¼
	"Small Reward"	111
	pt. "Spittle"	90
	pt. "Hogsdown"	25

James Kent Byrn	pt. "Neighbourhood"	26
	pt. "Prevent Danger"	100
Thomas Crumpton	"Jerusalem"	124
	pt. "Swinfen's Adventure"	25
	"Parker's Fortune" a/s "Chance"	263
	"Bigger"	1055
	pt. "Godsgrace"	100
	pt. "Morocco, Catterton's Lot, & Barbers Delight"	294
Rev. Thomas Claggett	pt. "Halls Craft" – for h/o (N) Smith	443⅓
Edmund Clare	pt. "Eltonhead Manor"	200
Gabriel Child	pt. "Letchworth's Chance"	336
Bennett Chew	"Chews Fortune"	49
Samuel Chew	pt. "Letchworth's Chance"	550
	pt. "Upper Bennett"	506
	"Lane & Gore"	51½
h/o Joseph Chilton	"Terra in Aqua"	4
Samuel Chew (AA)	"Popping Gay"	540
12:1770:4 ...		
Josias Crosby	pt. "Archers Hays"	30
	pt. "Goughs Purchase"	60
Michael Catterton	pt. "Lingans Purchase"	125
Henry Camden	pt. "Highland"	200
	"Chances"	70
Elizabeth Chesley w/o John	pt. "Batchelor's Quarter"	420
Michael Culpepper	"Venture"	16
Young Cox	pt. "Little Land"	17
	pt. "Cox's Inclosure"	65
	pt. "Cops Hall"	25
	pt. "Cox's Freehold"	120
	pt. "Merry Green Wood"	163
	pt. "Good Luck"	10
	"Hatchet"	25
Betty Clare	pt. "Lawreys Chance"	130
Mary Clare	pt. "Eltonhead Manor"	157
Calvert County School	"Security"	87
	pt. "Orchard"	100

Calvert County	pt. "Inland"	3
Isaac Clare	"Horse Path"	100
	pt. "Eltonhead Manor"	143
	"Concord"	161
	"Addition to Horse Path"	40
John Culpepper	"Wolf's Quarter"	40
Thomas Crutchely	"Addition"	50
John Cox	pt. "Smith's Lott"	33⅓
	pt. "Johnson's Farme, Good Prospect, & Lands Land"	87½
12:1770:5 ...		
Joseph Dawkins	"Dicks Cabin"	50
	pt. "Friendship"	25
	"Blinkhorn"	300
	"Fox's Road"	42
	"Joseph's Reserve"	196
Benjamin Duke	pt. "Rich Levells"	247
	pt. "Inland"	1
	pt. "Brooke Place Manor"	300
	pt. "Howard & Letchworth"	303
Henry Dixon	"Addition to Middlesex"	95
	"Fox's Walks"	5
Andrew Duke	"Middlesex"	100
	pt. "Gideon & Cleverlys Right" – from Cleverly Dare	19
h/o William Dorumple	"Hap at a Venture"	150
	pt. "Fox's Road"	158
h/o James Duke	pt. "Brooke Place"	171
	pt. "Lower Bennett"	211
	"Mackalls Desire"	78
Samuel Dare	pt. "Angle"	140
	pt. "Gideon & Cleverly's Right"	502
	pt. "Smiths Purchase"	119⅓
h/o James Dodson	"Huckleberry Hills"	50
	"Littleworth"	21

John Dossey	pt. "Mary Green"	63
	pt. "Dear Quarter"	62½
	pt. "Bennet's Desire"	10
	pt. "Robinson's Rest"	66⅓
Robert Day	pt. "No Name"	150
Benjamin Day	"Brandon"	57
	"Frampton"	50
William Dawkins	"Mary's Dukedom"	100
12:1770:6 ...		
James Dawkins	"Joseph's Place"	200
Susanna Dare	"Gideon & Cleverly's Right"	157
Nathaniel Dare	pt. "Gideon & Cleverly's Right" – from Susanna Dare	315
Philip Dossey	pt. resurvey of several tracts	104
	pt. "Tauney's Addition"	44
h/o William Day	pt. "No Name"	100
Cleverly Dare	pt. "Gideon & Cleverly's Right"	1174½
	pt. "Prestons Cliffs"	100
Ellis Dixon	"Hog Skin Cliffs"	100
Thomas Denton	pt. "Island Neck"	99
	"Puddlington"	50
John Dare	pt. "Gideon & Cleverly's Right"	100
Henry Dowell	pt. "Swinfen's Rest"	50
	pt. "Lingan's Purchase"	100
Richard Deale	pt. "Newington"	200
	pt. "Timberwell" – from James Deale	74
John Dossey s/o James	pt. "Garden"	100
	pt. "Robinson's Rest"	64
James Deale	pt. "Swinfen's Rest"	64½
Daniel Dossey	pt. "Garden"	67
Philip Dossey, Jr.	pt. "Robinson's Rest"	150
Francis Dossey	pt. "Bennetts Desire"	50
12:1770:7 ...		
Jacob Deale	pt. "Upper Bennett"	75
William Dare	pt. "Swinfens Rest"	250
	pt. "Lawrey's Chance" – from Mary Bond	36¼

Thomas Cleverly Dare	pt. "Agreement"	150
	"Bite the Biter"	112
	"Sampson's Dividend"	150
	pt. "Mannington"	25
	"Neglect"	50
Philip Dowell	pt. "Lingan's Purchase"	116
Alexander Deale	pt. "Newington"	46
	pt. "Islington"	25
John Dew	pt. "Archer's Hays"	43½
James Dossey, Jr.	pt. "Youngs Mount"	159
	pt. "Youngs Fortune"	40
James Dawkins s/o James	pt. "Hap Hazard"	90
Richard Everist	pt. "Highland"	50
Ann Elt	pt. "Eltonhead Manor"	336
Isaac Essex	pt. "Wolf Trap"	55
Robert Ethrington	pt. "Comsey"	92½
Barnaby Eagan	pt. "Brooke Place Manor"	400
Ezra Freeman	pt. "Forge"	50
h/o George Fowler	pt. "Tillington"	45½
James Fraizer	"Hills Hall"	100
	"White Marsh"	68
12:1770:8 ...		
Thomas Freeman	pt. "Rockhold"	135
h/o Joseph Freeman	pt. "Arnolds Purchase"	50
Col. William Fitzhugh	pt. "Eltonhead Manor"	2500
	pt. "Miles End"	399½
	pt. "Miles Run"	150
	"Hatton's Cove"	70
	"Staffords Freehold"	70
	"Round Ponds"	100
	"Leach" or "Smith's Hills"	100
	"Gore"	70
Jacob Freeland	pt. "Letchworths Chance"	179
	"Neglect"	125
	pt. "Fuller"	100

Robert Freeland	pt. "Trueman's Chance"	232
	"Dosseys Folly"	70
	"Burks Purchase"	50
	pt. "Dear Quarter"	100
	pt. "Fuller"	200
Peregrine Freeland	pt. "Mackall's Force"	323½
Frisby Freeland	pt. "Mackall's Force"	323½
John Ferguson	pt. "Govers & Griffiths Pasture"	40
	pt. "Skinner's Chance"	30
	pt. "Turner's Place"	126
Alexander Fraizer	"Sterlings Chance"	40
	"Sterling's Nest"	550
Jacob French	pt. "Danvin"	125
Richard Gibson	pt. "Swinfen's Rest"	72
	pt. "Lordships Favor"	50
h/o John Griffith	pt. "Welch Poole"	143¼
	pt. "Skinner's Chance"	90
12:1770:9 ...		
George Gantt	"Selbys Cliffs" – for h/o John Beckett	200
	pt. "Mears" – for h/o John Beckett	200
	pt. "Gunterton" – for h/o John Beckett	250
	pt. "Hardesty" – for h/o John Beckett	50
	"Poppy Gray" – for h/o John Beckett	40
John Gibson	pt. "Spittle"	90
	pt. "Additional Spittle"	22
John Gardner	pt. "Johnson's Lott"	100
Charles Grahame	pt. "Halls Craft"	521
	"Howard"	42
	"Bell"	68
	"Blackwall"	38
	pt. "Hardesty"	180
Joseph Galloway	pt. "Spittle"	20
	pt. "Additional Spittle"	28
Lewis Griffiths (cnp)	pt. "Welchpoole"	135
	pt. "Archers Hays"	231
	"Lewis's Slipe & Dews Purchase"	26

	"Long Lane"	31
	"All Points"	24
	pt. "Cooper"	86
James Gibson	pt. "Additional Spittle"	88
	pt. "Newington"	22
h/o Robert Gover	pt. "Archers Hays"	190
	"Goughs Purchase" a/s "Goughs Pasture"	50
	"Govers Addition"	167
	"Govers Meadows"	59
	pt. "Dunkirk"	150
	pt. "Exchange"	66
John Griffin	pt. "Robinson"	60
Edward Gantt	pt. "Ordinary"	606
	"Kingsburys Marsh"	130
	"Craft"	90
12:1770:10 ...		
Thomas Gray	pt. "Wolton & Hatch"	75
William Gray s/o Thomas	"Grays Addition"	109
John Gray (Patuxent)	"Marsh Land & Bushhead"	345
	"Hazard"	42
	pt. "Brooke Adventure"	100
	"Tonottle" a/s "Tuxbury"	100
	"Toddy"	138
William Gray	"Reserve"	50
	"Stennetts Ramble"	35
Howerton Games	pt. "Johnson's Lot"	50
	"Hazard"	25
Robert Gardiner	pt. "Johnson's Lott"	100
	"Wolf's Hole"	50
John Gardiner	pt. "Johnson's Lot"	100
Samuel Gray	"Norwood"	200
	"Theobush"	50
	pt. "Austin's Chance"	91
Driver Graves	pt. "Stevens Plains"	25
	"Graves's Rehobeth"	80

Edward Gardner	"Chilton" a/s "Chatham"	80
	pt. "Forked Neck" or "Dorington"	50
	"Short Neck"	76
Benjamin Gardiner	pt. "Round Pond Plains"	100
h/o James Trueman Greenfield	pt. "Aldermason"	150
	"Addition"	56½
Henry Gray	"Labour in Vain"	100
h/o Job Hunt	pt. "Upper Bennett"	195
12:1770:11 ...		
Mary Graves	pt. "Hap Hazard"	45
	"Batchelors Hall"	300
	"Timber Neck"	50
	"Clares Littleworth"	43
Esther Gray	"Fishing Creek"	165
	"Chaplain"	100
	"East Fishing Creek"	150
	"Nutt's Cliffs"	150
	"East Chaplain"	100
Thomas Hollingshead	pt. "Kents Freehold"	250
James Heighe	pt. "Beakly"	300
	"Forsters Purchase"	150
	pt. "Roberts Chance"	34
	"James's Chance"	40
	"Samuels Chance"	15
	"Clark's Hills"	19
	"Little Land"	11
	"Heighe's Addition"	15
	"James's Addition"	21
Thomas Holdsworth Heighe	pt. "Brooke Place"	300
William Harrison	pt. "Brook's Discovery"	200
	pt. "Lawrey's Reserve"	75
	pt. "Brothers Discovery"	126
	pt. "Cox's Freehold"	128
Joseph Hardesty	pt. "Den"	37½
	pt. "Nichols's Chance"	55
	"Nelson's Reserve"	22

William Hickman	pt. "Newington"	220
	pt. "Islington"	542
Thomas Hunt	pt. "Lordship's Favour"	50
h/o John Hance	pt. "Newington"	9
	"Johns Neglect"	128
	pt. "Illingsworth's Fortune"	65
12:1770:12 ...		
Henry Howes	pt. "Refuse"	50
	"Jensby's Lott"	46
	"Purchase"	23
Henry Hardesty	pt. "Den"	37
	pt. "Nichols's Chance"	55
William Hardesty	pt. "Lordship's Favour"	75
Henry Harrison	pt. "Swinfen's Rest"	150
Thomas Holland	pt. "St. James's Enlarged"	1138
	pt. "Alexanders Hope"	38
George Hall	pt. "Chance"	25
Abraham Hooper	pt. "Taylors Joy"	343
Walter Hoxton (CH)	pt. "Homesham"	117
Ann Holland	pt. "Abington"	150
William Harris	pt. "Durain"	200
	pt. "Illingsworth's Fortune"	100
	pt. "Littleworth"	150
	pt. "Tillington"	73
	pt. "Letchworth's Chance"	275
Dr. Leonard Holliday	"Buzzard Island"	700
	"Addition"	51
	pt. "Arnolds Purchase"	50
Newman Harvey	pt. "Turner's Place"	126
Benjamin Harris	pt. "Expectation"	100
	pt. "Whittle's Rest" – from Richard Johns	148
	pt. "Parker's Cliffs" – from Richard Johns	50
William Harris, Jr.	"Addition"	100
12:1770:13 ...		
Benjamin Hance (cnp)	"Parkers Clifts"	100
	pt. "Warrington"	175

	pt. "Agreement"	50
	"Bussey's Garden"	175
	pt. "Illington"	250
	"Hance Lane"	20
	pt. "Newington"	3
	"Purchase"	154
	"Warings Chance"	56
	resurvey of several tracts	119½
James Henley	"Smuggs Folly"	80
Joseph Hance	"Warbleton"	404
Kensey Hance	pt. "Stockley" a/s resurvey of several tracts – from Joseph Hance	100
Hannah Hungerford	pt. "Friendship" – from David Hellen s/o John	75
John Hungerford	pt. "Eltonhead Manor" – from David Hellen s/o John	200
	"Jermyn Quarter Enlarged" – from David Hellen s/o John	143
James Hellen	pt. "Truswell"	150
Samuel Hance	pt. "Theobush Manning"	189
Walter Hellen	pt. "Hoopers Neck"	275
Edmund Hellen	pt. "Waring"	121
	pt. "Bowdleys Chance"	75
	"Busseys Lot"	75
	"Hellens Lot"	12
Edmund Hungerford	pt. "Hogs Skin Neck"	100
	pt. "Stephens's Land"	100
	"Purchase"	24
	pt. "Desart"	100
Philip Hunt	pt. "Lordships Favour"	100
12:1770:14 ...		
Richard Hellen	pt. "Truswell"	150
	"Milton's Lott"	100
	"Persia"	100
	"Harrow the Hill Resurveyed"	77
	pt. "Rich Levell"	20
David Hellen s/o Richard	"Gully"	63½
Thomas Gosling Hutchins	pt. "Magruder"	175

Rebecca Hungerford	pt. "Friendship"	31¼
	pt. "Taylors Joy"	114
	pt. "Allens Neck"	36
Joseph Ireland	"Leach's Freehold" – from h/o James Leach	125
John Ivey	pt. "Stephens Plains" – from John Graves	25
Kensey Johns (AA)	pt. "Angelica"	200
	pt. "Mears"	200
	pt. "Inland"	1
Benjamin Johns	pt. "Angelica"	400
	pt. "Johns's Addition"	112
	pt. "Inland"	1
Richard Johns	pt. "Whittle's Rest"	188
	pt. "Devise"	75
	pt. "Parkers Cliffs"	130
h/o Joseph Isaac	"Plumb Point"	400
	pt. "Lordship's Favour"	205
	"Purchase"	100
Col. William Ireland	"Bridge"	100
	"George's Desire"	50
	"Addition"	43
	"Angle"	87
	pt. "Peahens Nest"	35
	pt. "Island Plains"	32
	"Lyons Creek"	300
	pt. "Dunkirk"	50
12:1770:15 ...		
William Johnson s/o George	pt. "Red Hall"	100
h/o Richard Johns	"Purchase"	100
	pt. "Youngs Desire"	12
William Ireland s/o Thomas	pt. "Halls Hills"	550
Mary Ireland	pt. "Eltonhead Manor"	200
	pt. "Preston's Cliffs"	108
	pt. "Angle"	88
	pt. "No Name"	100
	"Mill Marsh"	63

John Ireland	pt. "Tillington"	189
	"Wolf Trap"	45
Thomas Johnson	"Brewhouse"	260
w/o John Johnson	"Elizabeth"	200
	pt. "Gift"	70
Thomas Johnson	pt. "Prestons Cliffs" – from John Johnson	314
William Johnson s/o Jeremiah	pt. "Exchange"	150
Dr. Edward Johnson	"Preston"	200
	"Moffatts Mount"	200
	"Woods Adventure"	50
	"Hay Marsh"	18
	pt. "Poor Land"	185
	"Musqueto Point"	46
	"Turners Chance"	50
	"Addition to Wood's Venture"	33
Richard Ireland	"Ireland's Hope"	50
	pt. "Desart"	198
John Kent	pt. "Rockheld"	160
James Kirshaw	pt. "Prevent Danger"	100
John Kirshaw	pt. "Prevent Danger"	50
12:1770:16 ...		
Francis Kirshaw	pt. "Sharpes Outlet"	100
	pt. "Concord"	63
Joseph Kent	pt. "Timberwell"	326
	pt. "Additional Spittle"	50
Rev. Francis Lauder	pt. "Preston's Cliffs"	239
	pt. "Gore"	50
John Laurence	pt. "Laureys Addition"	145
	pt. "Islington"	50
William Lyles	pt. "Red Hall"	150
	pt. "Stripe"	8
	pt. "Turners Pasture"	170
	pt. "Long Lane"	32
h/o Lewis Lewin	pt. "Red Hall"	37½
John Laveal	pt. "Whittle's Rest"	210
Robert Lyles	pt. "Red Hall"	100

Capt. Richard Lane & Benjamin Lane	pt. "Homesham" – from Sarah Lane	233
Samuel Lyles	pt. "Laureys Chance"	50
Jeremiah Maulden	pt. "Parkers Cliffs"	250
John Mackall s/o John	pt. resurvey of several tracts	104
	pt. "Tauneys Addition"	44
James Mackall s/o John	pt. resurvey of several tracts	104
	pt. "Tauneys Addition"	44
Benjamin Mackall s/o John	"Schoolhouse"	100
	"Brigantine Adventure"	24
Elisabeth Marshall w/o Thomas	"Cox's Folly"	50
	pt. "Farm"	19
12:1770:17 ...		
William Thomas Marshall 3rd	pt. "Cox's Choice"	143
John Manning	pt. "Theobalds Manor"	112
	pt. "Gunsby"	168
	"Cold Harbour"	½
William Monnett	"Williams Purchase"	206
Jane Macdowell	pt. "Cole's Cliffs"	50
h/o James Mackall	"Cage"	50
	"Bussey's Lot"	100
	"Mackalls Desire"	10
h/o Thomas Morgan	pt. "Desire"	79
	pt. "Grays Chance"	350
	"Fellowship"	160
John Mackall (St. Leonards)	pt. "Morgan"	60
	pt. "Horse Range"	180
	"Claggetts Desire"	376
	"Desert"	350
	pt. "St. James's"	300
Benjamin Mackall (Holland Point) (cnp)	"Copartnership"	182
	pt. "Chance"	307
	"Hallowing Point"	400
	"Seamores Neck"	382
	pt. "Horse Range"	165
	pt. "Sharpe's Outlett"	100

	"Thoroughbridge"	250
	"Brooke Choice"	146
	pt. "Dividing Branch"	179
	pt. "Trouble"	27
	pt. "Morocco" – in corn	50
	"Addition to Sharpe's Outlett"	112
	pt. "Read"	46½
	pt. "Read & Magruder"	92½
	pt. "Coursey"	46½
h/o Barbara Mackall	pt. "Brooke Partition" – Thomas Bond	200
Rousby Miller	pt. "Orchard"	253
Ann Mills	pt. "Wolton"	25
	pt. "Catch"	50
12:1770:18 ...		
James Morsell	pt. "Rattlesnake Hills"	120
	"Chance"	70
	pt. "Littleworth"	60
	pt. "Mary Green"	55
James John Mackall (cnp)	pt. "Lower Bennett"	500
	pt. "Theobush Manor"	100
	"Cornhill"	350
	"Alexanders Hope"	200
	pt. "Grays Chance"	200
	pt. "Bone Road"	89
	pt. "Gunsbey"	38
	"Cold Harbour"	100
	pt. "Brooke Place"	432
	pt. "Stonesbay"	225
	"Piney Point"	50
	"Exchange"	350
	"Laureys Point" & pt. "Laureys Rest"	100
	"Littleworth"	77
	"Cold Carbey"	200
	pt. "Angle"	350
	pt. "Lawreys Rest"	295
	"Fox's Walks"	40

	"Bramhall"	500
	"Neglect"	30
	pt. "Godsgrace"	617
	"Meads"	166
	pt. "Evans's Land"	200
	pt. "Coles Cliffs"	150
	pt. "Preston's Cliffs"	63
	pt. "Cedar Branch"	240
	pt. "Sewalls Purchase"	30
	"Bramells Addition"	33
	"Angel" or "Angle"	87
John Norfolk	"Kidd's Levells"	84
	pt. "Island Plains"	27
	pt. "Ridge"	100
	pt. "Refuse"	100
	"Refuge"	14
James Norfolk	pt. "Peahens Nest"	50
William Powell	pt. "Gideon & Cleverly's Right" – from Cleverly Dare	5½
John Pardo	pt. "Rocky Neck"	50
	pt. "Foxes Walks"	70
12:1770:19 ...		
Mary Parker	"Clay Hammond"	380
	"Wilson's Commons"	29
Elizabeth Prindowell	pt. "Parkers Cliffs"	100
	pt. "Roberts Addition"	5
	pt. "Robert's Chance"	5½
	pt. "Beakly"	66⅔
Leonard Prindowell	pt. "Roberts Addition"	10
	pt. "Roberts Chance"	11
	pt. "Beakly"	133⅓
h/o John Peters	pt. "Kents Freehold"	50
	pt. "Lordship's Favour"	100
Robert Peters	pt. "Danvin & Clare's Hundred"	142
William Patterson	pt. "Stonesbay"	75
	pt. "Evans's Land"	65

h/o Alexander Parran	pt. "Patience"	360
	"Addition"	19
h/o Hutcheson Parker	pt. "St. Leonards" – in corn	175
	"Bulmore's Branch"	50
	pt. "Stones Hills"	25
Young Parran, Esq.	pt. "Desert"	349
	"Preston"	400
	pt. "Winfield's Resurvey"	207
	pt. "Bermingham"	25
	pt. "Parrans Park"	150
	pt. "Morgan"	45
	"Brooke Plains"	100
	pt. "Inland"	2
	"Discovery"	99
Samuel Parran	pt. "Winfields Resurvey"	207
	pt. "Bermingham"	25
	pt. "Morgan"	45
	pt. land without name	100
	pt. "Parrans Park"	150
12:1770:20 ...		
John Peters	pt. "Johnsons Farm"	150
	pt. "Turners Place"	66⅔
	pt. "Griffiths & Govers Pasture"	20
John Rawlings	pt. "Eltonhead Manor"	300
	"Cumpton" – from Margaret Parran	75
	"Rawlings's Purchase" – from Margaret Parran	60
Thomas Rhodes	"Black Robin"	38
Daniel Ross	pt. "Robinson's Rest"	200
Thomas Reynolds (cnp)	pt. "Robinson"	191
	pt. "St. Edmunds"	150
	pt. "Robinsons Rest"	518
	pt. "Good Luck"	100
	"Adjoinder" a/s "Adjunction"	10
	pt. "Brookes Discovery"	64
	"Crouder's Lot"	60
	"Reserve"	300

	"Fox's Chance"	72
	"Rich Bitt"	5½
	"Foxes Home"	30
	"Sterling's Perch"	300
	pt. "Lordship's Favour"	285
	pt. "Neglect"	60
	pt. "Cox's Inclosure"	70
	pt. "Cox's Freehold"	142
	"Troublesome"	150
	"Bennetts Refuge"	33
	pt. "Hopewell"	94
	pt. "Abington Manor"	769
	"Angles Lane"	37
	"Stallings Lot"	31
	pt. "Meadows"	186
	"Thomas & Williams Chance"	101
	pt. "Thatchcomb"	114
	pt. "Lingans Purchase"	8
	pt. "Brook Neck"	150
	"Stallings's Swamp"	10
	"Bite"	5
Samuel Robertson	"Emmerton's Addition"	20
	pt. "Halls Hills"	85
	pt. "Broughton Ashley"	73
Henry Scott	pt. "Highland"	50
12:1770:21 ...		
Daniel Rawlings	pt. "Eltonhead Manor"	200
	"Bathens Loss" – from Margaret Parran	50
	"Dearbought" – from Margaret Parran	200
Dr. John Hamilton Smith	"Branford"	150
	pt. "Hardesty's Choice"	150
	pt. "Henry Chew"	75
	1½ lots in Lower Marlbro	1½
	pt. "Dowdeswell Manor"	400
	pt. "Ordinary"	80½

Gavin Ham. Smith	"Little Ganery"	42
	pt. "Grantham"	220
	"Sam's Addition"	78
	"Hazard"	18½
Philemon Smith	"Soldiers Fortune"	200
	pt. "Ordinary"	75
Alexander Ham. Smith	pt. "Batchelors Quarter"	250
Walter Smith	pt. "Parkers Cliffs"	100
	"Fox's Road"	100
	"Wolf Quarter"	300
	"Smith's Hog Pen"	319
	pt. "St. Leonards" – in corn	175
	"Taylors Disposal"	270
	pt. "Stones Hills"	25
	"Purchase"	22
Isaac Simmons	pt. "Chance" – from Richard Johns	50
James Somerville	"Toby's Quarter"	100
	"Rocky Neck"	50
	pt. "Allens Neck"	164
	"Narrow Neck & Gore"	18
	"Swamp"	67
	pt. "Gore"	100
h/o Maryland Skinner	pt. "Newington"	94
	pt. "Miller's Folly"	250
h/o Leonard Skinner	"Borders"	77½
	pt. "Dodsons Desire"	25
	pt. "Chance"	27
	pt. "Reserve"	32¼
12:1770:22 ...		
John Simmonds	pt. "Rich Bottom"	25
	"Short Hills"	40
h/o George Smith	pt. "Desart"	52
	pt. "Round Bottom Plains"	100
Dorothy Sollers	"Forked Neck"	100
	"Hyam"	10

William Skinner	pt. "Scrap"	38
	pt. "Prestons Desire"	25
	pt. "Chance"	27
	pt. "Reserve"	32¼
	pt. "Border Enlarged"	77½
James Skinner	pt. "Border Enlarged"	77½
	pt. "Dodsons Desire"	25
	pt. "Chance"	27
	pt. "Reserve"	32¼
Robert Skinner	pt. "Blind Tom"	40
	"Addition"	60
	pt. "Tawneys Right"	150
Elizabeth Skinner	pt. "Tawney's Right"	150
	pt. "Scrap"	62
	pt. "Reserve"	121
	pt. "Newington"	94
h/o Adderton Skinner	pt. "Blind Tom"	32
	"Tawneys Delight"	70
	pt. "Mary Green"	36
	"Gore"	48
	pt. "Miller's Folly"	250
	"Neglect"	25
William Sly	pt. "Morocco" – in corn	100
Alexander Somerville	"Fox's Den"	50
	"Bartholomews Neck"	50
	pt. "Smith's Purchase"	238½
	pt. "Gore"	100
	"Goldens Folly"	75
Joseph Strickland	pt. "Robinson's Rest"	50
12:1770:23 **...**		
Josias Sunderland	pt. "Swinfen's Rest"	250
William Sollers	pt. "Dorington"	182½
	pt. "Bowdley's Chance"	34
Joshua Sedwick	pt. "Neighbourhood"	150
	"Adjoinder"	50
	pt. "Nortons Purchase"	83⅓

Joseph Skinner	pt. "Orchard"	50
	pt. "Border Enlarged"	77½
	pt. "Dodsons Desire"	25
	pt. "Chance"	27
	pt. "Reserve"	32¼
w/o Josias Sunderland, Jr.	pt. "Upper Bennett"	50
Phineas Stallings	pt. "Thatchcomb"	236
James Sewall	pt. "Dear Quarter"	62½
	pt. "Chance"	72½
	"Maidens Delight"	200
	pt. "Cops Hall"	80
	pt. "Parkers Cliffs"	50
	"Good Luck"	150
John Standforth	pt. "Poor Land"	104
h/o John Skinner	pt. "Halls Hills"	877½
	"Sneaking Point"	50
	pt. "Lingan's Purchase"	94
	pt. "Hamilton's Park"	33
William Sansbury	pt. "Archers Hays"	40
h/o Joseph Smith, Jr.	pt. "Turners Pasture"	50
	pt. "Smiths Pasture"	100
	pt. "Archers Hays"	15½
h/o William Smith	pt. "Smiths Chance"	50
	pt. "Turners Place"	50
	pt. "Mordyke"	50
12:1770:24 ...		
Mordecai Smith	pt. "Smiths Chance"	100
	pt. "Welchpoole"	72½
	pt. "Turners Place"	50
	pt. "Calender"	77
Joseph Smith	pt. "Mordyke"	50
w/o John Stone	pt. "Defence"	65
John Stallings	pt. "Upper Bennett"	25
Ellis Slater	pt. "Lawrey's Reserve"	100
Stephen Stamp	pt. "Red Hall"	125
	pt. "Turners Place"	144⅓

Capt. Henry Brooke	"Good Prospect" – from Mary Smith	50
	"Lands Land" – from Mary Smith	192
	"Addition" – from Mary Smith	28
Benjamin Skinner	\<n/g\>	\<n/g\>
Clement Smith	pt. "Halls Craft"	221
Patrick Smith	pt. "Halls Craft"	265
Nicholas Swamstead	pt. "Lordship's Favour"	100
Thomas Stallings	pt. "Swinfen's Rest"	64½
Stockett Sunderland	pt. "Lawreys Chance" or "Resurvey"	100
John Davis Scarth	pt. "Robinson's Rest"	50
Benjamin Sedwick	pt. "Bulmore's Branch" a/s "Right"	475
Jonathan Slater	pt. "Halls Revenge"	28
	1 lot in Lower Marlbro	1
Stephen Steward	pt. "Illingsworth's Fortune"	200
Eleanor Sly	pt. "Magruder"	150
12:1770:25 ...		
John Scott	pt. "Lordship's Favour"	100
Raphael Tauney	pt. "Stones Hills"	50
Jacob Tucker	"Tuckers Thickett"	200
	pt. "Chance"	50
h/o Philip Thomas, Esq.	"Majors Choice"	500
Joseph Talbutt, Jr.	pt. "Expectation"	100
John Tannehill	pt. "Calender"	123
	pt. "Cooper" & pt. "Friendship"	42
	pt. "Welchpoole"	86
Ann Tannehill	pt. "Cooper" & pt. "Friendship"	173
Joseph Talbutt	pt. "Freemans Chance"	123
	pt. "Tillington"	150
	"Batchelors Fortune"	200
John Talbutt	pt. "Expectation"	50
Edward Talbutt	pt. "Tillington"	415½
John Turner	pt. "Bowdley's Chance"	91
Thomas Talbutt	pt. "Expectation"	100
h/o Benjamin Tasker, Esq.	"Hard Travell"	300
John Tucker	pt. "Neighbourhood"	82½
William Vermilion	"Creeds Chance"	64

John Wilkinson	pt. "Youngs Attempt"	100
Ben Kid Wilson & Priscilla Gover	pt. "Aldermason"	150
	"Govers Expectation"	89
	pt. "Welchpoole"	2
12:1770:26 ...		
George Wheeler	"Berry" – for h/o (N) Tauney	600
	"Long Point" – for h/o (N) Tauney	100
	"Wooden Point" – for h/o (N) Tauney	25
	pt. "Letchworth" – for h/o (N) Tauney	50
	pt. "Angle" – for h/o (N) Tauney	3
John Ward	"Velchee's Rest"	50
Samuel Ward	"Goldson's Inheritance"	150
Aaron Williams, Jr.	pt. "Friendship Rectified"	200
	pt. "Swinfen's Adventure"	50
	pt. "Youngs Desire"	50
Hilleary Wilson	pt. "Robinson"	213
	pt. "Lordship's Favour"	9
Aaron Williams, Sr.	pt. "Williams's Hardship"	175
	"Williams's Rest"	50
	"Littlefield"	25
	pt. "Friendship Rectified"	25
	pt. "Swinfen's Adventure"	25
James Weems, Jr.	"Success, Tauneys Ease, & Stockley"	200
	"Partnership"	75
h/o Joseph Wilkinson	pt. "Godsgrace"	120
	pt. "Stockley"	70
John Waters	pt. "Stockley"	419
	pt. "Gunterton"	40
	"Myrtle Point"	7
John Willing	pt. "Taylors Joy" – 114⅓ a.	128
	"Jerusalem"	108
	pt. "Rich Bottom"	25
Francis Wolf, Jr.	pt. "Theobald Manor"	50
	pt. "Grays Chance"	50
Richard Ward	pt. "Swinfens Rest"	116
	pt. "Danvins & Clares Hundred"	138

12:1770:27 ...		
James Weems	pt. "Magruder"	450
	"Hogs Haunt"	50
	"Mauldens Luck"	25
	pt. "Busseys Orchard"	400
	pt. "Inland"	1
	pt. "Meadows Preserved"	46
	pt. "Bucks Chance"	150
	1 lot in Hunting Town	1
	pt. "Cuckholds Miss"	60
	pt. "Youngs Desire"	25
	pt. "Youngs Fortune"	60
	pt. "Youngs Attempt"	62
	"Penmanmaure"	50
	pt. "Reserve"	50
	pt. "Trouble"	10
James Weems s/o David	"Ringan"	200
	"Greenhouse"	155
	"Chews Purchase"	145
	pt. "Grantham"	45
	"Marshalls Addition"	70
Basil Williamson	pt. "Lingans Adventure"	310
Edward Wood	pt. "Woods Adventure"	150
	pt. "Titmarsh"	100
	pt. "Poor Land"	11
Jonah Winfield	pt. "Lands Land"	112
	pt. "Johnsons Farm"	100
Thomas Wells	pt. "Grantham Hall"	155
	"Arthur's Hall"	44
h/o James Williamson	"Den"	726
	"Fox's Nettles"	20
	pt. "Batchelors Quarter"	420
h/o Roger Wheeler (cnp)	pt. "Henry Chew"	237
	"Coxcomb"	150
	"Coxhead"	50
	pt. "Newington"	109

	"Smith's Conveyance"	60
12:1770:28 ...		
John Wilkinson	pt. "Henry Chew"	400
Thomas Wilson	pt. "St. Edmunds"	163
	pt. "Neglect"	16½
Leonard Wood	pt. "Woods Adventure"	100
Edward Wilson	"Dear Quarter"	25
	pt. "Robinsons Rest"	150
John Weems	pt. "Dowdeswell"	600
	pt. "Chance"	25
William White	pt. "Smith's Joy"	100
William Winnull	pt. "Nortons Purchase"	166⅔
William Hunton Wood	pt. "Arnolds Purchase"	100
Francis Whittington	pt. "Halls Hills"	100
Francis Williams	pt. "Inland"	100
	"Hutchings's Chance"	50
	pt. "Orchard"	40
Ithamor Williams	pt. "Swinfens Adventure"	50
	pt. "Williams's Hardship"	75
	pt. "Friendship Rectified"	125
h/o Joseph Wilson	"Tamot"	300
	pt. "Forsters Purchase"	150
	pt. "Robinson"	136
	pt. "Additional Spittle"	8
	pt. "Peahens Nest"	40
	pt. "Cedar Branch"	75
	"Letchworths Cypruss"	200
	pt. "Bowen" – for h/o (N) King	230
	pt. "Brookes Adventure"	150
	"Stones Lot"	50
	pt. "Arnolds Purchase"	50
	pt. "Youngs Attempt"	100
	pt. "Hap at a Venture"	50
	pt. "Horse Range"	125
12:1770:29 ...		

Philemon Young	pt. "Henry Chew"	175
	1 lot in Lower Marlbro	1
Joseph Wilson, Jr.	pt. "Lower Bennett"	189
Parker Young	"Hopyard"	150
	"Punch"	150
	pt. "Youngs Desire"	25
	pt. "Hoopers Neck"	275
Mary Yeo	pt. "Rattle Snake Hills"	100
Richard Hellen s/o Richard	pt. "Cedar Branch" – from Joseph Wilson	50
Peter Hellen	"Huckleberry Quarter Enlarged"	127¼
Recapitulation		
12:1770:<unnumbered>	**Recapitulation (continued)**	
Certification		

12:1771:1 ...		Acres
John Alton	pt. "Hardesteys Choice"	50
h/o David Arnold	pt. "Henrey Chew"	290
	pt. "Abingdon"	350
	pt. "Hardesteys Choice"	130
	pt. "Henrey Chew" – from Fillimon Young	110½
w/o Samuel Austin	pt. "Cox's Chance"	140
	pt. "Farme"	20
William Askew	pt. "Lowreys Chance"	118
James Alnutt	pt. "Freemans Choice"	150
William Alnutt	pt. "Freemans Choice"	156
	pt. "Agreement"	100
Samuel Austin	pt. "Cox's Chance"	117
Zeacheus Alnutt	pt. "Brooks Portion"	119
	pt. "Hog Down"	7
	pt. "Little Reward"	21
Roger Brooke	pt. "Brooks Place Manor"	1096
John & Isaac Baker	"Devels Woodyard"	150
Jacob Bourn	pt. "Eltonhead Manor"	300
John Beveridge	"Dearbought"	21
12:1771:2 ...		
Abraham Bowen	pt. "Devideing Branch"	169½
	pt. "Billingsleys Farme"	136
Isaac Bowen	pt. "Devideing Branch"	190
David Bowen	pt. "Devideing Branch"	189
John Brooke	pt. "Brooks Adventure"	116¾
	pt. "Ceder Branch"	25
	pt. "Arnolds Purchase"	150
Jesse Bourne	pt. "Eltonhead Manor"	1167
Jacob Bowen	pt. "Neighbourhood"	74
Henry Broome	pt. "Austins Chance"	65
	pt. "Howard & Letchworth"	200
	pt. "Broad Point"	10
	pt. "Austins Addition"	23
William Blackburn	pt. "Back Pasture"	50
James Bowen	pt. "Devideing Branch"	105

Thomas Bowen	pt. "Devideing Branch"	105
Col. Abraham Barnes	"Fishers Orchard"	253
	"Bran Fry"	100
Thomas Blackburn	"Readley"	100
12:1771:3 ...		
h/o Roger Brooke, Jr.	pt. "Bowen"	70
	pt. "Knowles Branch"	98
	"Tauneys Addition"	123
	"Brooke Battle"	230
	pt. "Brooks Adventure"	156
	pt. "Ceder Branch"	50
h/o Thomas Broome – tbc John Broome (124 a.) in 1773	"Rich Neck"	52
	"Marey Widowhood"	130
	"Addition to Island Neck"	130
John Broome	"Island Neck"	500
	pt. "Stone Bay"	200
	"Adventure"	82½
	"Broadpoint"	140
	pt. "Austings Addition"	23
Ann Bond	"Middle Fuller"	200
	"Lower Fuller"	200
	pt. "Lower Bennett"	250
Isabella Barton	pt. "Upper Bennett"	50
Jesse Bowen	"Lambeth"	94
h/o Richard Blake	pt. "Upper Bennett"	557
	pt. "St. Edmunds"	200
	pt. "Lordships Favour"	192
	pt. "Neglect"	50
Thomas Blake	pt. "Halls Craft"	221⅔
Mary Bond	pt. "Hogsdown"	275
	"Micham"	243
	pt. "Brooks Partition"	104
	pt. "Lowreys Chance"	98¼
12:1771:4 ...		
Richard Bond (cnp)	pt. "Lawreys Chance"	50
	"Small Land"	6¾

	"Small Reward"	54
	pt. "Spittle"	90
	pt. "Hogsdown"	25
James Kent Byrn	pt. "Neighbourhood"	26
	pt. "Prevent Danger"	100
Thomas Crumpton	"Jerusalem"	124
	pt. "Swinfens Adventure"	25
	"Parkers Fortune" a/s "Chance"	263
	"Bigger"	1055
	pt. "Godsgrace"	100
	pt. "Morocco, Catterton Lott, & Barbara Delight"	294
Rev. Thomas Claggett	pt. "Halls Craft" – for h/o (N) Smith	443⅓
Edmund Clare	pt. "Eltonhead Manor"	200
Gabriel Child	pt. "Letchworths Chance"	336
Bennett Chew	"Chews Fourtine"	49
Samuel Chew	pt. "Letchworth Chance"	550
	pt. "Upper Bennett"	506
	"Lane & Gore"	51½
h/o Joseph Chilton	"Terra in Aqua"	4
12:1771:5 ...		
Samuel Chew (AA)	"Popping Gray"	540
Josias Crossby	"Archers Hays"	30
	pt. "Goughs Purchase"	60
Michael Catterton	pt. "Lingams Purchase"	125
Henrey Camden	pt. "Highland"	200
	"Chance"	70
Elizabeth Chesley w/o John	pt. "Batchelors Quarter"	420
Michael Culpeper	"Venture"	16
Young Cox	pt. "Littleland"	17
	pt. "Cox's Inclosure"	65
	pt. "Cops Hall"	25
	pt. "Cox's Freehold"	120
	pt. "Merrey Greenwood"	163
	pt. "Good Luck"	10
	"Hatchet"	25
Betty Clare	pt. "Lawreys Chance"	130

Mary Clare	pt. "Eltonhead Manor"	157
Calvert County School	"Security" tbc William Hunter	87
	pt. "Orchard" tbc William Hunter	100
Calvert County	pt. "Inland"	3
12:1771:6 ...		
Isaac Clare	"Hard Travel" – originally "Horsepath"	150
	pt. "Eltonhead Manor"	143
	"Concord"	161
	"Addition to Horsepath"	40
John Culpeper	"Wolfs Quarter"	40
Thomas Crutchley	"Addition"	50
John Cox	pt. "Smiths Lott"	33⅓
	pt. "Johnsons Farme, Good Prospect, & Lands Land"	87¾
Charles Dawkins	"Dicks Cabin"	50
	"Blinkhorn" tbc Joseph Dawkins	300
	pt. "Foxs Road" tbc Joseph Dawkins	42
	"Joseph Reserve" tbc Joseph Dawkins	196
	pt. "Friendship" – from Hannah Hungerford	25
Benjamin Duke	pt. "Rich Levells" tbc Moses Duke	247
	pt. "Inland" tbc Moses Duke	1
	pt. "Brooks Place Mannor" tbc Moses Duke	300
	pt. "Howard & Letchworth" tbc Moses Duke	303
Henry Dixon	"Addition to Middlesex"	95
	"Fox's Walk"	5
Andrew Duke	"Middlesex"	100
	pt. "Gideon & Cleverleys Right"	19
h/o William Dorumple	"Hap at a Venture" tbc Elizabeth Dorumple	150
	pt. "Fox's Roads" tbc Elizabeth Dorumple	158
h/o James Duke	pt. "Broocks Place"	171
	pt. "Lower Bennett"	211
	"Mackall Desire"	78
12:1771:7 ...		
Samuel Dare	pt. "Angle"	140
	pt. "Gideon & Cleverley Right"	502
	pt. "Smith Purchase"	119⅓

h/o James Dodson	"Huckleberry Hills"	50
	"Littleworth"	21
John Dossey	pt. "Mary Green"	63
	pt. "Dear Quarter"	62½
	pt. "Bennett Desire"	10
	pt. "Robinsons Rest"	66⅔
Robert Day	pt. "No Name"	150
Benjamin Day	"Brandon"	57
	"Frampton"	50
William Dawkins	"Marys Dukedom"	100
James Dawkins	"Josephs Place"	200
Susanna Dare	pt. "Gideon & Cleverley Right"	157
Nathaniel Dare	pt. "Gideon & Cleverleys Right"	315
Philip Dossey	pt. resurvey of several tracts	104
	pt. "Tauneys Addition"	44
h/o William Day	pt. "No Name"	100
Cleverly Dare	pt. "Gideon & Cleverley Right"	1104½
	pt. "Preston Clift"	100
12:1771:8 ...		
Ellis Dixon	"Hogs Skin Cliftes"	100
Thomas Denton	pt. "Island Neck"	99
	"Puddington"	50
John Dare	pt. "Gideon & Cleverleys Right"	100
	pt. "Gideon & Cleverleys Right" – from Cleverley Dare	70
Henry Dowell	pt. "Swinfens Rest"	50
	pt. "Lingams Purchase"	100
Richard Deale	pt. "Newington"	200
John Dossey s/o James	pt. "Gardan"	100
	pt. "Robinsons Rest"	64
w/o James Deale	pt. "Swinfens Rest"	64½
	pt. "Timberwell" – from Richard Deale	74
Daniel Dossey	pt. "Garden"	67
Philip Dossey, Jr.	pt. "Robinsons Rest"	150
Francis Dossey	pt. "Bennett Desire"	50
Jacob Deale	pt. "Upper Bennett"	75

William Dear	pt. "Swinfins Rest"	250
	pt. "Lawreys Chance"	36¾
12:1771:9 **...**		
Thomas Cleverley Dare	pt. "Agreement"	150
	"Bite the Biter"	112
	"Sampsons Dividend"	150
	pt. "Mannington"	25
	"Neglect"	25
	pt. "Parkers Clifts" – from Richard Johns	21
	"Device" – from Richard Johns	75
	"Darby" – from Richard Johns	46
Philip Dowell	pt. "Lingans Purchase"	116
Alexander Deale	pt. "Newington"	46
	pt. "Islington"	25
John Due or h/o (N) Smith	pt. "Archers Hays"	43½
James Dossey, Jr.	pt. "Youngs Mount"	159
	pt. "Youngs Fourtune"	40
James Dawkins s/o James	pt. "Haphazard"	90
Richard Evrist	pt. "Highland"	50
Ann Elt	pt. "Eltonhead Manor"	336
Isaac Essex	pt. "Wolf Trap"	55
Robert Ethrington	pt. "Comsey"	92½
Barnaby Eagan	pt. "Brooks Place Mannor"	400
Ezra Freeman	pt. "Forge"	50
~~Barbara Dawkins~~	~~pt. "Smith Purchase" – from Alexander Somerville~~	~~119½~~
12:1771:10 **...**		
h/o George Fowler	pt. "Tillington"	45½
James Frazer	"Hills Hall"	100
	"White Marsh"	68
Thomas Freeman	pt. "Rockhold"	135
h/o Joseph Freeman	pt. "Arnolds Purchase"	50
Hon. Col. William Fitzhugh, Esq. (cnp)	pt. "Eltonhead Mannor"	2500
	pt. "Miles Ende"	399½
	pt. "Mile Run"	150
	"Hattons Cove"	70
	"Staffords Freehold"	70

	"Round Ponds"	100
	"Leach" or "Smith Hills"	100
	"Gore"	70
Jacob Freeland	pt. "Letchworths Chance"	179
	"Neglect"	125
	pt. "Fuller"	100
Robert Freeland	pt. "Truemans Chance"	232
	"Dosseys Folley"	70
	"Burks Purchase"	50
	pt. "Dear Quarter"	100
	pt. "Fuller"	200
Peregrine Freeland	pt. "Mackall Force"	323½
Frisby Freeland	pt. "Mackall Force"	323½
John Furguson	pt. "Govers & Griffiths Pasture"	40
	pt. "Skiners Chance"	30
	pt. "Turners Place"	126
12:1771:11 ...		
Alexander Fraizer	"Starlings Chance"	40
	"Starlings Nest"	550
Jacob French	pt. "Danvin" tbc Thomas French in 1773	125
Richard Gibson	pt. "Swinfens Rest"	72
h/o John Griffith	pt. "Welch Poole"	143¾
	pt. "Skinners Chance"	90
George Gantt	"Selbys Clift" – for h/o John Beckett	200
	pt. "Mears" – for h/o John Beckett	200
	pt. "Gunterton" – for h/o John Beckett	250
	pt. "Hardestey" – for h/o John Beckett	50
	"Poppy Gray" – for h/o John Beckett	40
John Gibson	pt. "Spittle"	90
	pt. "Additional Spittle"	22
John Gardiner	pt. "Johnsons Lott"	100
Charles Graham, Esq.	pt. "Halls Craft"	521
	"Howard"	42
	"Bell"	68
	"Blackwall"	30
	pt. "Hardesty"	180

Joseph Galloway	pt. "Spittle"	20
	pt. "Additional Spittle"	28
Lewis Griffith	pt. "Welch Poole"	135
	pt. "Arches Hays"	231
	"Lewis Stripe & Dues Purchase"	26
	"Long Lane" tbc William Lyles in 1773	31
	"All Points" tbc Robert Lyles in 1773	24
	pt. "Cooper"	86
12:1771:12 **...**		
James Gibson	pt. "Additional Spittle"	88
	pt. "Newington"	22
h/o Robert Gover	pt. "Archers Hays"	190
	"Goughs Purchase" a/s "Gough Pasture"	50
	"Govers Addition"	59
	pt. "Dunkirk"	150
	pt. "Exchange"	66
John Griffin	pt. "Robinson"	60
Edward Gantt	pt. "Ordinary"	606
	"Kingsburys Marsh"	130
	"Craft"	90
Thomas Gray	pt. "Wilton & Hatch"	75
	pt. "Throughbridge" – from Benjamin Mackall (Holland Point)	125
	pt. "Brooke Choice" – from Benjamin Mackall (Holland Point)	73
William Gray s/o Thomas	"Grays Addition"	109
John Gray (Patuxent)	"Marsh Land & Lushhead"	345
	"Hazard"	42
	pt. "Brooks Adventure"	100
	"Jonottle" a/s "Tuxbury"	100
	"Toddy"	138
William Gray	pt. "Stenneth Ramble"	35
	"Reserve"	50
Howerton Games	pt. "Johnsons Lott"	50
	"Hazard"	25

Robert Gardiner	pt. "Johnsons Lott"	100
	"Wolf Hole" tbc: • Kensey Gardener – 28⅔ a. in 1773 • John Gardener – 21⅓ a. in 1773	50
12:1771:13 ...		
John Gardiner	pt. "Johnsons Lott"	100
Samuel Gray	"Norwood"	200
	"Theobush"	50
	pt. "Austins Chance"	91
Driver Graves	pt. "Stevans Plaines"	25
	"Graves Rehobeth"	80
Edward Gardener	"Chilton" or "Chatham"	80
	pt. "Forked Neck" or "Dorington"	50
	"Short Neck"	76
Benjamin Gardiner	pt. "Round Pond Plains"	100
James Freeman	pt. "Aldermason" – for h/o (N) Greenfield	150
	"Addition" – for h/o (N) Greenfield	56½
Henry Gray	"Labour in Vain"	100
h/o Job Hunt	pt. "Uper Bennett" tbc Henry Hunt in 1773	195
Mary Graves	pt. "Hap Hazard" tbc Thomas Denton, Jr. in 1773	45
	"Batchelors Hall"	300
	"Timber Neck"	50
	"Cleves Littleworth"	43
Ester Gray	"Fishing Creek"	165
	"Chaplain"	100
	"East Fishing Creek"	50
	"Nutts Clifts"	150
	"East Chaplain"	100
Thomas Hollingshead	pt. "Kents Freehold"	250
12:1771:14 ...		
James Highe (cnp)	pt. "Beakley"	300
	"Forsters Purchase"	150
	pt. "Roberts Chance"	34
	pt. "James Chance"	40
	"Samuels Addition"	15
	"Clarks Hills"	19

	"Little Land"	11
	"Hughs Addition"	15
	"James Addition"	21
Thomas Holdsworth Highe	pt. "Brooks Place"	300
William Harrison	pt. "Brooks Discovery"	200
	pt. "Lawreys Reserve"	75
	pt. "Brothers Discovery"	126
	pt. "Cox's Freehold"	128
Joseph Hardesty	pt. "Den"	37½
	pt. "Nichol's Chance"	55
	"Nelsons Reserve"	22
William Hickman	pt. "Newington"	220
	pt. "Islington"	542
Thomas Hunt	pt. "Lordships Favour" tbc Elizabeth Hunt in 1773	50
h/o John Hance	pt. "Newington"	9
	"Johns Neglect"	128
	"Islingsworth Fortune"	65
Henry Howes	pt. "Refuse"	50
	"Jemsleys Lott"	46
	"Purchase"	23
Henry Hardesty	pt. "Den"	37
	pt. "Nichol's Chance"	55
12:1771:15 ...		
William Hardesty	pt. "Lordships Favour" tbc Hilleary Willson in 1773	75
Henry Harrison	pt. "Swinfens Rest"	150
Thomas Holland	pt. "St. James's Enlarged"	1138
	pt. "Alexander's Hope"	38
George Hall	pt. "Chance"	25
Abraham Hooper	pt. "Taylors Joy"	343
Walter Hoxton (CH)	pt. "Homesham"	117
Ann Holland	pt. "Abington"	150
William Harris (cnp)	"Durain"	200
	pt. "Illingworth Fortune"	100
	pt. "Littleworth" tbc James Morsell (60 a.) in 1773	150
	pt. "Illington"	73

	pt. "Letchworths Chance"	275
Dr. Leonard Holliday	"Buzzard Island"	700
	"Addition"	51
	pt. "Arnolds Purchase"	50
Newman Harvey	pt. "Turners Place"	126
Benjamin Harris	pt. "Expectation"	100
	pt. "Whittles Rest"	148
	pt. "Parkers Clifts"	50
William Harris, Jr.	"Addition"	100
James Henley	"Smuggs Folley"	80
12:1771:16 ...		
Benjamin Hance	pt. "Parkers Clifts"	100
	pt. "Warrington"	175
	pt. "Agreement"	50
	"Busseys Garden"	175
	pt. "Islington"	250
	"Hances Lane"	20
	pt. "Newington"	3
	"Purchase"	154
	"Warings Chance"	56
	resurvey of several tracts	119½
Joseph Hance	pt. "Warbleton"	404
Kensey Hance	pt. "Stockley" a/s resurvey of several tracts	100
Hannah Hungerford or John Ward	pt. "Friendship" tbc John Ward in 1773	50
John Hungerford	pt. "Eltonhead Manor"	200
	"Jermyn Quarter Enlarged"	143
James Hellen	pt. "Truswell"	150
Samuel Hance	pt. "Theobuck Manning"	189
	"Huckleburry Neck"	205
Walter Hellen	"Hooper Neck"	275
Edmund Hellen	pt. "Waring"	121
	pt. "Bowleys Chance"	75
	"Busseys Lott"	75
	"Hellens Lott"	12

Edmund Hungerford	pt. "Hogs Skin Neck"	100
	pt. "Stephens Land"	100
	"Purchase"	24
	pt. "Desart"	100
12:1771:17 ...		
Philip Hunt	pt. "Lordships Favour"	100
Richard Hellen	pt. "Trustwell"	150
	"Miltons Lott"	100
	"Persia"	100
	"Harrow the Hill"	77
	pt. "Rich Levell"	28
David Hellen s/o Richard	"Gully"	63½
Thomas Gosling Hutchings	pt. "Magruder" tbc Francis Hutchings in 1773	175
Rebecca Hungerford	pt. "Friendship"	39¼
	pt. "Taylors Joy"	114
	pt. "Allens Neck"	36
	pt. "Friendship" – from Charles Dawkins	25
Joseph Ireland	"Leachs Freehold"	125
John Ivey	pt. "Stephens Plains"	25
Kensey Johns (AA)	pt. "Angelica"	200
	pt. "Mears"	200
	pt. "Inland"	1
Benjamin Johns	pt. "Angelica"	400
	pt. "Johns Addition"	112
	pt. "Inland"	1
Richard Johns	pt. "Whittles Rest"	188
	pt. "Devise" tbc Cleveley Deare	<n/g>
	pt. "Parkers Clifts"	109
h/o Joseph Isaac	"Plumb Point"	400
	pt. "Lordships Favour"	205
	pt. "Purchase"	100
12:1771:18 ...		
Col. William Ireland (cnp)	"Bridge" tbc Joseph Ireland in 1773	100
	"Georges Desire" tbc Joseph Ireland in 1773	50
	"Addition" tbc Joseph Ireland in 1773	43
	"Angle" tbc Joseph Ireland in 1773	87

	pt. "Peahens Nest" tbc Joseph Ireland in 1773	35
	pt. "Island Plains" tbc Joseph Ireland in 1773	32
	"Lyons Creek"	300
	pt. "Dunkirt"	50
William Johnson s/o George	pt. "Read Hall"	100
h/o Richard Johns	"Purchase"	100
	pt. "Youngs Desire"	12
William Ireland s/o Thomas	pt. "Halls Hills"	550
Mary Ireland	pt. "Eltonhead Manor"	200
	pt. "Prestons Clifts"	108
	pt. "Angle"	88
	pt. "No Name"	100
	"Mill Marsh"	63
John Ireland	pt. "Tillington"	189
	"Wolf Trap"	45
Thomas Johnson	pt. "Brewhouse"	260
w/o John Johnson	"Elizabeth"	200
	pt. "Gift"	70
Thomas Johnson, Jr.	pt. "Preston Clifts"	314
William Johnson s/o Jere	pt. "Exchange"	150
Richard Ireland	pt. "Irelands Hope"	50
	pt. "Desart"	198
John Kent	pt. "Rockhold"	160
12:1771:19 ...		
Dr. Edward Johnson	"Prestons"	200
	"Moffats Mount"	200
	"Woods Adventure"	50
	"Hays Marsh"	18
	pt. "Poor Land"	185
	"Musquets Point"	46
	"Turners Chance"	50
	"Addition to Woods Venture"	33
James Kirshaw	pt. "Prevent Danger"	100
Sarah Kirshaw w/o John	pt. "Prevent Danger"	50
Francis Kirshaw	pt. "Sharps Outlett"	100
	pt. "Concord"	63

Joseph Kent	pt. "Timber Well"	326
	pt. "Additional Spittle"	50
Rev. Francis Lauder	pt. "Preston Clifts"	239
	pt. "Gore"	50
John Lawrence	pt. "Lowreys Addition"	145
	pt. "Islington"	50
	pt. "Small Reward" – from Richard Bond	57
William Lyles	pt. "Red Hall"	150
	pt. "Stripe"	8
	pt. "Turners Pasture"	170
	pt. "Long Lane"	32
h/o Lewis Lewin	pt. "Red Hall"	37½
John Leveal	pt. "Whittles Rest"	150
Robert Lyles	pt. "Red Hall"	100
12:1771:20 ...		
Capt. Richard Lane & Benjamin Lane	pt. "Homesham"	233
Samuel Lyles	pt. "Lawreys Chance"	50
Jeremiah Maulden	pt. "Parkers Clifts"	250
John Mackall s/o John	pt. resurvey of several tracts	104
	pt. "Tauneys Addition"	44
James Mackall s/o John	pt. resurvey of several tracts	104
	pt. "Tauneys Addition"	44
Benjamin Mackall s/o John	"Schoole House"	100
	"Brigantine Adventure"	24
Elizabeth Mackall w/o Thomas	"Cox's Folley"	50
	pt. "Farm"	19
William Marshall 3rd	pt. "Cox's Choice"	143
John Manning	pt. "Theobalds Manor"	112
	pt. "Gunsby"	168
	"Cold Kirby"	½
William Monnett	"Williams Purchase"	206
Jane Macdowell	pt. "Coles Clifts"	50
h/o James Mackall	"Cage" tbc Hannah Mackall in 1773	250
	"Busseys Lott" tbc Hannah Mackall in 1773	100
	"Mackalls Desire" tbc Hannah Mackall in 1773	10

h/o Thomas Morgan	pt. "Desire"	79
	pt. "Grays Chance" tbc Joseph Willson, Jr. in 1773	350
	"Fellowship"	160
12:1771:21 ...		
John Mackall (St. Leonards)	pt. "Morgan"	60
	pt. "Horse Range"	180
	"Claggetts Desire"	376
	pt. "Desart"	350
	"St. James"	300
Benjamin Mackall (Holland Point)	"Copartnership"	182
	pt. "Chance"	307
	"Hallowing Point"	400
	"Seamores Neck"	382
	pt. "Horse Range"	165
	pt. "Sharps Outlett"	100
	pt. "Devideing Branch"	179
	pt. "Trouble"	27
	pt. "Morocco" – in corn	50
	"Addition to Sharps Outlett"	112
	pt. "Read"	46½
	pt. "Read & Magruder"	92½
	pt. "Coursey"	46½
h/o Barbara Mackall	pt. "Brooke Partition" tbc Thomas Bond	200
Rousby Miller	pt. "Orchard"	253
Ann Mills	pt. "Wolton"	25
	pt. "Catch"	25
James Morsell	pt. "Rattlesnake Hills"	120
	"Chance"	70
	pt. "Littleworth"	60
	pt. "Mary Green"	55
h/o James John Mackall (cnp)	pt. "Lower Bennett"	500
	pt. "Thobucks Manor"	100
	"Corn Hill"	350
	"Alexanders Hope"	200
	pt. "Gooys Chance"	200
	pt. "Bone Road"	89

	pt. "Gunsbey"	38
	"Cold Harbour"	100
12:1771:22 ...		
h/o James John Mackall (continued)	pt. "Brook Place"	432
	pt. "Stone Bay"	225
	"Piney Point"	50
	"Laurey Point" & pt. "Lowrey Rest"	100
	"Littleworth"	77
	"Cold Carby"	200
	pt. "Angle"	350
	pt. "Lawreys Rest"	295
	"Fox Walks"	40
	"Bramhall"	500
	"Neglect"	30
	pt. "Godsgrace"	617
	pt. "Meads"	166
	pt. "Evans's Land"	200
	pt. "Cole Cliffs"	150
	"Prestons Cliffs"	63
	pt. "Ceder Branch"	240
	pt. "Sewell Purchase"	30
	pt. "Bramell Addition"	33
	"Angel" or "Angle"	87
John Norfolk	"Judds Levells"	84
	pt. "Island Plains"	27
	pt. "Ridge"	100
	pt. "Refuse"	100
	pt. "Refuge"	14
James Norfolk	pt. "Peahens Nest"	50
William Powell	pt. "Gideon & Cleverley Right" – from Cleverley Dare	5½
John Pardo	pt. "Rockey Neck"	50
	pt. "Fox's Walks"	70
Mary Parker	"Clay Hammond"	380
	"Wilsons Commons"	29

Elizabeth Prindowell	pt. "Parkers Cliffts"	100
	pt. "Roberts Addition"	5
	pt. "Roberts Chance"	5¼
	pt. "Beckley"	66⅔
12:1771:23 ...		
Leonard Prindowell	pt. "Roberts Addition"	10
	pt. "Roberts Chance"	11
	pt. "Beakley"	133⅓
h/o John Peters	pt. "Kent's Freehold" ~~tbc Robert Peters in 1773~~	50
	pt. "Lordships Favour" ~~tbc Robert Peters in 1773~~ tbc Hilleary Willson (70 a.)	100
Robert Peters	pt. "Danvin & Clares Hundred"	142
William Patterson	pt. "Stone Bay"	75
	pt. "Evans's Land"	65
h/o Alexander Parran	pt. "Patience"	368
	"Addition"	19
h/o Hutcheson Parker	pt. "St. Leonards" – in corn	175
	"Bulmores Branch"	50
	pt. "Stones Hills"	25
h/o Young Parran, Esq.	pt. "Desart"	349
	"Preston"	400
	"Preston Neglect"	200
	pt. "Bromogan" or "Bermingham"	50
	pt. "Parrans Park"	300
	"Brooks Plains"	100
	pt. "Inland"	2
	"Discovery"	99
	pt. "Winfield Resurvey"	207
	pt. "Morgan"	45
Samuel Parran	pt. "Winfields Resurvey"	207
	pt. "Birmingham"	25
	pt. "Morgan"	45
	pt. land without name	100
	pt. "Parrans Park"	150
John Peters (cnp)	pt. "Johnsons Farm"	150
	pt. "Turner's Place"	66⅔

	pt. "Griffiths & Govers Pasture"	20
12:1771:24 ...		
John Rawlings	pt. "Eltonhead Manor"	300
	"Crumpton" – from Margaret Parran	75
	"Rawlings Purchase" – from Margaret Parran	60
Thomas Rhodes	"Black Robin"	38
Daniel Ross	pt. "Robinson's Rest"	200
Thomas Reynolds	pt. "Robinson"	191
	pt. "St. Edmunds"	150
	pt. "Robinsons Rest"	518
	pt. "Good Luck"	100
	"Adjoinder" a/s "Adjunction"	10
	pt. "Brooks Discovery"	64
	"Crouders Lott"	60
	"Reserve"	300
	"Coxe's Chance"	72
	"Rich Bitt"	5½
	"Foxs Home"	30
	"Starling Perch"	300
	pt. "Lordship Favour"	285
	pt. "Neglect"	60
	pt. "Cox's Inclosure"	70
	pt. "Cox's Freehold"	142
	"Bennets Refuge" tbc Samuel Chew in 1773	33
	pt. "Hopewell"	94
	pt. "Abington Manor"	769
	"Angles Lane"	37
	"Stalling Lott"	31
	pt. "Meadows"	186
	"Thomas & Williams Chance"	101
	pt. "Tatchcumb"	114
	pt. "Lingan's Purchase"	8
	pt. "Brook Neck"	150
	"Stallings Swamp"	10
	"Bite"	5

Samuel Robinson	"Emmertons Addition"	20
	pt. "Halls Hills"	85
	pt. "Brougton Ashley"	73
Henry Scott	pt. "Highland"	50
12:1771:25 ...		
Daniel Rawlings	pt. "Eltonhead Manor"	200
	"Bethens Loss" – from Margaret Parran	50
	"Dearbought" – from Margaret Parran	200
Dr. John Hamilton Smith	"Bramford"	150
	pt. "Hardestys Choice"	150
	pt. "Henry Chew"	75
	1½ lot in Lower Marlbro	1½
	pt. "Dowdeswell Mannor"	400
	pt. "Ordinary"	80½
Gavin Ham. Smith	"Little Ganorey"	42
	pt. "Grantham"	220
	"Sam's Addition"	78
	"Hazard"	18½
Philemon Smith	pt. "Soldiers Fourtune"	200
	pt. "Ordinary"	75
Alexander Ham. Smith	pt. "Batcholors Quarter"	250
Walter Smith	pt. "Parkers Clifts"	100
	"Fox Road"	100
	"Wolf Quarter"	300
	"Smith Hog Pen"	309
	pt. "St. Leonards" – in corn	175
	pt. "Taylors Disposal"	270
	pt. "Stones Hall"	25
	"Purchase"	20
Isaac Simmonds	pt. "Chance" – from Richard Johns	50
James Somerville (cnp)	"Tobys Quarter"	100
	"Rocky Neck"	50
	pt. "Allens Neck" tbc John Ward in 1773	164
	"Narrow Neck & Gore" tbc Isaac Hooper (7 a.) in 1773	18
	"Swamp" tbc Isaac Hooper (6½ a.) in 1773	67

	pt. "Gore"	100
12:1771:26 ...		
h/o Maryland Skinner	pt. "Newington"	94
	pt. "Millers Folley"	250
h/o Leonard Skinner	"Borders"	77½
	pt. "Dodson's Desire"	23
	pt. "Chance"	27
	pt. "Reserve"	32¼
John Simmonds	pt. "Rich Bottom"	25
	"Short Hills"	40
h/o George Smith	pt. "Desart"	52
	pt. "Round Bottom Plains"	100
Dorothy Sollers	"Forked Neck"	100
	"Hyams"	10
William Skinner	pt. "Scrap" tbc Isaac Essex in 1773	38
	pt. "Prestons Desire"	25
	pt. "Chance"	27
	pt. "Reserve" tbc Isaac Simmonds in 1773	32¼
	pt. "Border Enlarged" tbc Isaac Simmonds in 1773	77½
James Skinner	pt. "Borders Enlarged"	77½
	pt. "Dodsons Desire"	25
	pt. "Chance"	27
	pt. "Reserve"	32¼
Robert Skinner	pt. "Blind Tom"	40
	"Addition"	60
	pt. "Tauneys Right"	150
Elizabeth Skinner	pt. "Tauneys Right"	150
	pt. "Scrap"	62
	pt. "Reserve"	121
	pt. "Newington"	94
Edward Wood (Holland Point)	pt. "Morocco" – from William Sly; in corn	100
	pt. "Magruder" – from Elinor Sly	150
12:1771:27 ...		
h/o Adderton Skinner (cnp)	pt. "Blind Tom"	32
	"Tauneys Delight"	70
	"Mary Green"	36

	pt. "Gore"	48
	pt. "Millers Folley"	250
	"Neglect"	25
Alexander Somerville	"Fox Den"	50
	"Bartholomews Neck"	50
	pt. "Smiths Purchase"	119¼
	pt. "Gore"	100
	"Golden Folley"	75
Barbara Dawkins	pt. "Smith Purchase" – from Alexander Somerville	119¼
Josias Sunderland	pt. "Swinfins Rest" tbc Benjamin Sunderland in 1773	250
Joseph Strickland	pt. "Robinsons Rest"	50
William Sollars	pt. "Dorrington"	182½
	pt. "Bowdleys Chance"	34
Joshua Sedwick	pt. "Neighbourhood"	150
	"Adjoinder"	50
	"Nortons Purchase"	83⅓
Joseph Skinner	pt. "Orchard"	50
	pt. "Border Enlarged"	77½
	pt. "Dodens Desire"	25
	pt. "Chance"	27
	pt. "Reserve"	32¼
w/o Josias Sunderland, Jr.	pt. "Uper Bennett"	50
Phineas Stallings	pt. "Thatchcomb"	236
John Sedwick	"Buck Hill"	21
12:1771:28 ...		
James Sewall	pt. "Dear Quarter"	62½
	pt. "Chance"	72½
	"Maidens Delight"	200
	"Cop Hall"	80
	pt. "Parkers Clifts"	50
	"Good Luck"	150
John Standforth	pt. "Poor Land"	104
h/o John Skinner (cnp)	pt. "Hall Hills"	877½
	"Sneaking Point"	50
	pt. "Lingans Purchase"	94

	pt. "Hamiltons Park"	33
William Stansby	pt. "Archers Hays" tbc Richard Stansbury in 1774	40
h/o Joseph Smith, Jr.	pt. "Turners Pasture"	50
	pt. "Smiths Pasture"	100
	pt. "Archers Hays"	15½
Mordecai Smith	pt. "Smiths Chance"	100
	pt. "Welch Poole"	72½
	pt. "Turners Place"	50
	pt. "Calender"	77
h/o William Smith	pt. "Smith Chance"	50
	pt. "Turners Place"	50
	pt. "Mordyke"	50
Joseph Smith	pt. "Mordyke"	50
w/o John Stone	pt. "Defence"	65
John Stalling	pt. "Uper Bennett"	25
Ellis Slater	pt. "Lowreys Reserve"	100
12:1771:29 ...		
Stephen Stamp	pt. "Read Hall"	125
	pt. "Turners Place"	144½
Capt. Henry Brooke	"Good Prospect" – from Mary Smith	50
	"Lands Land" – from Mary Smith	199
	"Addition" – from Mary Smith	28
Clement Smith	pt. "Halls Craft"	221
Patrick Smith	pt. "Halls Craft"	265
Nicholas Swamstead	pt. "Lordships Favour"	100
Thomas Stalling	pt. "Swinfins Rest"	64½
Stockett Sunderland	pt. "Lawreys Chance" or "Resurvey"	100
John Davis Sarth	pt. "Robinsons Rest"	50
Benjamin Sedwick	pt. "Bulmores Branch" a/s "Right"	475
Jonathan Slater or Elizabeth Countee	pt. "Halls Revenge"	28
	1 lot in Lower Marlbro	1
Stephen Steward	pt. "Illingsworth Fortune"	200
John Scott	pt. "Lordships Favour"	100
Clement Skinner	pt. "Whittles Rest" – from John Lovall	60
Raphell Tauney	pt. "Stones Hills"	50
12:1771:30 ...		

Jacob Tucker	"Tuckers Thickett"	200
	pt. "Chance"	50
h/o Phillip Thomas, Esq.	"Majors Choice" tbc Benjamin Mackall (381 a.) in 1773	500
Joseph Talbutt, Jr.	pt. "Expectation"	100
John Tannehill	pt. "Callender"	123
	pt. "Cooper" & pt. "Friendship"	42
	pt. "Welch Poole"	86
Ann Tannehill	pt. "Cooper" & pt. "Friendship"	173
Joseph Talbutt	pt. "Freemans Chance"	123
	pt. "Tillington"	150
	"Batcholors Fortune"	200
Edward Talbutt	pt. "Tillington"	415½
John Talbutt	pt. "Expectation"	50
John Turner	pt. "Bowdleys Chance"	91
Thomas Talbutt	pt. "Expectation"	100
h/o Benjamin Tasker, Esq.	"Hard Travell"	300
John Tucker	pt. "Neighbourhood"	82½
William Vermilion	"Creeds Chance"	64
John Wilkinson	pt. "Youngs Attempt"	100
12:1771:31 ...		
Ben Kid Wilson & Priscilla Gover	pt. "Aldermason"	150
	"Govers Expectation"	89
	pt. "Welch Pool"	2
George Wheeler	"Barry" – for h/o (N) Tauney	600
	"Long Point" – for h/o (N) Tauney	100
	"Wooden Point" – for h/o (N) Tauney	25
	pt. "Letchworth" – for h/o (N) Tauney	50
	pt. "Angle" – for h/o (N) Tauney	3
John Ward	"Velchee Rest"	50
	pt. "Friendship" – from Hannah Hungerford	50
Samuel Ward	"Goldson's Inheritance"	150
Aaron Williams, Jr.	pt. "Friendship Rectified"	200
	pt. "Swinfen's Adventure"	50
	pt. "Young's Desire"	50

Hilleary Wilson	pt. "Robinson"	213
	pt. "Lordship Favour"	9
Aaron Williams, Sr.	pt. "Williams's Hardship"	175
	"Littlefield"	25
	"Williams's Rest"	50
	pt. "Friendship Rectified"	25
	pt. "Swinfens Adventure"	25
James Weems, Jr.	"Success, Tauneys Ease, & Stockly"	200
	"Partnership"	75
12:1771:32 ...		
h/o Joseph Wilkinson	pt. "Gods Grace"	120
	pt. "Stockley"	70
John Waters	pt. "Stockley" tbc James Somerville in 1773	419
	pt. "Gunterton" tbc James Somerville in 1773	40
	"Myrtle Point"	7
John Willing	pt. "Taylors Joy"	128
	"Jerusalem"	108
	pt. "Rich Bottom"	25
Francis Wolf, Jr.	pt. "Theobald Manor"	50
	pt. "Gray's Chance"	50
Richard Ward	pt. "Swinfen's Rest"	116
	pt. "Danvins & Clares Hundred"	138
James Weems	pt. "Magruder"	410
	"Hogs Haunt"	50
	"Mauldens Luck"	25
	pt. "Busseys Orchard"	400
	pt. "Inland"	1
	pt. "Meadows Preserved"	46
	1 lot in Hunting Town	1
	pt. "Cuckholds Miss"	65
	pt. "Young's Desire"	25
	pt. "Youngs Fortune"	60
	pt. "Youngs Attempt"	62
	"Enmanmure"	50
	pt. "Reserve"	50
	pt. "Trouble" "Hucklebury Hills"	50

12:1771:33 ...		
James Weems s/o David	"Ringar"	200
	"Green House"	155
	"Chews Purchase"	145
	pt. "Grantham"	45
	"Marshall Addition"	70
Basil Williamson	pt. "Langans Adventure"	310
Edward Wood	pt. "Woods Adventure"	150
	pt. "Titmarsh"	100
	pt. "Poor Land"	11
	pt. "Brook Adventure" – from h/o Roger Brooke, Jr.	78
Jonah Winfield	"Johnsons Farm"	100
Thomas Wells & Jane Wells	pt. "Grantham Hall"	155
	"Arthurs Hall"	44
h/o James Williamson	"Den"	726
	"Fox's Nettle"	20
	pt. "Batchelors Quarter"	420
h/o Roger Wheeler	pt. "Henry Chew"	237
	"Coxcomb"	150
	"Cox Head"	50
	pt. "Newington"	109
	"Smiths Conveyance"	60
	pt. "Bucks Chance" – from James Weems	150
12:1771:34 ...		
John Wilkinson	pt. "Henry Chew"	400
Thomas Wilson	pt. "St. Edmunds"	163
	pt. "Neglect"	16½
	"Letchworth Cyprus" – from h/o Joseph Wilson	200
	"Youngs Atemp" – from h/o Joseph Wilson	100
	pt. "Horse Range" – from h/o Joseph Wilson	125
	pt. "Hap at a Venture" – from h/o Joseph Wilson	30
Leonard Wood	pt. "Woods Adventure"	100
Edward Wilson	"Dear Quarter"	25
	pt. "Robinsons Rest"	150

John Weems	pt. "Dowdeswell"	600
	pt. "Chance"	25
William White	pt. "Smiths Joy"	100
William Winnull	pt. "Nortons Purchase"	166⅔
William Hunton Wood	pt. "Arnold's Purchase"	100
Frances Whittington	pt. "Halls Hills"	100
Frances Williams	pt. "Inland"	100
	pt. "Hutchings's Chance"	50
	pt. "Orchard"	40
12:1771:35 ...		
Ithamor Williams	pt. "Swinfens Adventure"	50
	pt. "Williams Hardship"	75
	pt. "Friendship Rectified"	125
h/o Joseph Wilson	"Tamot"	300
	pt. "Forsters Purchase"	150
	pt. "Robinson"	136
	pt. "Additional Spittle"	8
	pt. "Peahens Nest"	40
	pt. "Cedar Branch"	75
	pt. "Bowen" – for h/o (N) King	230
	pt. "Brookes Adventure"	150
	"Stones Lott"	50
	pt. "Arnold's Purchase"	50
	~~pt. "Hap at a Venture"~~	⟨n/g⟩
Philemon Young	pt. "Henry Chew"	64½
	1 lot in Lower Marlbro	1
Joseph Wilson, Jr.	pt. "Lower Bennett"	189
Parker Young	"Hop Yard"	150
	"Punch"	150
	pt. "Young's Desire"	25
	pt. "Hoopers Neck"	275
Mary Yeo	pt. "Rattle Snake Hills"	100
Richard Hellen s/o Richard	"Cedar Branch" – from Joseph Wilson	50
12:1771:36 ...		
Peter Hellen	"Hucklebury Quarter Enlarged"	127¼

John Mills	pt. "Throughbridge" – from Benjamin Mackall (Holland Point)	125
	pt. "Brooks Choice" – from Benjamin Mackall (Holland Point)	73
Richard Winfield	pt. "Lordships Favour" – from Richard Gibson	50
John Winfield	pt. "Lands Land"	112
12:1771:<unnumbered>	Recapitulation	
12:1771:<unnumbered>	Certification	

12:1773:1 ...		Acres
John Allon	pt. "Hardestys Choice"	50
David Arnold	pt. "Henry Chew"	290
	pt. "Abbington"	350
	pt. "Hardestys Choice"	130
	pt. "Henry Chew"	110½
Elizabeth Austin	pt. "Cox's Chance"	140
	pt. "Farme"	20
William Askew	pt. "Lowreys Chance"	118
William Alnut	pt. "Foremans Chance'"	156
	pt. "Agreement"	100
William Alnut, Jr.	pt. "Foremans Chance"	153
Samuel Austin	pt. "Cox's Chance"	117
Roger Brook	pt. "Brook Place Manor" tbc: • Elizabeth Brooke – 241 a. • John Brooke – 430 a. • Basil Brooke – 225 a.	1096
John & Isaac Baker	"Devils Woodyard"	150
Jacob Bourne	pt. "Eltonhead Manor" – apply to Esther Bourne tbc Jesse Jacob Bourne	300
John Beveridge	"Dear Bought"	21
Abraham Bowen	pt. "Dividing Branch"	169½
	pt. "Billingsleys Farm"	136
Isaac Bowen	pt. "Dividing Branch"	190
12:1773:2 ...		
David Bowen	pt. "Dividing Branch"	189
John Brooke	pt. "Brooks Adventure"	116¾
	pt. "Cedar Branch"	25
	pt. "Arnolds Purchase"	150
Jesse Bourne	pt. "Eltonhead Manor"	1167
Jacob Bowen	pt. "Neighbourhood"	74
Henry Broome	pt. "Austins Chance"	65
	pt. "Howard & Letchworth"	200
	pt. "Broad Point"	10
	pt. "Austins Addition"	23
Eleanor Blackburn	pt. "Back Pasture"	50
James Bowen	pt. "Dividing Branch"	105

Thomas Bowen	pt. "Dividing Branch"	105
Col. Abraham Barns	"Fishers Orchard" tbc James Fraizer	255
	"Branfry" tbc James Fraizer	100
h/o Roger Brook, Jr.	pt. "Bowen" tbc Thomas Mackall	70
	"Knoles's Branch" tbc h/o James Duke	98
	"Tauneys Addition" tbc Thomas Mackall	123
	"Brooks Battle"	106
	pt. "Brooks Adventure" tbc Thomas Mackall	156½
	pt. "Cedar Branch"	50
Thomas Blackburn	"Roadly"	100
12:1773:3 ...		
h/o Thomas Broom	"Rich Neck"	52
	"Marys Widowhood"	30
	"Addition to Island Neck"	30
Ann Bond	"Lower Fuller"	200
	"Middle Fuller"	200
	pt. "Lower Bennet"	250
Issabella Barton	pt. "Upper Bennett"	50
Jesse Bowen	"Lambeth"	94
h/o Richard Blake	pt. "Upper Bennet"	557
	pt. "St. Edmunds"	200
	pt. "Lordships Favour"	192
	pt. "Neglect"	\<n/g\>
Thomas Blake	pt. "Halls Craft"	221⅔
Mary Bond	pt. "Hogsdown" tbc h/o Thomas Bond	275
	"Micham" tbc h/o Thomas Bond	243
	pt. "Brook Partition" tbc h/o Thomas Bond	104
	pt. "Lawreys Chance" tbc h/o Thomas Bond	98¼
Richard Bond	pt. "Lawreys Chance"	50
	"Small Land"	6¾
	"Small Reward"	54
	pt. "Spittle"	90
	pt. "Hogsdown"	25
James Kent Bryan	pt. "Neighbourhood"	26
	pt. "Prevent Danger"	100
12:1773:4 ...		

Richard Bond	pt. "Lawreys Chance"	50
	"Small Reward"	6¾
	"Small Reward"	54
	pt. "Spittle"	90
	pt. "Hogsdown"	25
h/o Thomas Crumpton	"Jeresalem"	124
	pt. "Swinfens Adventure"	25
	"Parkers Chance" a/s "Chance"	263
	"Bigger"	1055
	pt. "Godsgrace"	100
	pt. "Cottertons Lott & Barbers Delight"	294
Rev. Thomas Claggett	pt. "Halls Craft" – for h/o (N) Smith	443⅓
Edmund Clare	pt. "Eltonhead Manor"	200
Gabriel Child	pt. "Letchworth Chance"	336
Bennet Chew	"Chews Fortune"	49
h/o Joseph Chilton	"Terra in Aqua"	4
Samuel Chew	pt. "Letchworth Chance"	550
	pt. "Upper Bennett"	506
	"Lane & Grove"	51½
	pt. "Bennets Refuge"	33
Josias Crosby	pt. "Archers Hays"	30
	pt. "Goughs Purchase"	60
Michael Catterton	pt. "Lingans Purchase"	125
12:1773:5 ...		
Henry Camden	pt. "Highland"	200
	"Chances"	70
Elizabeth Chesley w/o John	<n/g>	420
Michael Culpepper	"Venture"	16
Young Cox	pt. "Little Land"	17
	pt. "Cox's Inclosure"	65
	pt. "Cops Hall" tbc John Norfolk	25
	pt. "Cox's Freehold"	120
	pt. "Merry Greenwood"	166
	pt. "Good Luck"	10
	"Hatchet"	25
Samuel Chew (AA)	"Poping Gray"	540

Betty Clare	pt. "Lawreys Chance" • "Lawreys Rest" tbc James Mackall, Jr.	130
Mary Clare	pt. "Eltonhead Manor" tbc John Clare, Jr.	157
Calvert County School – William Hunter	"Security"	87
	pt. "Orchard"	100
Calvert County	pt. "Inland"	3
Isaac Clare	"Hard Travel" – originally "Horse Path"	150
	pt. "Eltonhead Manor"	143
	"Concord"	161
	"Addition to Horse Path"	40
John Culpepper	"Wolfs Quarter" tbc Michael Culpepper	40
12:1773:6 ...		
Thomas Crutchley	"Addition"	50
h/o John Cox	pt. "Smiths Lott"	33⅓
	pt. "Johnsons Farm, Good Prospect, & Lands Land"	87½
Charles Dawkins	pt. "Friendship"	25
	pt. "Taylors Joy" – from Abraham Hooper	114
Moses Duke	pt. "Rich Levell"	247
	pt. "Inland"	1
	pt. "Brooke Place Manor"	300
	pt. "Howard & Letchworth"	303
Henry Dixon	"Addition to Middlesex"	95
	"Fox's Walks"	5
Andrew Duke	"Middlesex"	100
	pt. "Gideon & Cleverlys Right"	19
Elizabeth Dorumples	"Hop at a Venture" tbc: • William Dorrumple – 50 a. • Henry Dorrumple – 100 a.	150
	pt. "Fox's Road" tbc: • Bryan Taylor – 108 a. • William Dorrumple – 50 a.	158
h/o James Duke	pt. "Brookplace"	171
	pt. "Lower Bennett"	211
	"Mackalls Desire"	78
Samuel Dare (cnp)	pt. "Angle"	140
	pt. "Gideon & Claverlys Right"	502

	pt. "Smiths Purchase"	119⅓
h/o James Dodson	"Huckleberry Hills"	50
	"Littleworth"	21
12:1773:7 ...		
John Dossey	pt. "Marys Green"	63
	pt. "Dear Quarter"	62½
	pt. "Bennets Desire"	10
	pt. "Robinsons Rest"	66⅔
Robert Day	pt. "No Name" or pt. "Elisha Halls Resurvey"	150
Benjamin Day	"Brandom"	57
	"Frampton"	50
James Dawkins	"Joseph Place" tbc Charles Dawkins	200
William Dawkins	"Marys Dukedom"	100
Nathaniel Dare	pt. "Gideon & Claverlys Right"	315
Philip Dossey	pt. resurvey of several tracts	104
	pt. "Tauneys Addition"	44
h/o William Day	pt. "No Name"	100
Susanna Dare	pt. "Gideon & Claverlys Right" tbc Nathaniel Dare	157
Cleverly Dare	pt. "Gideon & Cleverlys Right"	1104
	pt. "Prestons Clift" tbc Thomas Johnson, Jr.	100
Ellis Dixon	"Hogskin Clift"	100
Thomas Denton	pt. "Island Neck"	99
	"Puddington"	50
12:1773:8 ...		
John Dare	pt. "Gideon & Cleverlys Right"	100
	pt. "Gideon & Cleverlys Right"	70
Henry Dowell	pt. "Swinfens Rest"	50
	pt. "Lingans Purchase"	100
Richard Deale	pt. "Newington"	200
John Dossey s/o James	pt. "Garden"	100
	pt. "Robinsons Rest"	64
James Deale	pt. "Swinfens Rest"	64½
	pt. "Timberwell"	74
Daniel Dossey	pt. "Garden"	67
Philip Dorsey, Jr.	pt. "Robinsons Rest"	150
Francis Dorsey	pt. "Bennets Desire"	50

Jacob Deale	pt. "Upper Bennett"	75
William Dare	pt. "Swinfens Rest"	250
	pt. "Lawreys Chance"	36¾
Philip Dowell	pt. "Lingans Purchase"	116
Alexander Deale	pt. "Newington" tbc John Weems	46
	pt. "Islington" tbc John Weems	26
12:1773:9 ...		
Thomas Cleverly Dare	pt. "Agreement"	150
	"Bite the Biter"	112
	"Sampsons Dividend"	150
	pt. "Mannington"	25
	"Neglect"	50
	pt. "Parkers Clifts"	21
	"Devise"	75
	"Darby"	46
John Dew or h/o (N) Smith	pt. "Archers Hays"	43⅓
James Dossey, Jr.	pt. "Youngs Mount"	159
	pt. "Youngs Fortune"	40
James Dawkins s/o James	pt. "Hap Hazard"	90
Richard Everist	pt. "Highland"	50
Ann Elt	"Eltonhead Manor"	336
Isaac Essex	pt. "Wolf Trap"	55
	pt. "Scrap"	38
Robert Etherington	pt. "Comsey" tbc Benjamin Mackall	92½
Barnaby Eagan	pt. "Brook Place Manor"	400
Ezza Freeman	pt. "Forge"	50
h/o George Fowler	pt. "Tillington" tbc: • Edward Talbutt – 22¾ a. • Edward North – 22¾ a.	45½
12:1773:10 ...		
James Frazier	"Hills Hall"	100
	"White Marsh"	68
Thomas Freeman	pt. "Rockhold"	135
h/o Joseph Freeman	pt. "Arnolds Purchase"	50
Col. William Fitzhugh (cnp)	pt. "Eltonhead Manor"	2500
	pt. "Miles End"	399½

	pt. "Miles Run"	150
	"Hattons Cove"	70
	"Staffords Freehold"	70
	"Round Ponds"	100
	"Leach" or "Smiths Hills"	100
	"Gore"	70
Jacob Freeland	pt. "Letchworth Chance"	179
	"Neglect"	125
	pt. "Fuller"	100
Robert Freeland	"Foremans Chance"	232
	"Dosseys Folly"	70
	"Burks Purchase"	50
	pt. "Dear Quarter"	100
	pt. "Fuller"	200
Peregrine Freeland	pt. "Makalls Force"	323½
John Furgeson	"Gover & Griffiths Pasture"	40
	pt. "Skinners Chance"	30
	pt. "Turners Place"	126
12:1773:11 ...		
Alexander Frazier	"Sterlings Chance"	40
	"Sterlings Nest"	550
Thomas French	pt. "Danvin"	125
Richard Gibson	pt. "Swinfens Rest"	72
	pt. "Lordships Favour"	50
h/o John Griffith	pt. "Welsh Pool"	143¾
	pt. "Skinners Chance"	90
George Grant	"Selbys Cliffs" – for h/o John Bicket	200
	pt. "Mears" – for h/o John Bicket	200
	pt. "Guntertons" – for h/o John Bicket	250
	pt. "Hardesty" – for h/o John Bicket	50
	"Poppy Gray" – for h/o John Bicket	40
John Gibson	pt. "Spittle"	90
	pt. "Additional Spittle"	22

John Gardiner	pt. "Johnsons Lott"	100
	pt. "Johnsons Lott" – from Robert Gardiner	100
	pt. "Johnsons Lott" tbc Hawerton Games & John Gardner, Jr. in 1774	174
	pt. "Wolfs Hole"	21⅓
Charles Graham	pt. "Halls Craft"	521
	"Howard"	42
	"Bell"	68
	"Black Wall"	38
	pt. "Hardesty"	180
Joseph Galloway	pt. "Spittle"	20
	pt. "Addition Spittle"	28
12:1773:12 ...		
James Gibson	pt. "Additional Spittle"	88
	pt. "Newington"	22
h/o Robert Gover	pt. "Archers Hays"	190
	"Goughs Purchase" a/s "Goughs Pasture"	50
	"Govers Addition"	167
	"Govers Meadow"	59
	pt. "Dunkirk"	150
	pt. "Exchange"	66
Lewis Griffith	pt. "Welch Pool"	135
	pt. "Archers Hays"	231
	"Lewis's Slipe & Davis Purchase"	26
	pt. "Cooper"	86
Edward Gant	pt. "Ordinary"	606
	"Kingsburys Marsh"	130
	"Craft"	90
John Griffin	pt. "Robinson"	60
Thomas Gray	pt. "Wolton & Catch"	75
	pt. "Thorough Bridge"	125
	pt. "Brooks Choice"	73
William Gray s/o Thomas	"Grays Addition"	109
John Gray (Patuxent) (cnp)	"Marsh Land & Bickhead" tbc George Gray	345
	"Hazard"	42
	pt. "Brooke Adventure"	100

	"Jontle" a/s "Tuxbury"	100
	"Toddy"	138
12:1773:13 ...		
William Gray	"Reserve"	50
	"Jennets Ramble"	35
Howerton Games	pt. "Johnsons Lott" tbc John Gardiner, Jr.	50
	"Hazard" tbc John Gardiner, Jr.	25
h/o Samuel Gray	"Norwood"	200
	"Theobush"	50
	pt. "Austins Chance"	91
Driver Graves	pt. "Stevens Plains"	25
	"Graves Rehobeth"	80
Edward Gardiner	"Chilton" or "Chatham"	80
	pt. "Forked Neck" or "Dorrington"	50
	"Short Neck"	76
Benjamin Gardiner	pt. "Round Pond Plains"	100
h/o James Trueman Greenfield	pt. "Aldermason" tbc Michael Catterton	150
	"Addition" tbc Michael Catterton	56½
Henry Gray	"Labour in Vain"	100
Henry Hunt	pt. "Upper Bennet"	195
Mary Graves	"Batchelors Hall"	300
	"Timber Neck"	50
	"Clares Littleworth"	43
12:1773:14 ...		
Esther Gray	"Fishing Creek"	165
	"Chaplain"	100
	"East Fishing Creek"	50
	"Nuts Clifts"	150
	"East Chaplain"	100
Thomas Hollingshead	pt. "Kents Freehold"	250
James Heighe (cnp)	pt. "Beakley"	300
	pt. "Roberts Chance"	34
	"Forsters Purchase"	150
	pt. "James's Chance"	40
	"Samuels Addition"	15
	"Clarks Hills"	19

	"Little Land"	11
	"Heighs Addition"	15
	"James's Addition"	21
h/o Thomas Holdsworth Heighe	pt. "Brook Place"	300
William Harrison	pt. "Brooks Discovery"	200
	pt. "Laureys Reserve"	75
	pt. "Brothers Discovery"	126
	pt. "Cox's Freehold"	128
Joseph Hardersty	pt. "Den"	37½
	pt. "Nicholsons Chance"	55
	"Nelsons Reserve"	22
12:1773:15 ...		
William Hickman	pt. "Newington"	220
	pt. "Islington"	308
Elizabeth Hunt	pt. "Lordships Favour"	50
h/o John Hance	pt. "Newington" tbc Thomas McKinsey	9
	"John's Neglect" tbc Thomas McKinsey	128
	pt. "Islingworths Fortune" tbc Thomas McKinsey	65
Henry Howes	pt. "Refuge" tbc Sarah Howes	50
	"Jenstys Lott" tbc John Weems	46
	"Purchase" tbc John Weems	23
Henry Hardesty	pt. "Den"	37
	pt. "Nicholsons Chance"	55
William Hardesty	pt. "Lordships Favour"	75
Henry Harrison	pt. "Swinfens Rest"	150
Thomas Holland	pt. "St. James's Enlarged"	1138
	pt. "Alexanders Hope"	38
George Hall	pt. "Chance" tbc John Weems	25
Abraham Hooper	pt. "Taylors Joy"	228
12:1773:16 ...		
Walter Hoxton (CH)	pt. "Hormesham"	117
Ann Holland	pt. "Abbington"	150
William Harris (cnp)	"Durain"	200
	pt. "Hillingsworth Fortune"	100
	pt. "Littleworth"	77

	pt. "Tillington"	73
	pt. "Letchworths Chance"	275
Dr. Leonard Hollyday	"Buzz & Island"	700
	"Addition"	51
	pt. "Arnolds Purchase"	50
Newman Harvey	pt. "Turners Place"	126
Benjamin Harris	pt. "Expectation"	100
	pt. "Whites Rest"	148
	pt. "Parkers Clifts"	50
William Harris, Jr.	"Addition"	100
James Henley	"Smuggs Folly"	80
Joseph Hance	"Warbleton"	404
Isaac Hickman	pt. "Islington"	234
12:1773:17 ...		
Benjamin Hance	"Taskers Clifts"	100
	"Warrington"	175
	pt. "Agreement"	50
	"Buseys Garden"	175
	pt. "Islington"	250
	"Hance Lane"	20
	pt. "Newington"	3
	"Purchase"	154
	"Wareing Chance"	56
	resurvey of several tracts	119½
Kensey Hance	pt. "Stockley" a/s resurvey of several tracts	100
John Hungerford	pt. "Eltonhead Manor"	200
	"Jermyn Quarter Enlarg'd"	143
James Hellen	pt. "Truswell"	150
Samuel Hance	"Theobusk Manning"	189
	"Huckleberry Neck"	205
Walter Hellen	pt. "Hoopers Neck"	275
Edmund Hellen	pt. "Waring"	121
	pt. "Bowdleys Chance"	75
	"Buseys Lott"	75
	"Hellens Lott"	12
Philip Hunt	pt. "Lordships Favour"	100

12:1773:18 ...		
h/o Edmund Hungerford	pt. "Hogskin Neck"	100
	pt. "Shepherds Land"	100
	"Purchase"	24
	pt. "Desart"	100
Richard Hellen	pt. "Farewell"	150
	"Miltons Lott"	100
	"Porsia"	100
	"Hairs Hill Resurveyed"	77
	pt. "Rich Levill"	20
David Hellen s/o Richard	"Gully"	63½
Fran. Hutchings	pt. "Magruder"	175
Rebecca Hungerford	pt. "Friendship"	31¼
	pt. "Taylors Joy" tbc Charles Dawkins	114
	pt. "Allens Neck" tbc Charles Dawkins	36
	"Dicks Cabin"	50
	pt. "Friendship" tbc John Ward	25
Joseph Ireland	"Leach's Freehold"	125
John Ivey	pt. "Stevens Plains"	25
Kensey Johns (AA)	pt. "Angelica"	200
	pt. "Mears"	200
	pt. "Inland"	1
12:1773:19 ...		
Benjamin Johns	pt. "Angelica" tbc Charles Owens (196 a.)	400
	pt. "John's Addition"	112
	pt. "Inland"	1
Richard Johns	pt. "Whites Rest" tbc John Laveale	188
	pt. "Parkers Clifts"	109
h/o Joseph Isaac	"Plumb Point"	400
	pt. "Lordships Favour"	205
	"Purchase"	100
Col. William Ireland	"Lyons Creek"	300
	pt. "Dunkirk"	50
Joseph Ireland (cnp)	"Bridge"	100
	"Georges Desire"	50
	"Addition"	43

	"Angle"	87
	pt. "Peahens Nest"	35
	"Island Plains"	32
William Johnson s/o George	pt. "Red Hall"	100
h/o Richard Johns	"Purchase"	100
	pt. "Youngs Desire"	12
William Ireland s/o Thomas	pt. "Halls Hills" tbc Francis Whittington (25 a.)	550
12:1773:20 ...		
Mary Ireland	pt. "Eltonhead Manor"	200
	pt. "Prestons Clifts" tbc Richard Ireland	108
	pt. "Angle" tbc Richard Ireland	88
	pt. "No Name"	100
	"Middle Marsh" tbc Richard Ireland	63
John Ireland	pt. "Tillington"	189
	"Wolf Trap"	45
Thomas Johnson	"Brewhouse"	260
w/o John Johnson	"Elizabeth"	200
	pt. "Gift"	70
Thomas Johnson, Jr.	pt. "Prestons Clifts"	314
William Johnson s/o Jere	pt. "Exchange"	150
Dr. Edward Johnson	"Preston"	200
	"Moffatt Mount"	200
	"Woods Adventure"	50
	"Hay Marsh"	18
	pt. "Poor Land"	185
	"Musqueto Point"	46
	"Turners Chance"	50
	"Addition to Wood Venture"	33
Richard Ireland	"Irelands Hope"	50
	pt. "Desart"	198
12:1773:21 ...		
John Kent	pt. "Rockhold"	160
James Kirshaw	pt. "Prevent Danger"	100
Sarah Kirshaw	pt. "Prevent Danger"	50
Francis Kirshaw	pt. "Sharpers Out Lett"	100
	pt. "Concord"	63

Joseph Kent	pt. "Timberwell"	326
	pt. "Additional Spittle"	50
Rev. Fran. Lawder	pt. "Prestons Clifts"	239
	pt. "Gore"	50
John Lawrence	pt. "Lawreys Addition"	145
	pt. "Islington"	50
	pt. "Small Reward"	57
William Lyles	pt. "Red Hall"	150
	pt. "Stripe"	8
	pt. "Turners Pasture"	170
	pt. "Long Lane"	31
h/o Lewis Levin	pt. "Red Hall"	37½
John Laveal	pt. "Red Hall"	150
12:1773:22 ...		
Robert Lyles	pt. "Red Hall"	100
	"All Point" – from Lewis Griffith	24
Capt. Richard Lane & Benjamin Lane	pt. "Homisham"	233
Samuel Lyles	pt. "Lawreys Chance"	50
Jeremiah Maulden	pt. "Parkers Clifts"	250
John Mackall s/o John	pt. resurvey of several tracts	104
	pt. "Tauneys Addition"	44
James Mackal s/o John	resurvey of several tracts	104
	pt. "Tauneys Addition"	44
Benjamin McKall s/o John	"School House"	100
	"Brigantine Adventure"	24
Elizabeth Marshall w/o Thomas	"Cox's Folly"	50
	pt. "Farme"	19
William Marshall 3rd	pt. "Cox's Choice"	143
John Manning	pt. "Theobalds Manor"	112
	pt. "Gimsby"	168
	"Cold Kirby"	½
William Monnett	"Williams Purchase"	206
w/o James McDowell	pt. "Coles Clifts"	50
12:1773:23 ...		

Hannah Mackall	"Cage"	250
	"Buseys Lott"	100
	"Mackalls Desire"	10
h/o Thomas Morgan	pt. "Desire"	79
	pt. "Grays Chance"	350
	"Fellow Ship"	160
John Mackall (SM)	pt. "Morgan"	60
	pt. "Horse Range"	180
	"Caggets Desire"	376
	pt. "Desart"	350
	"St. James's"	300
Benjamin Mackall (Holland Point)	"Copartnership"	182
	pt. "Chance"	307
	"Hollow Point"	400
	"Seamores Neck"	382
	pt. "Horse Range"	165
	pt. "Sharpes Out Lett"	100
	pt. "Dividing Branch"	179
	pt. "Trouble"	27
	pt. "Morocco" – in corn	50
	"Addition to Sharps Out Lett"	112
	pt. "Reed"	46½
	pt. "Majors Choice"	381
h/o Thomas Bond	pt. "Brooke Partition" tbc Zacheus Alnutt	200
Rousby Miller	pt. "Orchard"	250
Ann Mills	pt. "Wolton"	25
	pt. "Catch"	50
12:1773:24 ...		
James John Mackall (cnp)	pt. "Lower Bennett" tbc Mary Mackall	500
	pt. "Theobusk Manor" tbc Mary Mackall	100
	"Corn Hill" tbc Benjamin Mackall	350
	"Alexanders Hope" tbc Mary Mackall	200
	pt. "Grays Chance" tbc Mary Mackall	200
	pt. "Bone Road" tbc Mary Mackall	89
	pt. "Gunsby" tbc Mary Mackall	38
	"Cold Harbour" tbc Mary Mackall	100

	pt. "Brooke Place" tbc Mary Mackall	432
	pt. "Stones Bay" tbc Mary Mackall	225
	"Piney Point" tbc James Mackall	50
	"Exchange" tbc Thomas Mackall	350
	"Lawreys Point" & pt. "Lawreys Rest" tbc James Mackall	100
	pt. "Littleworth" tbc Mary Mackall	77
	"Cold Karbey" tbc Mary Mackall	200
	pt. "Angle" tbc Mary Mackall	350
	pt. "Lawreys Rest" tbc James Mackall	295
	"Fox's Walks" tbc Mary Mackall	40
	"Bramhall" tbc James Mackall	500
	"Neglect" tbc Mary Mackall	30
	pt. "Godsgrace" tbc Benjamin Mackall	617
	"Meads" tbc James Mackall	166
	pt. "Evans's Land" tbc Mary Mackall	200
	pt. "Coles Clifts" tbc Mary Mackall	150
	pt. "Prestons Clifts" tbc Mary Mackall	63
	pt. "Cedar Branch" tbc Thomas Mackall	240
	pt. "Sewells Purchase" tbc Thomas Mackall	30
	"Bramels Addition" tbc Mary Mackall	33
	"Angle" tbc Mary Mackall	87
John Norfolk	"Kids Levell"	84
	pt. "Island Plains"	27
	pt. "Ridge"	100
	pt. "Refuge"	100
	pt. "Refuge"	14
	pt. "Cap Hall" – from Young Cox	125
12:1773:25 ...		
James Morsell	pt. "Rattle Snake Hill"	120
	"Chance"	70
	pt. "Littleworth"	60
	pt. "Mary Green"	55
James Norfolk	pt. "Peahens Nest"	50
h/o John Peters	pt. "Kents Freehold"	50
	pt. "Lordships Favour"	30

William Powell	pt. "Gideon & Cleverly Right"	5½
John Pardo	pt. "Rockey Neck"	50
	pt. "Fox's Walks"	70
Mary Parker	"Clay Hammond"	380
	"Wilsons Commons"	29
Elizabeth Prindowell	pt. "Parkers Clifts"	100
	pt. "Roberts Addition"	5
	pt. "Beakley"	66⅔
	pt. "Roberts Chance"	5½
Leonard Prindowell	pt. "Roberts Addition"	10
	pt. "Roberts Chance"	11
	pt. "Beakley"	133⅓
Robert Peters	pt. "Danvin & Clares Hundred"	142
William Patterson	pt. "Stones Bay"	75
	pt. "Evans Land"	65
h/o Alexander Paran	pt. "Patience"	360
	"Addition"	19
12:1773:26 ...		
h/o Hutcheson Parker	pt. "St. Leonards" – in corn	175
	pt. "Bulmores Branh"	50
	pt. "Stones Hills"	26
Richard Parran	pt. "Desart"	349
	"Preston"	400
	"Preston Neglect"	200
	pt. "Bromogan"	50
	pt. "Parans Park"	300
	"Brooks Plains"	100
	pt. "Inland"	2
	"Discovery"	99
Samuel Paran	pt. "Winfields Resurvey"	207
	pt. "Burmingham"	25
	pt. "Morgan"	45
	pt. land without name	100
	pt. "Parans Park"	150
John Peters (cnp)	"Johnsons Farm" tbc David Car	150
	pt. "Turners Place" tbc David Car	66⅔

	pt. "Griffith & Govers Pasture" tbc David Car	20
John Rawlings	pt. "Stonhead Manor"	300
	"Crumpton"	75
	"Rawlings Purchase"	60
Thomas Rodes	"Block Robin"	38
Daniel Ross	pt. "Robinsons Rest"	200
12:1773:27 ...		
Thomas Reynolds	pt. "Robinson"	191
	pt. "St. Edmunds"	150
	pt. "Robinsons Rest"	518
	pt. "Good Luck"	100
	"Adjoinder" a/s "Adjuction"	10
	pt. "Brooks Discovery"	64
	"Crouch's Lott"	60
	"Reserve"	300
	"Fox's Chance"	72
	"Rich Bitt"	5½
	"Foxes Home"	30
	"Sterlings Perch"	110
	pt. "Lordships Favour"	285
	pt. "Neglect"	44
	pt. "Cox's Inclosure"	70
	pt. "Cox's Freehold" tbc Young Cox	142
	"Troublesome"	150
	pt. "Hopewell"	35
	pt. "Abbington Manor"	769
	"Angles Lane"	37
	pt. "Meadows"	132
	"Thomas & Williams Chance"	101
	pt. "Thatchcomb"	114
	pt. "Lingans Purchase"	8
	pt. "Brook Neck"	130
	"Stallings Swamp"	10
	"Bite"	5
Samuel Robertson (cnp)	"Emertons Addition"	20
	pt. "Halls Hills"	85

	pt. "Broughton Ashley"	73
Henry Scott	pt. "Highland"	50
Daniel Rawlings	pt. "Eltonhead Manor"	200
	"Bathens Loss"	50
	"Dear Bought"	200
12:1773:28 ...		
Dr. John Hamilton Smith	"Branford"	150
	pt. "Hardestys Choice"	150
	pt. "Henry Chew"	75
	1½ lots in Lower Marlbrough	1½
	pt. "Dowdswell Manor"	400
Gavin Hamilton Smith	"Little Genory"	42
	pt. "Grantham"	220
	"Sams Addition"	78
	"Hazard"	18½
	pt. "Ordinary"	80½
h/o Philemon Smith	"Soldiers Fortune"	200
	pt. "Ordinary"	75
Alexander Hamilton Smith	pt. "Batchelors Quarter"	250
Walter Smith	pt. "Parkers Clifts"	100
	"Fox's Road"	100
	"Wolfs Quarter"	300
	"Smiths Hog Pen"	309
	pt. "St. Leonards" – in corn	175
	"Taylors Disposal"	270
	pt. "Stones Hill"	25
	"Purchase"	20
h/o James Somervill	"Tobys Quarter"	21
	"Rocky Neck"	50
	pt. "Allens Neck"	12
	"Swamp"	60
	"Narrow Neck & Gore"	11
	pt. "Gore"	100
	pt. "Stockley"	419
	pt. "Gunterton"	40
12:1773:29 ...		

h/o Maryland Skinner	pt. "Newington"	94
	pt. "Millers Folly"	250
h/o Leonard Skinner	"Borden"	77½
	pt. "Dodsons Desire"	25
	pt. "Chance"	27
John Simmonds	pt. "Rich Bottom"	25
	"Short Hills" tbc William Powell (23½ a.)	40
h/o George Smith	pt. "Desart"	52
	pt. "Round Bottom Plains"	100
Dorothy Sollars	"Forked Neck"	100
	"Hyam"	10
William Skinner	pt. "Prestons Desire"	25
	pt. "Chance"	27
James Skinner	pt. "Border Enlarg'd"	77½
	pt. "Dodsons Desire"	25
	pt. "Chance"	27
	pt. "Reserve"	32¼
Robert Skinner	pt. "Blind Tom"	40
	pt. "Tauneys Right"	150
	"Addition" tbc George Gant for h/o John Beckett	60
Elizabeth Skinner	pt. "Tauneys Right"	150
	pt. "Scrap"	62
	pt. "Reserve"	121
	pt. "Newington"	94
12:1773:30 ...		
h/o Adderton Skinner	"Blind Tom"	32
	"Tawneys Delight"	70
	pt. "Mary Green"	36
	"Gore"	48
	pt. "Millers Folly"	250
	"Neglect"	25
Edward Wood	pt. "Morocco" – in corn	100
Alexander Somervill (cnp)	"Fox's Denn"	50
	"Bartholomews Neck"	50
	pt. "Smiths Purchase"	119¼
	pt. "Gore"	100

	"Goldins Folly"	75
Joseph Strickland	pt. "Robinsons Rest"	50
Benjamin Sunderland	pt. "Swinfens Rest"	250
William Sollars	pt. "Dorrington"	182½
	pt. "Bordleys Chance"	34
Joshua Sedwick	pt. "Neighbourhood"	150
	"Adjoinder"	50
	"Nortons Purchase"	83⅓
w/o Josias Sunderland, Jr.	pt. "Upper Bennett"	50
Phineas Stallings	pt. "Thatchcomb"	236
12:1773:31 ...		
Joseph Skinner	pt. "Orchard"	50
	pt. "Border Enlarged"	77½
	pt. "Chance"	27
	pt. "Dodsons Desire"	25
	pt. "Reserve"	32¼
	"Chance"	8
James Sewell	pt. "Dear Quarter"	62½
	pt. "Chance"	72½
	"Maidens Delight"	200
	pt. "Cops Hall"	80
	pt. "Parkers Clifts"	50
	"Good Luck"	150
John Standforth	pt. "Poor Land"	104
h/o John Skinner	pt. "Halls Hills" tbc John Lee Webster	877½
	"Sneaking Point" tbc John Lee Webster	50
	pt. "Lingans Purchase" tbc Thomas Cheney & Richard Wells	94
	pt. "Hamiltons Park" tbc Thomas Cheney & Richard Wells	33
Richard Stansbury	pt. "Archers Hays"	40
h/o Joseph Smith, Jr.	pt. "Turners Pasture"	50
	pt. "Smiths Pasture"	100
	pt. "Archers Hays"	15½
	pt. "Archers Hays" – from John Dew	30½

h/o William Smith	pt. "Smiths Chance"	50
	pt. "Turners Place"	50
	pt. "Mordyke"	50
Joseph Smith	pt. "Mordyke"	50
12:1773:32 ...		
Mordecai Smith	pt. "Smiths Chance"	100
	pt. "Welch Poole"	72½
	pt. "Turners Place"	50
	pt. "Claander"	77
w/o John Stone	pt. "Defence"	65
John Stallings	pt. "Upper Bennett"	25
Ellis Slater	pt. "Lawreys Reserve"	100
Stephen Stamp	pt. "Read Hall"	125
	pt. "Turners Place"	144⅓
Col. Henry Brooke	"Good Prospect" – for Mary Smith	50
	"Lanes Land" – for Mary Smith	192
	"Addition" – for Mary Smith	28
Benjamin Skinner	pt. "Smiths Lott & Johnsons Farm" & pt. "Good Prospect & Lands Land"	\<n/g\>
Clement Smith	pt. "Halls Craft"	221
Patrick Smith	"Halls Craft"	265
Nicholas Swamstead	pt. "Lordships Favour"	100
Thomas Stallings	pt. "Swinfens Rest"	64½
John Sedwick	"Buck Hill"	21
12:1773:33 ...		
Stocket Sunderland	pt. "Lawreys Chance" or "Resurvey"	109
John Davis Scarth	pt. "Robinsons Rest"	50
Benjamin Sedwick	pt. "Bulmores Branch" a/s "Right" tbc Dr. John Hamilton Smith	475
Elizabeth Countee	pt. "Halls Revenge"	28
	1 lot in Lower Marlbro tbc John Lee Webster	1
Stephens Stewards	pt. "Islingsworth Fortune"	200
John Scott	pt. "Lordships Favour" tbc Thomas Reynolds	100
Raphael Tauney	pt. "Stones Hills"	50
Jacob Tucker	"Tuckers Thicket" tbc William Harrison	200
	pt. "Chance" tbc John Weems	50

h/o Philip Thomas, Esq.	"Majors Choice" tbc John Mackall (AA)	119
Joseph Talbut, Jr.	pt. "Expectation"	100
John Tannehill	pt. "Callender"	123
	pt. "Cooper" & pt. "Friendship"	42
	pt. "Welsh Poole"	86
Ann Tannehill	pt. "Cooper" & pt. "Friendship"	173
Joseph Talbutt	pt. "Freemans Chance"	123
	pt. "Tillington"	150
	"Batchelors Fortune"	200
12:1773:34 ...		
John Tabutt	pt. "Expectation"	50
Edward Talbutt	pt. "Tillington"	415½
John Turner	pt. "Bowdleys Chance"	91
Thomas Talbutt	pt. "Expectation"	100
h/o Benjamin Tasker, Esq.	"Hard Travill"	300
John Tucker	pt. "Neighbourhood"	82½
William Vermelion	"Creeds Chance"	64
John Wilkinson	pt. "Youngs Attempt"	100
Ben Kid Wilson & Priscilla Gover	pt. "Aldermason"	150
	"Govers Expectation"	89
	pt. "Welsh Poole"	2
John Ward	"Welsh's Rest" tbc Edmund Hellen	50
	pt. "Friendship" – from Hannah Hungerford	50
h/o Samuel Ward	"Goldsons Inheritance"	150
Aaron Williams, Jr.	pt. "Friendship Rectified"	200
	pt. "Swinfens Adventure"	50
	pt. "Youngs Desire"	50
James Weems, Jr.	"Success, Tauneys Ear, & Stockley"	200
	"Partnership"	75
12:1773:35 ...		
Aaron Williams, Sr.	pt. "William's Hardship"	175
	"Williams Rest"	50
	"Littlefield"	25
	pt. "Friendship Rectified"	25
	pt. "Swinfens Adventure"	25

h/o Joseph Wilkins	pt. "Godsgrace"	120
	pt. "Stockley"	70
John Waters	"Mirtle Point"	7
John Willing	pt. "Taylors Joy" tbc Abraham Hooper	128
	"Jerusalem"	108
	pt. "Rich Bottom"	25
Francis Wolf, Jr.	pt. "Theobald Manor"	50
	pt. "Grays Chance"	50
Richard Ward	pt. "Swinfens Rest"	116
	pt. "Danvin & Clares Hundred"	138
James Weems s/o David	"Ringan"	200
	"Greenhouse"	155
	"Chews Purchase"	145
	pt. "Grantham"	45
	"Marshals Addition"	70
Basil Williamson	pt. "Langans Adventure"	310
Edward Wood	pt. "Woods Adventure"	150
	pt. "Titmarsh"	100
	pt. "Poor Land"	11
	pt. "Brook Adventure"	78
George Wheelor	"Barry" – for h/o (N) Tauney	600
	"Long Point" – for h/o (N) Tauney	100
	"Wooden Point" – for h/o (N) Tauney	25
	pt. "Letchworth" – for h/o (N) Tauney	50
	pt. "Angle" – for h/o (N) Tauney	3
12:1773:35a ...		
h/o Roger Wheelor	"Henry Chew"	237
	"Coxcomb"	150
	"Coxhead"	109
	"Smith Contrivance"	60
	pt. "Buck Chance" – from James Weems	150
12:1773:36 ...		
Jonah Winfield	pt. "Johnsons Farm"	100
Thomas & Jane Wells	pt. "Grantham Hall"	155
	"Arthurs Hall"	44

h/o James Williamson	"Den"	726
	"Fox's Nettles"	20
	pt. "Batholars Quarter"	420
John Wilkinson	pt. "Henry Chew"	400
Leonard Wood	pt. "Woods Adventure"	100
h/o Edward Wilson	"Dear Quarter"	25
	"Robinsons Rest"	150
John Weems	pt. "Dowdswell"	600
	pt. "Chance"	25
William White	pt. "Smiths Joy"	100
William Winnull	pt. "Nortons Purchase"	166⅔
William Hunton Wood	pt. "Arnolds Purchase"	100
Francis Whittington	pt. "Halls Hills"	100
	~~pt. "Halls Hills" – from William Ireland~~	~~25~~
Francis Williams	pt. "Inland"	100
	"Hutchings Chance"	50
	pt. "Orchard"	40
John Winfield	pt. "Lands Land"	112
12:1773:37 ...		
Ithamar Williams	pt. "Swinfins Adventure"	50
	pt. "Williams Hardship"	75
	pt. "Friendship Rectified"	125
h/o Joseph Wilson	"Tamot" tbc h/o Ed. Wilson	300
	pt. "Forsters Purchase" tbc h/o Ed. Wilson	150
	pt. "Robinsons" tbc Hillary Wilson	136
	pt. "Additional Spittle" tbc h/o Ed. Wilson	8
	pt. "Peahens Nest" tbc Jos. Ireland	40
	pt. "Cedar Branch"	75
	pt. "Bowen" – for h/o (N) King tbc John Brooke	230
	pt. "Brooks Adventure" tbc John Brooke	150
	"Stones Lott" tbc Nathaniel Wilson	50
	pt. "Arnolds Purchase" tbc John Brooke	50
Philemon Young	pt. "Henry Chew"	59½
	1 lot in Lower Marlbro	1
Joseph Wilson, Jr.	pt. "Garey Chance"	150
	"Lower Bennett"	189

Parker Young	"Hopyard"	150
	"Punch"	150
	pt. "Youngs Desire"	25
	pt. "Hoopers Neck"	275
Mary Yoe	pt. "Rattle Snake Hills"	100
Richard Hellen s/o Richard	pt. "Cedar Branch"	50
Peter Hellen	"Huckleberry Quarter Enlarg'd"	127¼
12:1773:38 ...		
John Mills	pt. "Thorough Point"	125
	pt. "Brooks Choice"	73
James Weems	pt. "Magruder"	410
	"Buseys Orchard"	400
	"Hogs Hunt"	50
	"Mauldens Luck"	25
	"Meadows Preserved"	46
	"Huckleberry Hill"	50
	pt. "Cuckolds Miss"	60
	"Youngs Attempt"	62
	"Youngs Fortune"	60
	"Youngs Desire"	25
	"Penman Mure"	50
	"Reserve"	50
	"Inland"	1
	1 lot in Hunting Town	1
Richard Winfield	pt. "Lordships Favour"	50
John Sedwick	"Buck Hill" – charged on f. 32	21
Edward Wood	"Brooks Adventure"	77¾
Joseph Dawkins	pt. "Blinkhorn" tbc William Dawkins, Jr.	300
	"Fox's Road" tbc William Dawkins, Jr.	42
	"Josephs Refuse" tbc William Dawkins, Jr.	196
Hilleary Wilson	pt. "Robinson"	213
	pt. "Lordships Favour"	9
	pt. "Lordships Favour"	75
	pt. "Lordships Favour"	70
12:1773:39 ...		
Thomas Denton, Jr.	"Hap Hazard"	45

Richard Hellen s/o Richard	pt. "Cedar Branch" – charged on f. 37	50
Barbary Dawkins or Bryan Taylor	pt. "Smiths Purchase"	119¼
Isaac Simmonds	pt. "Chance"	50
	pt. "Borders Enlarg'd" pt. "Reserve"	210
John Broome	pt. "Island Neck"	500
	pt. "Stones Bay"	200
	"Adventure"	82½
	"Broad Point"	140
	pt. "Austins Addition"	23
	pt. "Brooks Battle"	124
Thomas Wilson	pt. "St. Edmunds"	163
	pt. "Neglect"	16½
	"Letchworth"	200
	"Youngs Attempt"	100
	pt. "Horsepath"	125
	pt. "Hop at a Venture"	25
Isaack Hickman	pt. "Islington" – charged on f. 16	234
John Ward	"Velches Rest"	50
	pt. "Friendship"	50
	pt. "Allens Neck"	164
12:1773:40 ...		
Isaac Hooper	pt. "Tobys Quarter"	79
	pt. "Swamp"	6½
	pt. "Narrow Neck & Gore"	7
John Gardiner	pt. "Johnsons Lott" – charged on f. 11	200
	pt. "Wolfs Hole" – charged on f. 11	21⅓
Kensey Gardiner	pt. "Wolfs Hole"	28⅔
	pt. "Johnsons Lott"	26⅓
	pt. "Johnsons Lott"	100
Zacheus Alnutt	pt. "Brook Partition"	119
	pt. "Hog Down"	7
	pt. "Little Reward"	21
Clement Skinner	pt. "Whittles Rest"	60
Edward Wood	pt. "Magruder"	150

12:1774:1 ...		Acres
h/o John Alton	pt. "Hardestys Choice"	50
David Arnold	pt. "Henry Chew"	290
	pt. "Abbington"	350
	pt. "Hardesty's Choice"	130
	pt. "Henry Chew"	110½
Elizabeth Austin	pt. "Cox's Chance"	140
	pt. "Farm"	20
William Askew	pt. "Lawrey's Chance"	118
William Alnutt	pt. "Foremans Chance"	156
	pt. "Agreement"	100
William Alnutt, Jr.	pt. "Foremans Chance"	153
Samuel Austin	pt. "Cox's Chance"	117
Roger Brooke	pt. "Brooke Place Manor" – from Roger Brooke	200
Elizabeth Brooke	pt. "Brooke Place Manor" – from Roger Brooke	241
John Brooke	pt. "Brooke Place Manor" – from Roger Brooke	430
Basil Brooke	pt. "Brooke Place Manor" – from Roger Brooke	225
h/o John & Isaac Baker	"Devils Woodyard"	150
Esther Bourne	pt. "Eltonhead Manor" – from Jacob Bourn	150
Jesse Jacob Bourne	pt. "Eltonhead Manor" – from Jacob Bourn	156
<t> Beveridge	<t>	<t>
12:1774:2 ...		
Abraham Bowen	pt. "Dividing Branch"	169½
	pt. "Billingsleys Farm"	136
Isaac Bowen	pt. "Dividing Branch"	190
David Bowen	pt. "Dividing Branch"	189
h/o John Brooke	pt. "Brooks Adventure"	116¾
	pt. "Cedar Branch"	25
	pt. "Arnolds Purchase"	150
	pt. "Bowen" – from Joseph Wilson	230
	pt. "Brooks Adventure" – from Joseph Wilson	150
	pt. "Arnolds Purchase" – from Joseph Wilson	50
Jesse Bourne	pt. "Eltonhead Manor"	1167
Jacob Bowen	pt. "Neighbourhood"	74
h/o Henry Broome (cnp)	pt. "Austin Chance"	65
	pt. "Howard & Letchworth"	200

	pt. "Broad Point"	10
	pt. "Austins Addition"	23
Eleanor Blackburn	pt. "Back Pasture"	50
James Bowen	pt. "Dividing Branch"	105
Thomas Bowen	"Dividing Branch"	105
h/o Roger Brooke, Jr.	"Brook Battle"	106
	pt. "Cedar Branch"	50
Thomas Blackburn	pt. "Readly"	100
h/o Thomas Broom	"Rich Neck"	52
	"Marys Widowhood"	30
	"Addition to Island Neck"	30
12:1774:3 ...		
Ann Bond	"Lower Fuller"	200
	"Middle Fuller"	200
	pt. "Lower Bennett"	250
Issabella Barton	pt. "Upper Bennett"	50
Jesse Bowen	"Lambeth"	94
h/o Richard Blake	pt. "Upper Bennett"	557
	pt. "St. Edmunds"	200
	pt. "Lordships Favour"	192
	"Neglect"	\<n/g\>
Thomas Blake	pt. "Halls Craft"	221⅔
h/o Thomas Bond	pt. "Hogsdown" – from Mary Bond	275
	"Micham" – from Mary Bond	243
	pt. "Brook Partition" – form Mary Bond	104
	pt. "Lawreys Chance" – from Mary Bond	98¼
Richard Bond	pt. "Lawreys Chance"	50
	"Small Land"	6¾
	"Small Reward"	54
	pt. "Spittle"	90
	"Hogs Down"	25
James Kent Bryan	pt. "Neighbourhood"	26
	pt. "Prevent Danger"	100
h/o Thomas Crumpton (cnp)	"Jeresalem"	124
	pt. "Swinfens Adventure"	25
	"Parkers Chance" a/s "Chance"	263

	"Biggar"	1055
	pt. "Godsgrace"	100
	pt. "Cottertons Lott & Barbers Delight"	294
Rev. Thomas Clagett	"Halls Craft" – for h/o (N) Smith	443⅓
Edmund Clare	pt. "Eltonhead Manor"	200
12:1774:4 ...		
Gabriel Childs	"Letchworth Chance"	336
Bennet Chew	"Chew Fortune"	49
h/o Joseph Chilton	"Terra in Aqua"	4
Samuel Chew	pt. "Letchworth Chance"	550
	pt. "Upper Bennett"	506
	"Lane & Gore"	51½
	pt. "Bennetts Refuge"	33
Josias Crosby	pt. "Archers Hays"	30
	pt. "Goughs Purchase"	60
Michael Catterton	"Lingans Purchase"	125
	pt. "Aldermason" – from h/o James T. Greenfield	150
	"Addition" – from h/o James T. Greenfield	56½
h/o Henry Camden	pt. "Highland"	200
	"Chances"	70
Elizabeth Chesley w/o John	pt. "Batchelor's Quarter"	420
Michael Culpeper	"Venture"	16
	"Wolfs Quarter" – from John Culpeper	40
Young Cox	pt. "Little Land"	17
	"Cox's Inclosure"	65
	pt. "Cox's Freehold"	120
	pt. "Merry Greenwood"	166
	pt. "Good Luck"	10
	"Hacket"	25
	pt. "Cox's Freehold" – from Thomas Reynolds	142
Samuel Chew (AA)	"Poping Gray"	540
John Clare, Jr.	pt. "Eltonhead Manor" – from Mary Clare	157
12:1774:5 ...		
Calvert County School – William Hunter	"Security"	87
	pt. "Orchard"	100
Calvert County	pt. "Inland"	3

Isaac Clare	"Hard Travil" – originally "Horse Path"	150
	pt. "Eltonhead Manor"	143
	"Concord"	161
	"Addition to Horsepath"	40
Thomas Crutchley	"Addition"	50
h/o John Cox	pt. "Smiths Lott"	33⅓
	pt. "Johnson Farm, Good Prospect, & Lands Land"	87½
Charles Dawkins	pt. "Friendship"	25
	pt. "Taylors Joy"	114
	"Joseph Place" – from James Dawkins	200
	pt. "Allen Neck" – from Rebecca Hungerford	36
	"Dicks Cabin" – from Rebecca Hungerford	50
Moses Duke	pt. "Rich Levell"	247
	pt. "Inland"	1
	pt. "Brooks Place Manor"	300
	pt. "Howard & Letchworth"	303
Henry Dixon	"Addition to Middlesex"	95
	"Fox's Walks"	5
Andrew Duke	"Middlesex"	100
	pt. "Gideon & Cleverly Right"	19
William Dorumple	pt. "Hop at a Venture" – from Elizabeth Dorumple	50
	pt. "Fox's Road" – from Elizabeth Dorumple	50
12:1774:6 ...		
Henry Dorumple	pt. "Hop at a Venture" – from Elizabeth Dorumple	100
h/o James Duke	pt. "Brook Place"	171
	pt. "Lower Bennett"	211
	"Mackalls Desire"	78
	"Knolers Branch" – from Roger Brooke, Jr.	98
Samuel Dare	pt. "Angle"	140
	pt. "Gideon & Cleverly Right"	502
	pt. "Smith Purchase"	119⅓
h/o James Dodson	"Huckleberry Hills"	50
	"Littleworth"	21
John Dossey (cnp)	pt. "Marys Green"	63
	"Dear Quarter"	62½
	pt. "Bennetts Desire"	10

	pt. "Robinson Rest"	66⅔
Robert Day	pt. "No Name" or pt. "Elisha Hall Resurvey"	150
Benjamin Day	"Brandom"	57
	"Frampton"	50
William Dawkins	"Marys Dukedom"	100
Nathaniel Dare	pt. "Gideon & Cleverly Right"	315
	pt. "Gideon & Cleverly Right" – from Susanna Dare	157
Philip Dossey	pt. resurvey of several tracts	102
	pt. "Tauneys Addition"	44
12:1774:7 ...		
h/o William Day	pt. "No Name"	100
Ellis Dixon	"Hogskin Clift"	100
Thomas Denton	pt. "Island Neck"	99
	"Puddington"	50
John Dare	pt. "Gideon & Cleverly Right"	100
	pt. "Gideon & Cleverly Right"	70
Henry Dowell	pt. "Swinfens Rest"	50
	pt. "Lingans Purchase"	100
Richard Deale	pt. "Newington"	200
John Dossey s/o James	pt. "Garden"	100
	pt. "Robinson Rest"	64
h/o James Deale	pt. "Swinfin Rest"	64½
	pt. "Timberwell"	74
Daniel Dossey	pt. "Garden"	67
Philip Dossey, Jr.	pt. "Robinson Rest"	150
Francis Dossey	pt. "Bennets Desire"	50
Jacob Deale	pt. "Upper Bennett"	75
	pt. "Davin" – from Thomas French	125
William Dare	pt. "Swinfins Rest"	250
	"Lawreys Chance"	36¾
12:1774:8 ...		
Philip Dowell	"Lingans Purchase"	116
Thomas Cleverly Dare (cnp)	pt. "Agreement"	150
	"Bite the Biter"	112
	"Sampson Dividend"	150

	"Mannington"	25
	"Neglect"	50
	pt. "Parkers Clifts"	21
	"Devise"	75
	"Darby"	46
John Dew or h/o (N) Smith	pt. "Youngs Mount"	159
	pt. "Youngs Fortune"	40
James Dawkins s/o James	pt. "Hap Hazard"	90
	pt. "Hap Hazard" – from Thomas Denton, Jr.	45
Richard Everest	pt. "High Land"	50
Ann Elt	pt. "Eltonhead Manor"	336
Isaac Essex	pt. "Wolf Trap"	55
	pt. "Scrap"	38
Barnaby Eagan	pt. "Brooke Place Manor"	400
Ezza Freeman	pt. "Forge"	50
James Fraizer	"Hills Hall"	100
	"White Marsh"	68
	"Fishers Orchard" – from Abraham Barns	255
	"Branfly" – from Abraham Barns	100
12:1774:9 ...		
Thomas Freeman	pt. "Rockhold"	135
h/o Joseph Freeman	pt. "Arnolds Purchase"	50
Col. William Fitzhugh	pt. "Eltonhead Manor"	2500
	pt. "Miles End"	399½
	pt. "Miles Run"	150
	"Hattons Cove"	70
	"Staffords Freehold"	70
	"Rounds Ponds"	100
	"Leacher Smiths Hills"	100
	"Gore"	70
Jacob Freeland	"Leatchworth Chance"	179
	"Neglect"	125
	pt. "Fuller"	100
Robert Freeland (cnp)	"Foremans Chance"	232
	"Dossey's Folly"	70
	"Burks Purchase"	50

	pt. "Dear Quarter"	100
	pt. "Fuller"	200
Peregrine Freeland	pt. "Mackalls Force"	323½
Frisby Freeland	pt. "Mackalls Force"	323½
John Furgeson	"Gover & Griffiths Pasture"	40
	pt. "Skinners Chance"	30
	pt. "Turners Place"	126
Alexander Fraizer	"Sterlings Chance"	40
	"Sterlings Nest"	550
12:1774:10 ...		
Richard Gibson	pt. "Swinfin's Rest"	72
	pt. "Lordships Favour"	50
h/o John Griffith	pt. "Welsh Pool"	143¾
	"Skinners Chance"	90
George Gantt	"Selbys Clifts" – for h/o John Beckett	200
	pt. "Mears" – for h/o John Beckett	200
	"Gunterstons" – for h/o John Beckett	250
	pt. "Hardesty" – for h/o John Beckett	50
	"Poppy Gray" – for h/o John Beckett	40
	"Addition" – for h/o John Beckett from Robert Skinner	60
John Gibson	pt. "Spittle"	90
	pt. "Addition to Spittle"	22
John Gardener	"Johnsons Lott"	100
	pt. "Johnsons Lott"	100
	pt. "Johnson Lott"	174
	pt. "Wolfs Hole"	21⅓
	"Short Neck" – from Edward Gardener	76
Charles Grahame	"Halls Craft"	521
	"Howard"	42
	"Bell"	68
	"Black Wall"	38
	pt. "Hardesty"	180
Joseph Gallaway	pt. "Spittle"	20
	pt. "Addition Spittle"	28

James Gibson	pt. "Addition Spittle"	88
	pt. "Newington"	22
12:1774:11 ...		
h/o Robert Gover	"Archers Hays"	190
	"Goughs Purchase" a/s "Goughs Pasture"	50
	"Govers Addition"	167
	"Govers Meadow"	59
	pt. "Dunkirk"	150
	pt. "Exchange"	66
Lewis Griffith	pt. "Welch Pool"	135
	pt. "Archers Hays"	231
	"Lewis's Slip & Davis Purchase"	26
	pt. "Cooper"	86
Edward Gantt	pt. "Ordinary"	606
	"Kingsburys Marsh"	130
	"Craft"	90
John Griffin	pt. "Robinson"	60
Thomas Gray	"Wolton & Catch"	75
	pt. "Thorough Bridge"	125
	pt. "Brook Choice"	73
William Gray s/o Thomas	"Grays Addition"	109
	"Creed Chance" – from William Vermilion	64
George Gray	"Marsh Land & Birkhead" – from John Gray	345
	"Hazard"	42
	"Brooke Adventure"	100
	"Jonotle" a/s "Tuxbury"	100
	"Toddy"	138
William Gray	"Reserve"	50
	"Sumits Ramble"	35
12:1774:12 ...		
John Gardener, Jr.	pt. "Johnson Lott" – from Howerton Games	50
	"Hazard" – from Howerton Games	25
h/o Samuel Gray	"Norwood"	200
	"Theobush"	50
	pt. "Austin Chance"	91

Driver Graves	"Stephens Plains"	25
	"Graves Rehobeth"	80
h/o Benjamin Gardener	pt. "Round Ponds Plains"	100
h/o James Truman Greenfield	pt. "Aldermanson"	150
	"Addition"	56½
Henry Gray	"Labour in Vain"	100
Henry Hunt	pt. "Upper Bennett"	195
Mary Graves	"Batchelors Hall"	300
	"Timber Neck"	50
	"Clares Littleworth"	43
Esther Gray	"Fishing Creek"	165
	"Chaplain"	100
	"East Fishing Creek"	50
	"Nuts Clifts"	150
	"East Chaplain"	100
Thomas Hollingshead	"Kents Freehold"	250
12:1774:13 ...		
James Heighe	pt. "Beakley"	300
	pt. "Roberts Chance"	34
	"Forsters Purchase"	150
	pt. "James's Chance"	40
	"Samuel Addition"	15
	"Clarks Hills"	19
	"Little Land"	11
	"Heighs Addition"	15
	"James's Addition"	21
h/o Thomas Holdsworth Heighe	pt. "Brooke Place"	300
William Harrison	pt. "Brooks Discovery"	200
	pt. "Lawreys Reserve"	75
	pt. "Brothers Discovery"	126
	"Cox's Freehold"	128
	"Tuckers Thickett" – from Jacob Tucker	200
Joseph Hardesty	pt. "Den"	37½
	pt. "Nicholson Chance"	55
	"Nelson Reserve"	22

William Hickman	pt. "Newington"	220
	pt. "Islington"	308
Sarah Howes	pt. "Refuge" – from Henry Howes	50
Henry Hardesty	pt. "Den"	37
	pt. "Nicholson Chance"	55
Henry Harrison	pt. "Swinfens Rest"	150
Elizabeth Hunt	pt. "Lordships Favour"	50
Thomas Holland	pt. "St. James's Enlarged"	1138
	"Alexanders Hope"	38
12:1774:14 ...		
Abraham Hooper	pt. "Taylors Joy"	228
	pt. "Taylors Joy" – from John Willing	128
Walter Hoxton (CH)	"Homesham"	117
Ann Holland	pt. "Abbington"	150
William Harris	"Durain"	200
	pt. "Hillingsworth Fortune"	100
	pt. "Littleworth"	77
	pt. "Tillington"	73
	pt. "Letchworth Chance"	275
Dr. Leonard Hollyday	"Buzz & Island"	700
	"Addition"	51
	pt. "Arnolds Purchase"	50
Newman Harvey	pt. "Turners Place"	126
Benjamin Harris	pt. "Expectation"	100
	pt. "Whites Rest"	148
	pt. "Parkers Clifts"	50
William Harris, Jr.	"Addition"	100
James Henley	"Smuggs Folly"	80
Joseph Hance	"Warbelton"	404
Isaac Hickman	pt. "Islington"	234
Kensey Hance	pt. "Stockley" a/s resurvey of several tracts	100
John Hungerford	pt. "Eltonhead Manor"	200
	"Jermyn Quarter Enlarged"	143
12:1774:15 ...		
Benjamin Hance (cnp)	"Taskers Clifts"	100
	"Warrington"	175

	pt. "Agreement"	50
	"Buseys Garden"	175
	"Hance Lane"	20
	"Islington"	250
	pt. "Newington"	3
	"Purchase"	154
	"Wareing Chance"	56
	resurvey of several tracts	119½
Samuel Hance	"Theobush Manning"	189
	"Huckleberry Neck"	205
Walter Hellen	pt. "Hooper Neck"	275
Edmund Hellen	"Wareing"	121
	pt. "Bowdleys Chance"	75
	"Buseys Lott"	75
	"Hellen Lot"	12
	"Vitches Rest" – from John Ward	50
Philip Hunt	pt. "Lordships Favour"	100
h/o Edmund Hungerford	pt. "Hogskin Neck"	100
	pt. "Sheperds Land"	100
	"Purchase"	24
	pt. "Desart"	100
Richard Hellen	pt. "Farewell"	150
	"Meltons Lott"	100
	"Porsia"	100
	"Hairs Hill Resurveyed"	77
	pt. "Rich Levell"	20
David Hellen s/o Richard	"Gully"	60½
Francis Hutchings	"Magruder"	175
12:1774:16 ...		
Joseph Ireland (cnp)	"Leach's Freehold"	125
	"Bridge"	100
	"Georges Desire"	50
	"Addition"	43
	"Angle"	87
	"Peahens Nest"	35
	"Island Plains"	32

	pt. "Peahens Nest" – from h/o Joseph Wilson	40
William Johnson s/o George	pt. "Read Hall"	100
h/o Richard Johns	"Purchase"	100
	pt. "Youngs Desire"	12
William Ireland s/o Thomas	pt. "Halls Hills"	525
John Ivey	pt. "Stephens Plains"	25
Kensey Johns	"Angelica"	200
	"Mears"	200
	"Inland"	1
Benjamin Johns	"Angelica"	204
	pt. "John's Addition"	112
	pt. "Inland"	1
Charles Owens	pt. "Angelica" – from Benjamin Johns	196
Richard Johns	~~pt. "Whites Rest"~~	~~188~~
	pt. "Parkes Clifts"	109
h/o Joseph Isaac	"Plump Point"	400
	pt. "Lordships Favour"	205
	"Purchase"	100
Col. William Ireland	"Lyons Creek"	300
	pt. "Dukirk"	50
12:1774:17 ...		
Mary Ireland	pt. "Eltonhead Manor"	200
	pt. "No Name"	100
John Ireland	pt. "Tillington"	198
	"Wolfs Trap"	45
Thomas Johnson	"Brewhouse"	260
w/o John Johnson	"Elizabeth"	200
	pt. "Gift"	70
Thomas Johnson, Jr.	pt. "Prestons Clifts"	314
	pt. "Gideon & Cleverly Right" – from Cleverly Dare	104
	pt. "Prestons Clifts" – from Cleverly Dare	100
William Johnson s/o Jere	pt. "Exchange"	150
Dr. Edward Johnson (cnp)	"Preston"	200
	"Moffath Mount"	200
	"Hay Marsh"	18

	"Woods Adventure"	50
	pt. "Poor Land"	185
	"Musquito Point"	46
	"Turners Chance"	50
	"Addition to Woods Adventure"	33
Richard Ireland	"Ireland Hope"	50
	pt. "Desart"	198
	pt. "Prestons Clifts" – from Mary Ireland	108
	pt. "Angle" – from Mary Ireland	88
	"Middle Marsh" – from Mary Ireland	63
John Kent	pt. "Rockhold"	160
James Kirshaw	pt. "Prevent Danger"	100
12:1774:18 **...**		
Sarah Kirshaw	pt. "Prevent Danger"	50
Francis Kirshaw	pt. "Sharpers Outlet"	100
	pt. "Concord"	63
Joseph Kent	pt. "Timberwell"	326
	pt. "Addition to Spittle"	50
Rev. Francis Lauder	pt. "Prestons Clifts"	239
	pt. "Gore"	50
John Lawrence	pt. "Lawreys Addition"	145
	pt. "Islington"	50
	pt. "Small Reward"	57
William Lyles	"Red Hall"	150
	"Stripe"	8
	"Turners Pasture"	170
	pt. "Long Lane"	31
h/o Lewis Lewin	pt. "Read Hall"	37½
John Laveal	"Read Hall"	150
	"Whites Rest" – from Richard Johns	188
Robert Lyles	pt. "Red Hall"	100
	"All Point"	24
Capt. Richard & Benjamin Lane	pt. "Homesham"	233
Samuel Lyles	pt. "Lawreys Chance"	50

Thomas Mackensey	pt. "Newington" – from h/o John Hance	9
	"John's Neglect" – from h/o John Hance	128
	"Islingsworth Fortune"	65
12:1774:19 ...		
Jeremiah Maulden	pt. "Parkers Clifts"	250
John Mackall s/o John	pt. resurvey of several tracts	104
	pt. "Tauneys Addition"	44
James Mackall s/o John	pt. resurvey of several tracts	104
	pt. "Tauneys Addition"	44
Benjamin Mackall s/o John	"Schoolhouse"	100
	"Brigantine Adventure"	24
	"Chilton" or "Chatham" – from Edward Gardener	80
	pt. "Forked Neck" or "Dorrington" – from Edward Gardener	50
Elizabeth Marshall	"Cox's Folly"	50
	pt. "Farme"	19
William Marshall 3rd	"Cox's Choice"	143
John Manning	pt. "Theobalds Manor"	112
	"Gunsby"	168
	"Cold Kerby"	½
w/o James McDowell	pt. "Coles Clifts"	50
Hannah Mackall	"Cage"	250
	"Buseys Lott"	100
	"Mackalls Desire"	10
h/o Thomas Morgan	pt. "Gray Chance"	350
	"Fellowship"	160
John Mackall (SM)	pt. "Morgan"	60
	pt. "Horse Range"	180
	"Clagetts Desire"	376
	pt. "Desart"	350
	"St. James's"	300
12:1774:20 ...		
Benjamin Mackall (Holland Point) (cnp)	"Copartnership"	182
	pt. "Chance"	307
	"Hollon Point"	400
	"Seamorse Neck"	382

	pt. "Horse Range"	165
	"Sharpes Out Lett"	100
	pt. "Dividing Branch"	179
	pt. "Trouble"	27
	pt. "Morocco" – in corn	50
	"Addition to Sharpes Out Lett"	112
	pt. "Reed"	46½
	pt. "Major Choice"	381
	pt. "Comsey" – from Robert Etherington	92½
Rousby Miller	pt. "Orchard"	253
Ann Mills	pt. "Wolton"	25
	pt. "Catch"	50
James Mackall	"Piney Point" – from James John Mackall	50
	"Lawreys Pont" & pt. "Lawreys Rest" – from James John Mackall	100
	"Bramhall" – from James John Mackall	500
	"Meads" – from James John Mackall	166
	pt. "Lawreys Chance" – from Betty Clare	130
	pt. "Lawreys Rest" – from James John Mackall	295
Benjamin Mackall s/o James John	"Cornhill" – from J. J. Mackall	350
	"Godsgrace" – from J. J. Mackall	617
Thomas Mackall	"Exchange" – from James John Mackall	350
	pt. "Cedar Branch" – from James John Mackall	240
	pt. "Sewells Purchase" – from James John Mackall	30
	pt. "Bowen" – from h/o Roger Brooke, Jr.	70
	"Tauneys Addition" – from h/o Roger Brooke, Jr.	123
	"Brooke Adventure" – from h/o Roger Brooke, Jr.	156
James Morsell	pt. "Rattle Snake Hill"	120
	"Chance"	70
	pt. "Littleworth"	60
	"Mary Green"	55
12:1774:21 ...		
Mary Mackall (cnp)	pt. "Lower Bennett" – from James John Mackall	500
	"Theobush Manor" – from James John Mackall	100
	"Grays Chance" – from James John Mackall	200
	pt. "Bone Road" – from James John Mackall	89

	"Gunsby" – from James John Mackall	38
	"Cold Harbour" – from James John Mackall	100
	"Brooke Place" – from James John Mackall	432
	"Stones Bay" – from James John Mackall	225
	pt. "Littleworth" – from James John Mackall	77
	"Cold Karby" – from James John Mackall	200
	pt. "Angle" – from James John Mackall	350
	"Fox's Walks" – from James John Mackall	40
	"Neglect" –f rom James John Mackall	30
	pt. "Evans's Land" – from James John Mackall	200
	"Coles Clifts" – from James John Mackall	150
	pt. "Preston Clifts" – from James John Mackall	63
	"Bramels Addition" – from James John Mackall	33
	"Angle" – from James John Mackall	87
John Norfolk	"Kidds Levell"	84
	"Inland Plains"	27
	"Ridge"	100
	pt. "Refuge"	100
	pt. "Refuge"	14
	pt. "Cap Hall" – form Young Cox	25
James Norfolk	pt. "Peahens Nest"	50
h/o John Peters	pt. "Kents Freehold"	50
	pt. "Lordships Favour"	30
William Powell	pt. "Gideon & Cleverly Right"	5½
	pt "Short Hills" – from John Simmonds	23½
John Pardo	pt. "Rockey Neck"	50
	pt. "Fox's Walks"	70
Mary Parker	"Clay Hammond"	380
	"Wilson's Commons"	29
12:1774:22 ...		
Elizabeth Prindowell	pt. "Parkers Clifts"	100
	"Roberts Addition"	5
	pt. "Beakley"	66⅔
	pt. "Roberts Chance"	5½
Leonard Prindowell (cnp)	pt. "Roberts Addition"	10
	pt. "Roberts Chance"	11

	"Beakley"	133⅓
	pt. "Desire" – from h/o Thomas Morgan	79
Robert Peters	"Davin & Clares Hundred"	142
William Patterson	"Stones Bay"	75
	"Evans Land"	65
h/o Alexander Parran	pt. "Point Patience"	360
	"Addition"	19
h/o Hutcheson Parker	pt. "St. Leonards" – in corn	175
	"Bulmores Branch"	50
	"Stones Hills"	26
Richard Parran	pt. "Desart"	349
	"Preston"	400
	"Preston Neglect"	200
	pt. "Bismogan"	50
	pt. "Parran Park"	300
	"Brooks Plains"	100
	pt. "Inland"	2
	"Discovery"	99
Samuel Parran	pt. "Winfields Resurvey"	207
	"Burmingham"	25
	"Morgan"	45
	pt. land without name	100
	pt. "Parrans Park"	150
Capt. David Caucard	"Johnson Farm" – from John Peters	150
	pt. "Turner Place" – from John Peters	66⅔
	pt. "Griffiths & Gover Pasture" – from John Peters	20
12:1774:23 ...		
Edward Reynolds	"Alexanders Hope" – from James John Mackall	200
John Rawlings	pt. "Eltonhead Manor"	300
	"Crumpton"	75
	"Rawlings Purchase"	60
Thomas Rhodes	"Block Robin"	38
Daniel Ross	pt. "Robinsons Rest"	200
Thomas Reynolds (cnp)	pt. "Robinson"	191
	pt. "St. Edmunds"	150
	pt. "Good Luck"	100

	pt. "Robinsons Rest"	518
	"Adjoinder" a/s "Adjuction"	10
	"Brooks Discovery"	64
	"Crouch's Lott"	60
	"Reserve"	300
	"Fox's Chance"	72
	"Rich Bitt"	5½
	"Fox's Home"	30
	"Sterling Perch"	110
	pt. "Lordships Favour"	285
	"Neglect"	44
	"Cox's Inclosure"	70
	"Troublesome"	150
	pt. "Hopewell"	35
	pt. "Abbington Manor"	769
	"Angles Lane"	37
	pt. "Meadows"	132
	"Thomas & Williams Chance"	101
	pt. "Thatchcomb"	114
	pt. "Lingans Purchase"	8
	pt. "Brook Neck"	130
	"Stallings Swamp"	10
	"Bite"	5
	pt. "Lordships Favour" – from John Scott	100
Samuel Robertson	"Emortons Addition"	20
	pt. "Hall Hills"	85
	pt. "Broughton Asply"	73
12:1774:24 ...		
Daniel Rawlings	pt. "Eltonhead Manor"	200
	"Bathens Loss"	50
	"Dear Bought"	200
Henry Scott	pt. "High Land"	50
Dr. John Hamilton Smith (cnp)	"Branford"	150
	pt. "Hardesty Choice"	150
	"Henry Chew"	75
	1½ lots in Lower Marlbro	1½

	pt. "Dowdswell Manor"	400
	"Mill Swamp"	54
	pt. "Bulmores Branch" a/s "Right" – from Benjamin Sedwick	475
Gavin Hamilton Smith	"Little Genory"	42
	pt. "Grantham"	220
	"Sams Addition"	78
	"Hazard"	18½
	pt. "Ordinary"	80½
h/o Philemon Smith	"Soldiers Fortune"	200
	pt. "Ordinary"	75
Alexander Hamilton Smith	pt. "Batchelors Quarter"	250
Walter Smith	pt. "Parkers Clifts"	100
	"Fox's Road"	100
	"Wolfs Quarter"	300
	"Smiths Hogpen"	309
	pt. "St. Leonards" – in corn	175
	"Taylors Disposal"	270
	"Stones Hills"	25
	"Purchase"	20
12:1774:25 ...		
h/o James Somervell	"Tobys Quarter"	21
	"Rockey Neck"	50
	pt. "Allen Neck"	12
	"Swamp"	60
	"Narrow Neck & Gore"	11
	pt. "Gore"	100
	pt. "Stockly"	419
	pt. "Gunterton"	40
h/o Maryland Skinner	pt. "Newington"	94
	pt. "Millers Folly"	250
	pt. "Williams Purchase" – from William Monnett	103
Leonard Skinner	"Borden"	77½
	pt. "Dodson Desire"	25
	pt. "Chance"	27

John Simmonds	pt. "Rich Bottom"	25
	"Short Hills"	16½
h/o George Smith	pt. "Desart"	52
	pt. "Round Bottom Plains"	100
Rezin Sollers	"Forked Neck" – from Dorothy Sollers	100
	"Hyam" – from Dorothy Sollers	10
William Skinner	pt. "Preston Desire"	25
	pt. "Chance"	27
James Skinner	pt. "Border Enlarg'd"	77½
	"Dodson Desire"	25
	pt. "Chance"	27
	pt. "Reserve"	32¼
Robert Skinner	pt. "Blind Tom"	40
	pt. "Tauneys Right"	150
12:1774:26 ...		
Elizabeth Skinner	pt. "Tauneys Right"	150
	pt. "Scrap"	62
	pt. "Reserve"	121
	"Newington"	94
	pt. "Williams Purchase" – from William Monnett	103
h/o Adderton Skinner	"Blind Tom"	32
	"Tauneys Delight"	70
	pt. "Mary Green"	36
	"Gore"	48
	"Neglect"	25
Richard Skinner	pt. "Millers Folly" – from h/o Adderton Skinner	52½
Alexander Sommervell	"Fox's Denn"	50
	"Bartholomew Neck"	50
	pt. "Smiths Purchase"	119¼
	pt. "Gore"	100
	"Goldens Folly"	75
Joseph Strickland	pt. "Robinsons Rest"	50
Benjamin Sunderland	pt. "Swinfens Rest"	250
William Sollers	pt. "Dorrington"	182½
	pt. "Bordleys Chance"	34

Joshua Sedwick	pt. "Neighbourhood"	150
	"Adjoinder"	50
	"Nortons Purchase"	83⅓
w/o Josias Sunderland, Jr.	pt. "Upper Bennett"	50
Phineas Stallings	pt. "Thatchcomb"	236
12:1774:27 ...		
Joseph Skinner	pt. "Orchard"	50
	pt. "Border Enlarged"	77½
	pt. "Chance"	27
	pt. "Dodson Desire"	25
	pt. "Reserve"	32¼
	"Chance"	8
James Sewell	pt. "Dear Quarter"	62½
	pt. "Chance"	72½
	"Maidens Delight"	200
	pt. "Cap Hall"	80
	pt. "Parkers Clifts"	50
	"Good Luck"	150
John Standforth	pt. "Poor Land"	104
John Lee Webster (BA)	pt. "Halls Hills" – from h/o John Skinner	877½
	"Sneaking Point" – from h/o John Skinner	50
	"Halls Revenge" – from Elizabeth Contee	28
	1 lot in Lower Marlbro – from Elizabeth Contee	1
Thomas Cheney & Richard Wells	pt. "Lingans Purchase" – form h/o John Skinner	94
	pt. "Hamilton Park" – from h/o John Skinner	33
Richard Stansbury	pt. "Archers Hays"	40
h/o Joseph Smith, Jr.	pt. "Turners Pasture"	50
	pt. "Smiths Pasture"	100
	pt. "Archers Hays"	15½
	pt. "Archers Hays"	30½
h/o William Smith	pt. "Smith Chance"	50
	pt. "Turner Place"	50
	pt. "Mordyke"	50
Joseph Smith	pt. "Mordyke"	50
12:1774:28 ...		

Mordica Smith	pt. "Smith Chance"	100
	pt. "Welsh Poole"	72½
	pt. "Turners Place"	50
	"Calander"	77
w/o John Stone	pt. "Defence"	65
John Stallings	pt. "Upper Bennett"	25
Ellis Slater	pt. "Lawreys Reserve"	100
Stephen Stamp	pt. "Read Hall"	125
	pt. "Turners Place"	144⅓
Capt. Henry Brooke	"Good Prospect"	50
	"Lands Land"	192
	"Addition"	28
Benjamin Skinner	pt. "Smith Lott, Johnson Farm, Good Prospect, & Lands Land"	\<n/g\>
Clement Smith	pt. "Halls Craft"	221
	pt. "Halls Craft" – from Partrick Smith	9
Partrick Smith	pt. "Halls Craft"	256
Nicholas Swamstead	pt. "Lordships Favour"	100
Thomas Stallings	pt. "Swinfens Rest"	64½
John Sedwick	"Buck Hill"	21
	"Hard Travell" – from h/o Benjamin Tasker	300
w/o Stockett Sunderland	pt. "Lawreys Chance" or "Resurvey"	100
John Davis Scarth	pt. "Robinsons Rest"	50
12:1774:29 ...		
Stephen Steward	"Islingworth Fortune"	200
Raphael Tauney	pt. "Stone Hills"	50
James Gray	pt. "Expectation" – from Joseph Talbutt, Jr.	100
John Tannehill	pt. "Callender"	123
	pt. "Cooper" & pt. "Friendship"	42
	pt. "Welsh Poole"	86
Ann Tannehill	pt. "Cooper" & pt. "Friendship"	173
Joseph Talbutt	pt. "Freemans Chance"	123
	pt. "Tillington"	150
	"Batchelors Fortune"	200
John Talbutt	pt. "Expectation"	50
	pt. "Expectation" – from Thomas Talbutt	25

Edward Talbutt	pt. "Tillington"	415½
	pt. "Tillington" – from h/o George Fowler	22¾
Edward North	pt. "Tillington" – from h/o George Fowler	22¾
John Turner	pt. "Bowdleys Chance"	91
Philip Talbutt	pt. "Expectation" – from Thomas Talbutt	75
John Tucker	pt. "Neighbourhood"	82½
John Wilkinson	pt. "Youngs Attempt"	100
Ben Kid Wilson & Priscilla Gover	pt. "Aldermason"	150
	"Govers Expectation"	89
	pt. "Welch Poole"	2
12:1774:30 ...		
John Ward	pt. "Friendship"	50
	pt. "Allen Neck"	164
	pt. "Friendship" – from Rebeca Hungerford	25
h/o Samuel Ward	"Goldsons Inheritance"	150
Aron Williams, Jr.	pt. "Friendship Rectified"	200
	pt. "Swinfens Adventure"	50
	pt. "Youngs Desire"	50
James Weems, Jr.	"Success, Tauneys Ear, & Stockley"	200
	"Partnerships"	75
Aron Williams, Sr.	pt. "Williams's Hardship"	175
	"Williams Rest"	50
	"Little Field"	25
	pt. "Swinfens Adventure"	50
	pt. "Friendship Rectified"	25
h/o Joseph Wilkinson	pt. "Godsgrace"	120
	pt. "Stockley"	70
John Waters	"Mirtle Point"	7
John Willing	"Jerusalem"	108
	pt. "Rich Bottom"	25
	"Willen Swamp"	11
	"Content"	6½
Francis Woolf, Jr.	pt. "Theobald Manor"	50
	"Grays Chance"	50
Richard Ward	pt. "Swinfens Rest"	116
	"Davin & Clares Hundred"	138

12:1774:31 ...		
James Weems s/o David	"Ringan"	200
	"Greenhouse"	155
	"Chew Purchase"	145
	pt. "Grantham"	45
	"Marshall Addition"	70
	"Fall Short"	56
Basil Williamson	pt. "Lingans Adventure"	310
Edward Wood	pt. "Wood Adventure"	150
	pt. "Titmarsh"	100
	pt. "Poor Land"	11
	pt. "Brook Adventure"	78
Michael Tayney	"Berry" – from George Wheelor	600
	"Long Point" – from George Wheelor	100
	"Wooden Point" – from George Wheelor	25
	pt. "Letchworth" – from George Wheelor	50
	pt. "Angle" – from George Wheelor	3
h/o Roger Wheelor	"Henry Chew"	237
	"Coxcomb"	150
	~~"Coxhead"~~	~~50~~
	pt. ~~"Newington"~~ "Cox Head"	109
	"Smith Contrivance"	60
	pt. "Burk Chance"	150
Jonah Winfied	pt. "Johnson Farm"	100
Thomas & Jane Wells	pt. "Grantham Hall"	155
	"Arthurs Hall"	44
h/o James Williamson	"Den"	726
	"Fox's Nettles"	20
	pt. "Batchelors Quarter"	420
John Wilkinson	pt. "Henry Chew"	400
12:1774:32 ...		
Leonard Wood	pt. "Wood Adventure"	100
h/o Edward Wilson (cnp)	"Dear Quarter"	25
	"Robinson Rest"	150
	"Tamot" – from h/o Jos. Wilson	300
	pt. "Forsters Purchase" – from h/o Jos. Wilson	150

	pt. "Addition Spittle"	8
Nathaniel Wilson	"Stone Lott" – from h/o Jos. Wilson	50
John Weems	pt. "Dowdswell"	600
	pt. "Chance"	25
	pt. "Chance" – from Jacob Tucker	50
	pt. "Chance" – from George Hall	25
	pt. "Newington" – from Alexander Deale	46
	pt. "Islington" – from Alexander Deale	26
	"Tensley Lott" – from Henry Howes	46
	"Purchase" – from Henry Howes	23
William White	pt. "Smith Joy"	100
William Winnull	pt. "Nortons Purchase"	166⅔
Francis Whittington	pt. "Halls Hills"	100
	pt. "Halls Hills" – from William Ireland	25
William Hutton Wood	pt. "Arnolds Purchase"	100
Francis Williams	pt. "Inland"	100
	"Hutchings Chance"	50
	pt. "Orchard"	40
John Winfield	pt. "Lands Land"	112
Ithamar Williams	pt. "Winfens Adventure"	50
	"Williams Hardship"	75
	pt. "Friendship Rectified"	125
12:1774:33 ...		
Philemon Young	pt. "Henry Chew"	59½
	1 lot in Lower Marbrough	1
Joseph Wilson	pt. "Garey Chance"	150
	"Lower Bennett"	189
Parker Young	"Hop Yard"	150
	"Punch"	150
	pt. "Youngs Desire"	25
	pt. "Hooper Neck"	275
Mary Yoe	pt. "Rattle Snake Hill"	100
Richard Hellen s/o Richard	pt. "Cedar Branch"	50
Peter Hellen	"Huckleberry Quarter Enlarg'd"	127⅓
John Mills	pt. "Thorough Point"	125
	pt. "Brook Choice"	73

James Weems	pt. "Magruder"	410
	"Buseys Orchard"	400
	"Hogs Hant"	50
	"Mauldens Luck"	25
	"Meadows Preserv'd"	46
	"Huckleberry Hill"	50
	"Cockolds Miss"	60
	"Youngs Attempt"	62
	"Youngs Fortune"	60
	"Youngs Desire"	25
	"Penman Mure"	50
	"Reserve"	50
	"Inland"	1
	1 lot in Hunting Town	1
Richard Winfield	pt. "Lordships Favour"	50
12:1774:34 ...		
Edward Wood	pt. "Brooks Adventure"	77¾
William Dawkins, Jr.	pt. "Blinkhorn" – from Jos. Dawkins	300
	"Fox's Road" – from Jos. Dawkins	42
	"Josephs Refuse" – from Jos. Dawkins	196
Hillary Wilson	pt. "Robinson"	213
	pt. "Lordships Favour"	9
	pt. "Lordships Favour"	75
	pt. "Lordships Favour"	70
	pt. "Robinson" – from h/o Jos. Wilson	136
Bryan Taylor	pt. "Smiths Purchase"	119¼
	pt. "Fox's Road" – from Elizabeth Dorrumple	108
Isaac Simmonds	pt. "Chance"	50
	pt. "Borders Enlarg'd" pt. "Reserve"	210
	pt. "Millers Folly" – from h/o Adderton Skinner	145
John Broome	pt. "Island Neck"	500
	pt. "Stones Bay"	200
	"Adventure"	82½
	pt. "Broad Point"	140
	pt. "Austin Addition"	23
	pt. "Brooks Battle"	124

Thomas Wilson	pt. "St. Edmunds"	163
	pt. "Neglect"	16½
	"Letchworth"	200
	"Youngs Attempt"	100
	pt. "Horsepath"	125
	pt. "Hop at a Venture"	25
Isaac Hooper	pt. "Tobys Quarter"	79
	pt. "Swamp"	6½
	"Narrow Neck & Gore"	7
~~John Gardiner~~	<n/g>	<n/g>
12:1774:35 ...		
Kensey Gardener	pt. "Wolfs Hole"	28⅔
	pt. "Johnson Lott"	26⅓
	pt. "Johnson Lott"	100
Zacheus Alnutt	pt. "Brook Partition"	119
	pt. "Hogg Down"	7
	pt. "Little Reward"	21
	pt. "Brook Partition" – from Thomas Bond	119
Clement Skinner	pt. "Whittles Rest"	60
	pt. "Millers Folly" – from h/o Adderton Skinner	52½
Edward Wood	pt. "Magruder"	150
	pt. "Morocco" – in corn	100
William Allen	"Second Thought"	<n/g>
John Mackall	pt. "Majors Choice" – from h/o Philip Thomas	119
Edward Johnson	"Musketa Point" – vacancy added on resurvey	5½
h/o Edward Hungerford	"Doe Hill"	25
Samuel Parran	"Halls Resurvey" – vacancy added	4
Edward Gardner	"Shelton" – vacancy added on resurvey	43
William Dawkins	"Heighes Fancy" – disclaimed for upward of 20 years	79½
12:1774:<unnumbered>	**Allowances claimed by the Farmer of CV**	
James Truman Greenfield	double charge	<n/g>
John Gardiner	"Johnson Lott"	124
Isaac Clare	"Concord" tbc Francis Kirshaw	63
Richard Johns	"Purchase" tbc Jos. Isaac	100
h/o John Peters	"Kents Freehold" tbc Thomas Hollandhead	50

William Skinner	<n/g> tbc Isaac Simmonds	<n/g>
Edward Wood	"Brooke Adventure" – double charge	78
Thomas Morgan	"Garys Chance" tbc J. Wilson	150
Rebecca Hungerford	"Friendship" – overcharge	31¼
Roger Brooke	"Brook Battle" – lost in elder survey	106
Richard Johns	"Parkers Clifts" – taken by elder survey	109
Thomas Stallings	"Swinfens Rest" – taken by "Sterling Nest" an elder survey	61
12:1774:<unnumbered>	**Recapitulation**	
12:1774:<unnumbered>	**Certification**	

Jos. 112, 234
Joseph 4, 29, 54, 60, 78-80,
105, 132, 158, 207
Mary 5, 30, 80, 105
William 5, 29, 30, 54, 79,
106, 133, 159, 186,
207, 213, 234, 235
Day
Benjamin 5, 29, 54, 79, 106,
133, 159, 186, 213
Robert 5, 29, 54, 79, 106,
133, 159, 186, 213
William 5, 30, 55, 80, 106,
133, 159, 186, 213
Deal
Jacob 30
James 99
Deale
Alexander 6, 30, 55, 80, 107,
134, 160, 187, 233
Jacob 6, 55, 80, 106, 133,
159, 187, 213
James 5, 30, 55, 80, 106, 133,
159, 186, 213
Richard 5, 30, 55, 80, 106,
133, 159, 186, 213
Dear
William 160
Dear Bought 76, 91, 102, 117, 129, 182,
200, 226
Dear Quarter 5, 7, 19, 24, 29, 31, 45,
49, 54, 56, 79, 81, 95,
100, 106, 122, 126,
133, 135, 149, 153,
159, 161, 175, 179,
186, 188, 202, 206,
212, 215, 229, 232
Dearbought 1, 15, 26, 41, 51, 65, 146,
155, 173
Deare
Cleveley 166
Deer Quarter 69, 74
Defence 20, 45, 70, 96, 123, 149, 176,
203, 230
Den 10, 24, 34, 49, 59, 73, 84, 100,
110, 111, 126, 137,
138, 152, 164, 179,
191, 206, 217, 218,
232
Denit 16

Denton
Thomas 5, 30, 55, 80, 106,
133, 159, 163, 186,
207, 213, 214
Desart 1, 11, 18, 26, 36, 39, 41, 43, 51,
61, 66, 68, 86, 88, 92,
94, 112, 114, 118,
121, 139, 141, 147,
166, 167, 169, 171,
174, 193, 194, 196,
198, 201, 219, 221,
222, 225, 228
Desert 13, 63, 89, 115, 142, 145
Desire 36, 38, 89, 115, 142, 169, 196,
225
Devels Woodyard 155
Device 160
Devideing Branch 155, 156, 169
Devils Wood Yard 26
Devils Woodyard 1, 51, 76, 102, 129,
182, 209
Devise 13, 25, 61, 63, 87, 113, 140,
166, 187, 214
Dew
John 6, 31, 55, 80, 107, 134,
187, 214
Dicks Cabbin 4, 29, 105
Dicks Cabin 132, 158, 193, 212
Dick's Cabbin 54, 79
Discovery 16, 41, 66, 92, 118, 145, 171,
198, 225
Dividing Branch 1, 2, 14, 26, 39, 51, 64,
76, 89, 102, 116, 129,
143, 182, 183, 196,
209, 210, 223
Dixon
Benjamin 4, 29, 54, 79, 105
Ellis 5, 30, 55, 80, 106, 133,
159, 186, 213
Henry 105, 132, 158, 185,
212
Dobsons Desire 43
Dodens Desire 175
Dodson
James 5, 29, 54, 79, 106, 132,
159, 186, 212
Dodson Desire 227-229
Dodsons Desire 18, 19, 121, 122, 147-
149, 174, 201, 202
Dodson's Desire 68, 94, 95, 174

www.ingramcontent.com/pod-product-compliance
Lightning Source LLC
Chambersburg PA
CBHW050410280326
41932CB00013BA/1810